# Beyond Stereotypes in Black and White

# Beyond Stereotypes in Black and White

*How Everyday Leaders Can Build Healthier Opportunities for African American Boys and Men*

**Henrie M. Treadwell**

 PRAEGER

AN IMPRINT OF ABC-CLIO, LLC
Santa Barbara, California • Denver, Colorado • Oxford, England

**Library of Congress Cataloging-in-Publication Data**

Treadwell, Henrie M.
  Beyond stereotypes in black and white : how everyday leaders can build healthier opportunities for African American boys and men / Henrie Treadwell.
      p. cm.
  Includes bibliographical references and index.
  ISBN 978-1-4408-0399-4 (hbk. : alk. paper) — ISBN 978-1-4408-0400-7 (ebook)
1. African American men—Social conditions.   2. African American boys—Social conditions.   3. African American men—Health and hygiene.   4. African American boys—Health and hygiene.   5. Leadership—United States.   6. Community leadership—United States.   7. United States—Social conditions—21st century.
8. United States—Social policy.   I. Title.
  E185.86.T74   2013
  305.38'896073—dc23         2012036575

ISBN: 978-1-4408-0399-4
EISBN: 978-1-4408-0400-7

17  16  15  14  13     1  2  3  4  5

This book is also available on the World Wide Web as an eBook.
Visit www.abc-clio.com for details.

Praeger
An Imprint of ABC-CLIO, LLC

ABC-CLIO, LLC
130 Cremona Drive, P.O. Box 1911
Santa Barbara, California 93116-1911

This book is printed on acid-free paper ∞
Manufactured in the United States of America

# Contents

## PART ONE: Losing the Race

### Chapter 1: Addressing the Stereotypes   3

Meet Martin and Jamal, fictional representative African American men who put a face to the crisis.

### Chapter 2: Communities in Crisis   13

The crisis and how it affects African American communities, as well as communities of every stripe across the nation.

### Chapter 3: Sick and Tired: The Killer Disease of Racism   29

The real impact of racism on the life opportunities of men and boys of color.

### Chapter 4: Lost in Translation: "Access to Care" for Men of Color   43

Whether in the community or in the prisons, men and boys of color lack the kind of access to health services that help people live full and healthy lives.

### Chapter 5: A Deafening Silence   59

The devastating lack of attention and urgency in the face of the crisis. How and why silence, indeed, equals death for men and boys of color.

## Chapter 13: Opportunities for Success: What You Can Do and How 209

Concrete steps we can take at every level of leadership to make real change happen now.

Organizations around the country that are actually making a difference, where you can get more information or find opportunities to get involved and become a leader yourself.

# Prologue
## *Hear My Voice*

### "I fit into the stereotype as the person who got shot."

In February 2012, Trayvon Martin was gunned down in a gated town-house community in Florida. George Zimmerman, a neighborhood watch captain, had called the police because the boy looked "real suspicious," and proceeded to pursue Martin in a sport-utility vehicle. The boy's body was taken to the medical examiner's office and listed as a John Doe. Zimmerman claimed he acted in self-defense. Trayvon was "armed" with a bag of Skittles and a can of iced tea. Trayvon was 17 years old and black. Zimmerman was 28 years old at the time and Hispanic/white. As reported in the *New York Times*, one of the witnesses was a 13-year-old black boy, who ended his description of what he saw by saying, "I just think that sometimes people get stereotyped, and I fit into the stereotype as the person who got shot." If a 13-year-old boy can see what's happening, can feel the burden of black boys, why can't we?[1]

### All We Want Is a Different Life

*Fred Anderson and his wife sat with me one Saturday morning to share more of his story, his work, and his vision. Fred is an ex-offender who has come home after serving more than 8 years in prison. I have known him for 2 years now, and I always leave from seeing Fred inspired and moved. Such a talented man. I wonder, where would he be right now if only he had all of the right chances and made all of the right choices? Regardless, he leaves a large footprint. Fred's story . . .*

Can you imagine being stripped of everything, family, lifestyle, freedom, and even constitutional rights? Of becoming a victim of circumstances resorting to survival rather than success? Have you ever lived amongst murderers, rapists, thieves, angels, and demons? This living condition is obtained due to bad choices. Many of us are known as criminals, felons, or ex-cons, but honestly we are people like you who lost direction. To better society, as well as ourselves, we are punished by the law and never rebuild as productive citizens. The most important stage of our journey through the justice system is often overlooked. Being released back into a civilized world, after time in just the opposite, can be too much of an adjustment to be made without proper guidance. Our dreams of success are often turned into prayers of survival. Endless nights of imagining a new life trained our minds to change our direction. Our belief and ambition is constantly crushed by society, as we are denied, contained, and restricted to the lowest standards of this system. Jobs, housing, finances, and rights become obstacles, instead of being priorities. As a 38-year-old formerly incarcerated man, I fight a battle amongst millions like me searching for a new life filled with equality. Though most of us lack the proper tools, as well as the knowledge, to secure our visions, we all share the feeling of hope in its purest form. We hope for a secure purpose, we trust our passion, but our past often harbors our future. To break this system, one must re-create the mind and carefully navigate a new path to success.[2]

\* \* \*

## "The best way to promote change is to continue to speak out."

Nicholas Peart, a 23-year-old college student, has been stopped and frisked at least five times, for no reason. In a *New York Times* opinion piece, he described four of those instances. The first, he was celebrating his 18th birthday with his cousin and a friend. They were sitting on some benches "talking, watching the night go by, enjoying the evening, when suddenly, and out of nowhere, squad cars surrounded us. A policeman yelled from the window 'Get on the ground.' I was stunned, I was scared. Then I was on the ground—with a gun pointed at me," he writes. The next time, he was leaving his grandmother's home when he was stopped, frisked, searched, and then let go. The third time, he was walking home from the gym. And a fourth time, he was outside his apartment building on his way to the store "when two police officers jumped out of an unmarked car and told me to stop and put my hands up against the wall." He complied. "Without my permission, they removed my cellphone from my hand . . . looked through my wallet, then handcuffed me." With the keys they had taken from his pocket, they tried to get into his apartment, terrifying his 18-year-old sister and two younger siblings. Eventually, they "removed the handcuffs and simply drove off. I was deeply shaken," he writes.

When I interviewed Peart, he told me he became aware of the "dangers" when his mother warned him to always carry ID and to never argue with a policeman "when" (not "if") they stopped him. "I don't have a record," he told me, "but I am still stopped, and the only reason can be racial profiling." He filed a complaint with the Civilian Review Board about the gun held to his head, but the board did and said nothing in response to his complaint. Peart works with a neighborhood organization in Harlem that educates young people about their rights when stopped by the police and the best way to handle such situations. He is also acting as a witness in a lawsuit to stop racial profiling and harassment by police. Peart says he feels that the momentum for change is growing, but he observes that many young men do begin to respond negatively because they feel threatened. "Their response is never good for them and the psychological impact is probably very powerful . . . the best way to promote change is to just continue speaking out . . ."[3]

## "Why I'm Marching"

"Why I'm Marching" was the subject of Manhattan Borough President Scott Stringer's June 2012 email blast in reaction to the New York City Police Department's "Stop and Frisk" policy. In a previously published op-ed piece in *The Nation*, he noted, "Last year, the NYPD made over 680,000 stops—an increase of over 600 percent since 2002. Eighty-seven percent of those stopped were black or Latino, in a city where those groups comprise 54 percent of the population. And in 99.9 percent of those stops, no gun was recovered . . . in 94 percent of stops, no arrest is made. . . . Today, we cannot afford to wait any longer for reform while thousands among us suffer suspicion-less stops. We should not wait for the next Trayvon Martin."[4]

What was Stringer's immediate call to action to address this blatant form of stereotyping? A people's march in Harlem to advocate for reform of this unfair policy. As he concludes in his email, "We need to build bridges of trust and respect into every neighborhood by exploring innovative policing strategies that succeed in other cities—strategies that work with communities, not against them."[5]

Will you march? Is marching enough?

## Notes

1. Blow, Charles M. "The Curious Case of Trayvon Martin." *New York Times*. http://www.nytimes.com, May 16, 2012.
2. Author's personal communication with Fred Anderson, February 2012.

3. Pert, Nicholas K. "Why Is the N.Y.P.D. After Me?" *New York Times*. http://www.nytimes.com, December 17, 2011.

4. Stringer, Scott. "Beyond Stop-and-Frisk: Toward Policing That Works." *The Nation*. http://www.thenation.com, April 23, 2012.

5. Email communication from Scott Stringer's office, June 2012.

# Acknowledgments

This book has been a long time coming. My family has endured my search for what I call the "missing" men. My work in improving access to primary health care, prevention, and other needed health services to include oral and mental health services found traction among women and children, adolescents, and the senior citizen community. The men were not present. The insurance systems did not cover them; the hospitals and clinics did not want more bad debt from people who have no way to pay. When I "found" the men, their lives had been touched by the criminal justice system and whatever health care they received they found in jail or prison. Although family and friends know about my work in general, I know that they were puzzled about my growing interest in the prison system. I simply could not stop myself as the issue became one of justice— health justice—very much akin to the general struggle for civil rights and justice in other sectors. I thank my friends, family, and colleagues for suffering through my non-ceasing dialogue on this issue that I perceive as one of the most significant wedge political issues of our time, as well as perhaps the most stunning example of man's inhumanity to man, acted out principally against the poor and defenseless communities of color.

I also thank many others who have rallied to the cause throughout the years. Mary Northridge, the editor of the *American Journal of Public Health*, is first among many, and her faith in the mission gave it grounding. I also thank Georges Benjamin, Executive Director of the American Public Health Association, who has always lent an ear and provided wise counsel as I looked for ways to blend into the mainstream a population currently absent from health care services. I am also infinitely grateful to the Kellogg Foundation and its visionary Board of Trustees as they funded many intervention programs, often on my recommendation, to support efforts to remove the barriers to prevention health services. Others who have been an invaluable support and counsel throughout the years are Dr. Siegfried Merwyn, Editor Emeritus of the *Journal of*

*Men's Health*; Kellogg Foundation Trustee, Joe Stewart, who was always a thoughtful critic and cheerleader; Dr. Gail Christopher, Vice President of Programs at the Kellogg Foundation, for her help with strategic thinking; and Dr. John Maupin, President of the Morehouse School of Medicine, who gives me the space to work in often unchartered ways to bring attention to the issues. I also thank my colleagues in Community Voices who have embraced this cause across the nation and world and to numerous students who are now fanning across the nation, carrying the torch to extinguish damning and damaging stereotypes.

I am blessed to have had in my life Marguerite Ro, my co-conspirator and alter ego throughout many years, as well as Teresa Odden and Jareese Stroud. My sincere thanks to these three, who always found a way to make the impossible possible so the work could continue uninterrupted.

Along the way, in streets, in homes, in prisons or related facilities, in meetings, wonderful human spirits too numerous to mention have shared their personal stories or the stories of people they loved who were now in trouble. In many cases, the pain was evident. In too many cases, I could do nothing but listen, as there are just too many hurdles for even a committed advocate to remove. But I thank them for their faith and confidence in at least my advocacy. And I am equally grateful to those community leaders, those thinkers and doers, who dream a better world and who work each day, without fanfare or recognition, to move just one grain of sand, if that is all they can do within their space and place, out of the way of a poor boy or man of color striving to find his footing in a nation in which health justice remains elusive.

I do not know where the journey of all of us leads or if we are yet in sight of the end of the journey. But this I do know: As a result of your efforts, things may not yet be set right, but they will never be the same. You have made our world a more careful and nurturing space. The time will come when we are able to say, "Those days are gone and will never come again." Not today, but soon. That day will come, because we will WILL it into being and will not stop until African American boys and men take their rightful place as full members of our nation.

# Introduction

When you think of the typical African American boy or man, what images come to mind?

Someone who is involved with drugs? Undereducated? Unemployed? An absent father? In prison? A victimizer rather than a victim?

When you think of the typical "leader," what images come to mind? A politician? CEO? Local or state bureaucrat? Someone who says his or her hands are tied rather than someone who acts to redress critical social issues?

If these are your thoughts, it is time to move beyond these stereotypes.

African American boys and men are more victims than victimizers—yes, they are unemployed, underemployed, undereducated, and incarcerated at higher rates than any other group in the United States, but when the plight of these boys and men is discussed in the media, it is often from a "blame the victim" perspective. What is not acknowledged is the havoc their marginalization wreaks on them as individuals, on their children and families, on their neighborhoods, and on this potential workforce that could add to the overall growth of the U.S. economy.

For example, felony convictions of African American boys and men, coupled with a lack of education, leave them unemployable in many fields that offer a living wage. Additionally, this segment of the population experiences far greater health disparities than their white counterparts. Exacerbating this problem are the health policies that have left them without a source of payment for medical care, thus facilitating early morbidity and mortality.

With few options for employment and health care following a felony conviction, poor health, and low educational attainment, far too many African American boys and men are trapped in a downward spiral, which they are ill equipped to stop by themselves.

Concurrently, although there are many black and white American leaders who feel their hands are tied when it comes to making changes to the policies that allow the above to proliferate, there are enough who are taking effective action to circumvent the cynical hopelessness of the stereotypical powerless leader. These true leaders are often in the least expected positions, such as corrections officers, judges, teachers, governors, mayors, parents, and grocery clerks. They are found at every level of the community and are finding roles for themselves in redressing multiple critical social issues.

All over the country, there are pockets of hope moving the pendulum of change in a positive direction. A difference can be made in the lives of African American boys and men in education, employment, health, and incarceration prevention and re-entry programs when the common man and woman find a way to acknowledge and assert the power within them and become the new leaders.

*Beyond Stereotypes in Black and White* aims to identify and cultivate such new leaders.

I am Senior Social Scientist and Director of Community Voices and Men's Health Initiative, as well as Research Professor, Department of Community Health and Preventive Medicine at the Morehouse School of Medicine in Atlanta, Georgia. Community Voices: Healthcare for the Underserved, an initiative funded and initially operated by the W.K. Kellogg Foundation and now run through a program office at the Morehouse School of Medicine, has health justice as its fundamental mission. This initiative has matured over the past decade from a national network of learning laboratories into a program with distinctive and directive practice and policy goals. I have been working for 25 years to improve equity in access to health care and the full benefits of society that should be available to poor men of color, especially African Americans. In 2008, I was guest editor of a special legacy issue of the *American Journal of Public Health*, which focused on priorities of Community Voices: themes of prisons and health, as well as related themes, such as men's health and health care for the underserved.[1] I have learned that many people do not even know the basic facts that have brought us to this dark and fragile place in the history of our nation.

This book provides a concise presentation of the facts of this history and a voice from the vantage point of the boys and men themselves, as well as that of advocates in communities around the country. I give you a context for the policies that put African American boys and men on the downward spiral. I then set the parameters for new policies and new leadership on every level—from government officials to members of the media, from CEOs of large corporations to small business owners, from elite educators to single parents.

To move people to think and act beyond their stereotypes of other people and themselves is no easy task. If it were, all of us good-intentioned people would have done it by now. This book uses four powerful and innovative features: "Reality Check" to make certain we are all starting at the same place; "Take a Good Look," as a way for readers to check in with themselves around what they would do to change the lives of many who are marginalized; "History of Change" to place brave individuals' efforts along a historical spectrum; and, at the end of each chapter, "Leaders and Heroes"— the stories of some everyday people who are using their skills to make a difference, to shift a paradigm, and to create space for those who have been at the margins. These four features are designed to break through our preconceived notions. These features will motivate people from all walks of life to not only care, but to channel that caring toward practical ways to take action for this worthy cause in their everyday lives, as well as in their professional lives.

Here is one:

---

 **REALITY CHECK   Who's in Prison?**

**Likelihood of incarceration over a lifetime:**

African American males: 1 in 3
Hispanic males: 1 in 6
White males: 1 in 17

**Percentage of prison population:**

African American males: 38%
Hispanic males: 22%
White males: 32%

**Total** estimated prisoners rate per 100,000 U.S. residents – **1,005**

Rates
Black – 3,192 (3,059 males); 3.2% of blacks in the nation
White – 503 (456 males); 0.5% of whites in the nation
Hispanic – 1,329 (1,252 males); 1.3% of Hispanics in the nation[1]

---

1. Guerino, Paul, Paige M. Harrison, and William J. Sabol, "Prisoners in 2010." Dec. 15, 2011. Bureau of Justice Statistics. http://bjs.ojp.usdoj.gov/.

---

The time for this book is now, as frustration grows over the feeling that national, state, and local African American leadership has failed to advance the constituency this leadership represents.

As the years pass, the statistics regarding African American boys and men are growing extensively worse. Headlines after headlines across America have published the fact that, at current levels of incarceration, a black male in the United States today has greater than a 1 in 3 chance of going to prison during his lifetime, compared to 1 in 6 Hispanic males and 1 in 17 white males.[2]

Lesser known are the research findings that show the long-term detrimental effects of prison life on the incarcerated, as well as the families and communities to which they return. Of note, nationally, African Americans make up 40% of the prison population. Of this population, most never hold a decent job, which has rippling negative implications. How can these men obtain health insurance? How can they care for themselves and their families or future families? How can they educate themselves? How can they contribute to the tax base of their communities? How can they contribute to Social Security? The lack of answers to these questions is further evidence of the failure of current leadership to protect the people they are charged to represent and reinforces the need for new leaders.

This country is in a health care crisis of unprecedented proportions, one that threatens to eviscerate an entire community. However, the crisis is even direr in the prison system. In 2009, the Physicians for a National Health Program reported that, among the incarcerated, rates of chronic conditions, including diabetes, hypertension, and asthma, are much higher than in the national population. Among federal inmates, the rate of diabetes is more than 11% (nearly twice that of the age-adjusted general population). Here's another reality check for you:

After release, one-quarter to one-third of inmates with medical conditions are deprived of prescribed medication, either because of their financial inability to pay for the medication(s) or the insurance that covers it. Even if only sentenced to a short term in prison, coming home with tuberculosis, hepatitis, or HIV can be a life sentence not only for the ex-offender, but also to the women, children, and community to which they return.

The collateral damage of incarceration on ex-offenders as a result of a felony drug conviction is a lifetime sentence as well, which makes individual, family, and neighborhood recovery virtually impossible. These voices are muted by loss of the right to vote, loss of the ability to earn a living, loss of the ability to live in taxpayer-supported housing, and no rights to health care coverage. Where are *their* leaders who advocate for them?

*Beyond Stereotypes in Black and White* precisely documents how incarceration is but a symptom that emerges from a long line of inequitable policies.

Men and boys of color are born and remain at the bottom of the proverbial ladder in terms of chronic and continuing health inequities and

**REALITY CHECK  Increased Likelihood of Diseases and Traumatic Brain Injuries**

Compared with the general population, those in state prisons are:

- 31% more likely to have asthma

- 55% more likely to have diabetes

- 90% more likely to have suffered a heart attack

- more than 2 times more likely to have confirmed AIDS

- nearly 50% of inmates in state (and federal) prison suffer from some mental disorder[1]

. . . and 60% have had at least one traumatic brain injury (TBI) compared with 8.5% of nonincarcerated adults—that's 7 times more frequently![2] Symptoms, such as headache and irritability, can linger, affecting day-to-day functioning and quality of life. Furthermore, TBIs can alter behavior, emotion, and impulse control; prisoners may seem noncompliant or intentionally defiant. These symptoms, in turn, can provoke situations that help keep prisoners behind bars longer, as well as Increase the odds that they will return, in an endless cycle of injury and incarceration.[3]

1. Maruschak, Laura M. "Medical Problems of Prisoners." April 1, 2008. Bureau of Justice Statistics. http://bjs.ojp.usdoj.gov/index.

2. Harmon, Katherine. "Brain Injury Rate 7 Times Greater among U.S. Prisoners." February 4, 2012. http://www.scientificamerican.com.

3. Wald, Marlena M., Sheryl R. Helgeson, and Jean A. Langelois. "Traumatic Brain Injuries among Prisoners." http://www.brainline.org.

crushing denials of real life opportunities. Men and boys of color, especially resource-poor African Americans, struggle with limited opportunities for a healthy and fulfilling life at every turn.

According to the Children's Defense Fund's "Portrait of Inequality: Black Children in America, 2011,"[3] African American men and boys are:

- more likely to be raised in a poor environment and less likely to be raised in an affluent environment than their white counterparts

- more likely to be placed in foster care and less likely to be raised in a two-parent home

- more likely to be expelled from school and less likely to graduate

- more likely to eat unhealthy food and less likely to benefit from good nutrition
- more likely to be penalized by punitive public policy at every step they take to overcome their disadvantages

As reported by the Children's Defense Fund, it is clear that the health of black children begins to suffer at the moment of birth. The Defense Fund's 2011 fact sheet[4] states that babies born to black mothers are:

- almost twice as likely as those born to white mothers to be born at low birth weight
- 58% more likely to be born pre-term than white children
- 73% more likely than white children to have an unmet medical need
- 35% more likely than white children to have an unmet dental need
- almost 50% more likely to have asthma than white children[5]

As a result, a child born at low birth weight is more likely to have health, behavior, and learning problems as he or she gets older. Uncontrolled asthma can also affect a child's ability to learn, play, and sleep and can require hospital treatment or visits to the emergency department. What chance do these babies have to avoid incarceration?

These are awful statistics, and we need to hear them, but *Beyond Stereotypes in Black and White* is much more than an aggregation of disparities imposed on African American men and boys. It also serves as a vehicle that succinctly and compassionately opens the door to thought-provoking discussions about the plethora of inequities. My aim is to move beyond pondering the statistics to charting the course for solvable action.

I want to move toward resolution through stimulating the dormant leadership potential with the laypeople of this country. *Beyond Stereotypes in Black and White* describes and decries a kind of "power failure"—the vacuum in our current American leadership compounding the problem. I want to guide readers through the process to fill that vacuum by encouraging leadership at every socio-economic level, among people of every color and background. Of course, I target people in positions of authority, in government, with financial means, and those with a network of influence. However, no one is left out of the equation; everyone is invited to move beyond their tightly-held stereotypes and be part of the solution.

Our current leadership, which is among the most diverse in our nation's history, continues to leave us sitting in the echo of a deafening silence around the realities faced by millions of Americans stuck in a dead end cycle of poverty, incarceration, chronic disease, and early death. A complex set of public policy decisions has left a trail of destroyed lives, fractured families, and devastated communities in its wake.

It is long past time to stand up and turn the tide. The average person has the ability and capability to make real change happen—this book helps us get beyond the comfortable stereotypes we all have of others, and of ourselves, and creates new images of reality, hope, and action through a new wave of leaders.

I begin the book with the stories of two men, Martin and Jamal, who put faces on the crisis of disparity. In Chapter 6, a third man, Benjamin, helps tell another part of the story. I devote subsequent chapters to detailing the crisis, the real impact of racism, the inaccessibility of health care, the marginalization of progressive leadership, ways to avoid wasting money on ineffective programs, the public policies and financial investments underlying the crisis, and the role of the media in promoting and busting stereotypes. The final two chapters set forth innovative leadership models and present concrete steps that leaders across the country can take immediately. Finally, an Appendix provides resources for additional information and models of success.

In each chapter, I include four unique features designed to lead readers through a process of motivation through myth busting, inspiration through role models and historic milestones, and action through interactive introspection.

The four types of innovative, linked features throughout the book are:

- "Reality Check." Eye-opening "Reality Checks" dispel common myths that feed the stereotype by providing accurate facts. You have already seen two of these in this introduction.

- "Leaders and Heroes." Concise profiles of "Leaders and Heroes" present specific individuals in various audience groups making a difference. This diverse group of people is an example that readers can identify with, including role models to be inspired by.

- "History of Change." Throughout American history, there are endless stories of brave individuals who have worked for change. This book includes a selection of stories of people and events that have affected history and that particularly resonate with me.

- "Take a Good Look." Most unique of all, interactive "Take a Good Look" exercises urge readers to reflect on how it feels to use their power to change their actions and the lives of others.

Taken together, these powerful elements help readers understand how such a broad lack of healthy opportunities happened, as well as the source of the dilemma, and then offer a detailed process toward a solution.

## This Book Is for You

Just about everyone's lives are in some way touched by incarceration. And just about everyone can do something about the injustices this book discusses:

*Government administrators/bureaucracies at state, city, and county levels and individuals and units:* These people may be in community health (may include Medicaid), a Medicaid officer, or in Social Security (SSI programs), health and human services, behavioral health, public health departments, and public housing agencies/HUD.

*Elected officials:* Legislators are those who pass the laws that judges, lawyers, and criminal justice systems must enforce, even if they do not agree with them.

*Key personnel in schools of public health:* In particular, these are Department Chairs, who can mandate the book's use as a textbook for courses that have a theme of community development and health and in social work and psychology department courses.

*Presidents of academic institutions:* In particular, these are those with a mission of serving the underserved and who operate on our tax dollars (i.e., community colleges, technical schools, job corps programs, and all other types of educational institutions/postsecondary, including dental).

*Staff of jails, prisons, and other criminal justice systems, as well as the accrediting agencies:* These are judges, lawyers (prosecutors), Directors of Corrections, Directors of Reentry Services (probation and parole), and Commissioners of Public Safety.

*School personnel:* These are teachers/principals, school counselors (via American School Counselors Association), and school nurses (via National Assembly of School-based Health Centers).

*Private philanthropists:* This book offers critical opportunities for nongovernmental funding to make a real impact in the areas prioritized by the philanthropic community, as they have the ability to model new ways of attacking all problems.

*Media:* A critical segment of the primary market is traditional and new media (pundits, commentators, news reporters, and filmmakers who, to date, have ignored this story, which speaks of human devastation that compares favorably with, or exceeds, losses in wars or national disasters).

*Family, neighborhood, and community members:* I address, especially, those interested in history, politics, and racial and gender studies, as well as the millions who have recently stood up for social change, yet remain unsure of how to get involved.

*Beyond Stereotypes in Black and White* particularly speaks to those who care about the legacy we leave as individuals, as communities, and as a nation and those who place themselves in the lineage of sagacious, history-making risk-takers who make a difference. If you are a woman, a girl, or the parent of a young African American girl, you can see yourself and your future in these pages, by implication, since current estimates are that 42-45% of African American women will never marry and this is attributed to the hyper-incarceration of males.

## What You Will Get from This Book

The book will:

- Give you a sense of confidence and security by giving you the talking points needed to support your actions without fear of personal or political retribution.

- Dilute the hardened, engrained remnant that stereotypes men of color and is permissive of a system of separation and denigration.

- Counterbalance the political correctness that may be a major cause of the current travesties and may be embedded in racial profiling that has a disproportionate effect on African Americans.

- Give policymakers, who "perhaps" do not see the full impact of past policies, the means to use their influence and ability to act proactively and affirmatively to change policy.

- Help policymakers use the policies and windows of opportunity they have to make progress and not complain that they are constricted by the current system.

- Create opportunities for parents, teachers, community organizers, neighbors, co-workers, and all laypeople to redefine and develop themselves as new leaders who can create change.

- Provide readily available facts needed by those who work in government or who impact (or aspire to impact) governmental leadership.

- Tell compelling stories of the marginalization of African American boys and men and how health policy has historically excluded African American men and boys for reasons related to racial discrimination.

- Call attention to the need for public health to give greater attention to the health of poor men of color.

- Give policy makers and other decision-makers the opportunity to exercise leadership that will reverse the current trends of early morbidity and mortality seen in African American boys and men.

- Begin to reverse the catastrophic destruction of the African American family, cultivate family formation policy potential, and stem the tide of neighborhood disintegration.

- Provide a call to leadership that can assist municipalities in identifying those local and individual steps that improve the health and well-being of African American boys and men, as well as their families.

- Begin the reformation and dismantling of a criminal justice system of which benefits are based on the backs of African American boys and men and their families and communities.

- Move public conscience, one person at a time.

- Form the basis for a new civil rights struggle.

Poor black boys and men are the proverbial canaries in the coal mine not only for communities of color, but also for all Americans. Until we take a serious approach to our policy decisions as if everyone's health matters, we will continue to see the inequities visited on the families of this population and these inequities will . . . just as night follows day . . . slowly, but surely, negatively impact more and more of the majority population. When poor black boys and men are in ill health, the rest of us are not far behind if we do not get out of that coal mine together and begin to institute real change.

This book does not ask, "What should THEY do?" Rather, it probes the reader to ask, "What Should I do?" Genuine hope compels authentic local action. You do not have to be President of the United States, governor of one of the 50 states, or even a commissioner or legislator to make a substantive and permanent difference in the lives of those marginalized by poverty and adverse health and social policy.

You will notice that not all our heroes and leaders work directly with prisons or the incarcerated. Most, in fact, are in the "prevention" business, working to prevent black men and boys from being shuttled through the pipeline to prison in the first place. At the end of their stories, I have provided ways to find out more about their work. Why not start breaking through the stereotype of the person who is caring but silent by contacting them and telling them how much you admire their work? Perhaps you will even take the next step by offering to contribute to their work in some way. You do not need to re-invent the wheel or work for change alone.

Granted, when you do this kind of work, you run the risk of finding yourself in a lonely place. With every action there is a reaction, and the reaction might come from your friends, family, and colleagues; even the media separate from you or give you unwanted attention. Being an advocate, being tenacious, staying the course may bring you face to face with some who do not understand the issue or who are satisfied with the status quo. Persistence is everything in moving the needle on the issues, so you soldier on. Time changes all things, and, if you are patient, strategic, and even tactical in your work, you will achieve your goals and those who did not understand will once again be a part of your world. And along the path, you will add wonderful new friends and colleagues to your life. Believe me, I know!

In summary, *Beyond Stereotypes in Black and White* provides a voice from the vantage point of the boys and men themselves, as well as of leading key informants and advocates. *Beyond Stereotypes in Black and White* describes the situational and policy context, with data that have put African American boys and men on a perilous downward spiral and sets the parameters for leadership at every level of community, local and state bureaucracy, and national public policy to find a role for themselves in redressing this crucial and critical social issue. My major goal is a call to leadership and action versus more analysis of the issue and blaming the victim postures. Although "passing the buck" for the problem is the predominant response to the issue, this book evokes a new paradigm: Stand Up and Act in *your* space with the goal of ultimately changing the environment in which the current situation has been allowed to evolve.

This will not be a soothing book to read, but it will be a hopeful one. I ask you to ask yourself hard questions, to take a good, honest look at yourself and at others. I provide ways to help shatter your stereotypes of yourself, of people in power, and of African American boys and men. And then I guide you toward the specific steps you can take, no matter what your profession or standing in the community.

## Notes

1. *American Journal of Public Health*. Supplemental issue (Supplement 1), 2008; 98:S1–S202.
2. Bonczar, Thomas P. and Allen J. Beck. Bureau of Justice Statistics Special Report: Prevalence of Imprisonment in the U.S. Population, 1974–2001. August 2003.

3. "Portrait of Inequality: Black Children in America, 2011." Children's Defense Fund. http://www.childrensdefense.org/.

4. "Youth Development: Poverty and the Pipeline to Prison" and "Portrait of Inequality 2011: Black Children in America." Children's Defense Fund. http://www.childrensdefense.org/.

5. Ibid.

# PART ONE

# Losing the Race

# CHAPTER 1

# Addressing the Stereotypes

*"Every great dream begins with a dreamer. Always remember, you have within you the strength, the patience, and the passion to reach for the stars to change the world."*

—*Harriet Tubman*

*Meet Martin Jones.*

*Martin has a problem.*

*You may have seen Martin sitting near you during a typical long-slog wait to see a doctor in your local emergency room. A 79-year-old resident of the Vine City region of Atlanta, GA, he is well past retirement age, but Martin is unable to collect social security, because he has spent most of his working life in domestic service positions and his employers did not choose to contribute to the Social Security Administration and allow Martin to earn the federal retirement benefit. As a result, although he is a highly-skilled gardener, our most cherished safety net has no space for him, so he continues to work when he can get it.*

*In addition, Martin has no comprehensive health coverage, so Medicare and the emergency room are his best options to access any kind of medical care. He knows he is not getting the best treatment. Even after the notorious day-long wait for service, over-taxed doctors rush him in and out of their offices, make minimal efforts to listen to his concerns, and send him home in pretty much the same shape as when he walked in. Each trip to the waiting room leaves him swearing he will not return until his condition is again critical.*

*So, what is Martin's problem? It is not just his diabetes or the high blood pressure and chronic depression he carries through his days. Nor is Martin's problem easily summed up by simply glossing over such large concepts as "racial injustice," "systemic poverty," or "health disparities." Martin Jones' problem is "us." Those*

3

*of us, in what was called the Era of Hope based on the rhetoric surrounding the Obama election and presidency, who have so little hope to offer him as he approaches the end of his life.*

*As we reach the close of another decade of "change," our current cache of leaders, more racially and ethnically diverse than ever before in our nation's history, continue to have far too little to say about Martin's problems, other than to call them just that: "Martin's problems." The high profile, very visible national leaders and everyday people who are also leaders in their own place and space are saying even less that moves us toward the radical and transformative steps needed for a solution.*

*One of the worst aspects of Martin's story is that, although it is bleak, when placed in the context of his peers, Martin's got it pretty good. To wit:*

*Meet Jamal Mason.*

*He, too, has a problem.*

*Born nearly 50 years after Martin, in the same Vine City neighborhood of Atlanta, Georgia, Jamal Mason is a bright young man nearing 30 years of age and anxious to start his life over after having spent much of the past 18 years in and out of the criminal justice system. Jamal is not what you would call a violent man. What he is, however, according to many of those who would profess to be his leaders, is someone who has always been just a bit too impatient with the sorry set of cards he has been dealt.*

*Despite his smarts and keen intellectual curiosity, from the moment he entered kindergarten, Jamal was tracked into special education classes. Although Jamal entered school more than 30 years after the landmark* Brown vs. Board of Education *case mandated an end to school segregation, his kindergarten class was more than 90% African American children, most of whom were living well below the poverty line. At age 5, Jamal joined his cohort of the school's poorest boys who received very little formal training in anything but becoming streetwise and getting by, hustling, just trying to make a way out of a no way in system that seemed carefully catered to their exclusion.*

*After circling the track of suspensions, expulsions, and juvenile justice detentions, Jamal was finally convicted on a felony count of armed robbery. Although he was not actually armed, he served a minimum 10-year sentence, because he led the store owner to believe the pack of gum in his pocket was a gun. A week prior, with little education, no money, and a fractured family unable to support him, Jamal was released from Metro State Prison. As bad as Jamal's present situation is, his future looks even grimmer.*

*Jamal and Martin are about to meet each other in that same emergency waiting room. Jamal needs to see someone about the stabbing pain in his lower back. He can hardly stand for more than 10 minutes without pain. Martin woke up on his floor again this morning, feeling dizzy, with no memory of how he got there. Four hours into the wait, the two men strike up a conversation just outside the hospital doors over a cigarette: the only legal means of self-medication that Jamal can afford—and afford to share with Martin. They engage in friendly banter about who would wait longer and who should be treated first.*

## The More Things Change, the More They Stay the Same

Martin Jones and Jamal Mason are fictional characters, but they are based on very real people. Their experiences are not representative of all African American males, but they do point to a common set of circumstances and histories shared by men and boys of color, no matter what their social class. The past 60 years have witnessed a tremendous amount of change for people of color living in America, both male and female. In many ways, some groups are finding long-denied access to the American dream, but the sad reality for the majority of men and boys of color is that, despite a host of well-intentioned, well-publicized interventions, they are still left far behind.

The facts speak for themselves:

- Only 3 out of every 100 African American boys who enter kindergarten will graduate from college.[1]
- "Children who are struggling to read in the third grade are four times more likely to drop out of or not complete high school as classmates who are proficient readers. The dropout rate was highest for poor Black and Hispanic students at 31 and 33 percent respectively—or about 8 times the rate for all proficient readers." [2]
- African American men represent about 8% of 18- to 24-year-olds in the United States; however, in 2004, they made up only 2.8% of the undergraduates at the 50 leading public universities across the nation.[3]
- "53 percent of black male students drop out of high school without a diploma, compared to 22 percent of white males."[4]
- "75 percent of America's state prison inmates are high school dropouts." This includes an uncounted percentage who were either suspended, expelled, or otherwise never got the opportunity to either drop out or graduate because of interference from the criminal justice system.[5,6]

- A black boy born in 2001 has a 1 in 3 chance of going to prison during his lifetime, compared to the 1 in 17 chance faced by white boys born in the United States.[7,8]

- In impoverished urban areas, two-thirds of African American boys who reach their 15th birthday will not reach their 65th birthday—triple the average American rate of early death. The mortality rates of African American men who live in urban areas are in the range of men living in developing countries.[9]

- The "mortality rate from homicide for African American males ages 15-17 is 34.4 per 100,000, compared to a rate of 2.4 per 100,000 for non-Hispanic white males ages 15-17."[10]

- "Black children are more than three times as likely as white children to be born into poverty and to be poor, and are four times as likely to live in extreme poverty." In 2006, the net worth of black families was $6,100. The net worth of white families was $67,000.[11]

In spite of all the "progress" and money spent, the overall status of this population is not getting better. In fact, it is going in the wrong direction, even among the younger generations and the middle class. For example: in 1950, the cancer rate among African Americans was slightly lower than among whites (194.6/100,000 among whites compared to 176/100,000 among blacks), but, by 2000, the rate of cancer among African Americans was 30% higher (248.5/100,000) than for whites (197.2/100,000). And, even as American life expectancy continues to increase, progress remains slow for African Americans who now die at a rate comparable to that of whites 30 years ago.[12]

Those who would argue that the black middle class is exempt from these startling statistics would be sadly mistaken. Between 1960 and 1980, when African Americans saw the greatest rise in advancement compared with the pre-Civil Rights era, high school graduation rates climbed from 20% to greater than 50%. Yet, by 2001, those graduation rates had already slipped back down to 42.8%.[13]

In our American culture, it is generally accepted as a given that each generation will do better than the generation that preceded it. For young African American men and boys, this assumption is proving far from the truth. Although Jamal might have been somewhat better protected if he had come from a middle-class family, current research shows that his experiences would not have been significantly different. Some report that they have children entering kindergarten already reading and writing and African American boys who have never even held a pencil! All too often, African American boys are on what educators privately dub "the prison track."[14] They face much harsher discipline in public schools.[15] A recent report asserted that, in every state but Idaho, black students are suspended in numbers that far exceed their representation as a percentage of the student population. In 21 states, the percentage of black suspensions is more than double their percentage of the student body; nationally, on average, black students are suspended and expelled at nearly 3 times the rate of white students. More specifically, in "1999, 35 percent of all black students in grades 7-12 had been suspended or expelled" from school compared with 15% of white students.[16]

## Reality Check: Growing the American Economy: Jobs Anyone?

The private prison industry thrives on a steady supply of African American males, who account for 10% of all youth but 60% of incarcerated youth under 18 years of age. White males are incarcerated at a rate of 8.5 per 1,000, but that figure for African American males is 48.3 per 1,000. Consequently, the "school-to-prison" pipeline is often invoked as a metaphor to capture the seemingly inexorable progression of African American boys. The more African American preschool males there are in the United States, the more prisons will be needed when those young children become young adults. For the approximately 600,000 4-year-old African American males growing up in the United States in 2008, prisons are being planned to house 28,134 of them by 2029.[17]

Even those children who start life with a leg up often find themselves kicked back down the ladder. A pivotal report revealed that, of the sons and daughters of the black middle class, 45% of black children end up "near poor," compared with 16% of white families with similar socioeconomic advantages. The Pew report further showed that, although 68% of white children earn incomes above their parents, only 31% of African American children earn incomes greater than their parents. Contrary to the accepted American dream narrative, this trend of downward mobility has left the majority of middle-class black children looking forward to earning sharply lower incomes than those of their parents.[18]

Is it any wonder that a 2007 *ABC News/Washington Post* poll found that African American respondents, both male and female, of every age and social class were less optimistic about the future of black Americans than they were 20 years ago? *Every single group.*

This information is not shared to simply alarm. As Winston Churchill said, "Facts are better than dreams." Sometimes we need to know the facts, so we can be driven to act. The fact is that we are in the midst of

| ✔ REALITY CHECK  Income "Progress" |
|---|

Black Median Income as a Percentage of White Median Income:

| 2009: | 63% |
|---|---|
| 2007: | 65% |
| 2005: | 63% |
| 1995: | 62% |
| 1980: | 57%[1] |

1. U.S. Census Bureau. "Income Poverty and Health Insurance Coverage in the United States: 2009. Current Population Reports, P60-2238, and Historical Tables-Table H-5." September 2010. http://www.census.gov/.

a crisis that affects the growth and stability of *all* Americans. As was said during the Civil Rights movement, communities of color did not come this far by grace alone or even solely by the force of their own action or inaction. They have gotten a big push from the past 30 years of devastating public policy that has led to this spiraling crisis among men and boys of color—young and old, poor and not-so-poor. In 2009, even an internationally known and respected Harvard University professor, Henry Louis Gates, could be harassed and arrested in his own home for not addressing police officers with the proper amount of deference after they mistakenly accused him of breaking into what he informed them was his own home.[19]

The facts fly in the face of the "post-racial" society that we are quite pleased to pat ourselves on the back for having achieved; and we have achieved it. We have every right to be proud. But we cannot forget that, for every Barack Obama or Denzel Washington, there are millions of Jamal Masons caught in a policy-driven cycle of poverty, imprisonment, and disappearing opportunities that limit the life paths for young men of color. For every middle-aged African American man who has "made it" out of the spiral and away from a tough life in the inner city, nearly one-half of the children of such men are slowly finding themselves sucked back in.

## From Power Failure to Powerful Leadership

As our nation embraces the most racially and ethnically diverse leadership to ever reach the heights of power in history, what is reflected in the lives of far too many young men of color is the result of what I call a "power failure." Many African Americans who have managed to climb or be pushed up the ladder of success by those who believed in them are in position to know what is happening and to act . . . to use their power. Strangely, or even perversely, their very success may have made them less willing or able to speak up, act out, be different (other than in skin color), and sound a clarion call for action. Stereotyping holds them back. They fear, perhaps, being accused of focusing on and promoting issues of concern to the black community versus working solely on problems that face the majority of those in the nation. These African Americans who have escaped up the ladder of success from the mire of poverty and overt racial discrimination even come to believe that, if they act, they will be viewed as uncooperative, lacking leadership skills for the good of all. Although it is true that the patterns of the past that relied on "breaking" black men and women so they would conform were common practice, today, organizations want people who will lead to success. Speaking out without strategy, solid facts, and a strong network that may be outside of the workplace may be perilous. But being armed with tactics and political savvy, as well as undergirded by facts, will never redound harm to the individual. Fear of retribution directed toward a "pushy black woman" or so-called "threatening black man" emasculates both and undermines the future of everyone.

I have not written this book to repeat the sad stories that fill up nearly every street corner and jail cell in urban and rural America. Instead, I call on every one of us with the potential to lead in ways big and small, in our families and our communities, in our professional and civic lives. I want us to progress beyond stereotypical thinking—whether that relates to how we view others or how we view ourselves. The time has come for us to forcefully acknowledge and address the giant sucking sound created by a broken health care system, a predatory criminal justice system, a failing public education system, and a generation of leaders who have spent more time blaming the victims than engaging communities toward effective solutions.

This book exists to engage us all. What is the truth behind the false images and accusations flung daily by the media? For millions of young men of color living in America, theirs is not a land of promise and opportunity, but rather a painful and ongoing catastrophe, as the "Reality Checks" in each chapter attest. In the following chapters, I present "Leaders and Heroes"—role models for us to be inspired by and emulate. I also ask each of us to "Take a Good Look"—literally and figuratively—to face ourselves in the mirror, challenge our own culpability, and find out what we are doing that is working and what we are doing that is

**TAKE A GOOD LOOK   Getting beyond Stereotypes**

What stereotypes do you hold about young men of color? What stereotypes do you hold about yourself? Look in the mirror as you ask yourself the following questions:

- When I see a group of boys hanging out after school, what goes through my mind?

- Do I ever speak to them?

- If so, what do I say?

- If not, what do I wish I would said?

- What do I think and feel when a group of African American boys are walking toward me?

- Do I think differently about boys who are Latino or White?

- Am I less surprised when I hear about a crime in which an African American is accused?

- Am I more surprised when an African American receives an honor or is a well-regarded professional?

- What is the basis for my thoughts?

- What would I do if I were an African American boy and people usually crossed to the other side of the street when they saw me?

- What will I do or say the next time this happens?

widening the vacuum. Jamal and Martin are not actual people—but their lives are as real as can be. Their stories are heartbreaking and frustrating, but, as we will see, they are not without hope. Only when we honestly address our own stereotypes and prejudices, as well as the stark realities of a public policy legacy that continues to exact a crushing toll on an already vulnerable community, can we find the real power needed to engage in meaningful change.

You will learn about effective models for sustainable solutions, both current and historic, and explore the best practices in place around the country. You will discover in each chapter best opportunities for solution and success. This book is not the same old run-down of troubles already staring us all in the face. Nor is it simply a call to action. It is a chance to build, together, a roadmap for powerful leadership opportunities that will require us each to roll up our sleeves, individually and together, and buckle down to the radical work of solving Martin's and Jamal's problem. For as much as it is their problem, it is also our own problem.

Our most visionary leaders working on these issues today know that we are not going to have resolution over the next 2 years or 10 years. Protecting our young men and rebuilding our communities require a long-term committed focus, and that is what they have committed to doing. In this book, people like Joe Brooks, Doug Lomax, Tony Iton, and others talk about leadership in ways that only experienced leaders can. They focus on building supportive and effective networks, being flexible with the approach to intervention strategy, taking a panoramic view rather than isolating single symptoms and treating them out of context, and capitalizing on opportunities as they arise.

Whether we exercise leadership over no one but our own children or over millions of dollars in state-wide budgets, we can take a cue from their examples.

## Notes

1. Wynn, Mychal. "Black Male Acheivement." Rising Sun Publishing. 2007. www.rspublishing.
2. Baron, Kathryn. "Poverty + poor reading = dropout: 3rd grade reading is good predictor." Silicon Valley Education Foundation. http://toped.svefoundation.org.
3. Ross, Lawrence C. "One dropout every 26 seconds is ticking time bomb for blacks." The Grio. April 6, 2011. http://thegrio.com./
4. Ross, Lawrence C. "One dropout every 26 seconds is ticking time bomb for blacks." The Grio. April 6, 2011. http://thegrio.com/.
5. Karwath, Rob. "Study Links High Dropout Rate to State Prison Overcrowding." *Chicago Tribune*, September 15, 1991.
6. U.S. Department of Education. "Trends in High School Dropout and Completion Rates in the United States: 1972–2009." http://nces.ed.gov/pubs2012/2012006.pdf.
7. Children's Defense Fund. "Cradle to Prison Pipeline Campaign." www.childrensdefense.org.
8. Kerby, Sophia. "1 in 3 Black Men Go To Prison? The 10 Most Disturbing Facts about Racial Inequality in the U.S. Criminal Justice System." *The American Prospect*, March 17, 2012.
9. Geronimus, AT, Bound, J, Colen, CG. "Excess Mortality in the United States and in Selected Black and White High-Poverty Areas, 1980–2000." *American Journal of Public Health* 101(4), 2011.

10. The Henry J. Kaiser Family Foundation. "Race, Ethnicity & Health Care Fact Sheet." http://www.kff.org/minorityhealth/upload/7541 .pdf.
11. The Morehouse Male Initiative. "Statistics on African-American males." http://morehousemaleinitiative.com/?page_id=178.
12. The Office of Minority Health. "A Strategic Framework for Improving Racial/Ethnic Minority Health and Eliminating Racial/Ethnic Health Disparities." http://minorityhealth.hhs.gov
13. Greene, Jay P. "High School Graduation Rates in the United States." Manhattan Institute for Policy Research. http://www.manhattan institute.org/. Revised 2002.
14. Kirp, David L. "Bridging the Achievement Gap." *Los Angeles Times*, September 22, 2010.
15. Lewin, Tamar. "Black Students Face More Discipline, Data Suggests." *The New York Times*, March 6, 2012.
16. Witt, Howard. "School Discipline Tougher on African Americans." *Chicago Tribune*, September 25, 2007.
17. Barbarin, Oscar A. "Halting African American Boys' Progression from Pre-K to Prison: What Families, Schools, and Communities Can Do!" *American Journal of Orthopsychiatry* 80(2010):81–88.
18. Pew Research Center Publications. "Blacks See Growing Values Gap Between Poor and Middle Class." November 13, 2007. http://pew research.org/pubs.
19. Thompson, Krissah. "Harvard Scholar Henry Louis Gates Arrested." *Washington Post*, July 21, 2009. www.washingtonpost.com/.

CHAPTER 2

# Communities in Crisis

*"People are often afraid to talk about poverty, but I grew up in poverty and I'm not afraid to talk about it."*
        —*Donna Brazile, Democratic political strategist,*
                *syndicated columnist, political commentator,*
                *and Managing Director, Brazile & Associates, LLC*

*Martin and Jamal stub out their cigarettes with a last laugh and head back into the emergency room waiting area. They reclaim their seats, near each other but with a generous amount of space between them. As Martin begins to doze, Jamal looks around at the growing crowd that continues to fill the waiting room: mothers and children, men and women sitting alone or with friends, many holding blood-soaked t-shirts to open wounds.*

*The looks on the faces surrounding Jamal each express their own quiet version of defeat. The wait drags on and he watches Martin sleep, feeling protective of his new friend. Finally, he begins to lose himself in his thoughts, planting dreams for an uncertain future, to pass the time.*

Over the past few years, people across the country have been slowly waking to the reality of a growing crisis in our health care system. Discussions are taking place in public forums and around private kitchen tables about the frightening course of chronic disease, the high cost of health care, and the often-frustrating lack of quality, accessible, affordable treatment. The numbers of Americans going without basic access to prevention and treatment is growing faster than we can count. Yet, even as we try, there are large swaths of people who fall daily between the ever-widening cracks.

I started the Community Voices (www.communityvoices.org) initiative, with the generous support and assistance of the W.K. Kellogg

Foundation, in an effort to stem the tide that threatens to carry communities of color quickly past the point of no return. From research labs to funding offices to the direct programming that Community Voices provides, my commitment to working in support of health and wellness has brought me face-to-face with the realities of a community in crisis. At every turn, in neighborhood after neighborhood, from clinic sites to medical symposia, I began to notice the frequency with which my colleagues and myself would turn to each other with the same question: *Where are the men?*

They were not in the clinics accessing services. They were not at home with their families. They were neither in the schools receiving medical training nor learning to provide either critical care or technical support. They were neither in the meetings nor were they even on the agenda. Instead, what began to pile up was a troubling assortment of statistics. Men and boys of color, especially African American men and boys, have long been disproportionately represented among the underserved and uninsured. The numbers of uninsured African American men are quickly matched by those of Latino and Hispanic descent. As the demographics of our national community continue to shift, the numbers of uninsured, uncounted, and underserved in a variety of marginalized communities are on a steady upswing.

For years now, when I step outside of my door, I find myself greeted by the long hissing sound that fills the streets where I live, where I work, and where my programs carry out their outreach efforts. That sound, which has been audible all of my life, has been growing louder the past 20 years. This sound is neither one of opportunity or achievement, nor does it carry the gentle whistle of the promised land. Instead, it is the slow sucking vacuum pulling boys and men out of their communities and away from their own innate sense of hope for a life of opportunity and fulfillment.

## Disappearing Optimism

Millions of boys and young men of color quickly outgrow the optimism that should be the playground of every child raised in a society with advantages such as ours. When we consider that these are children who come from communities that have fought so hard and at such great cost for an equal shot at those opportunities, then the sense of despair only grows stronger. In the place of that optimism creeps a devastating disbelief in the self. It is here that violence, disease, and early death quickly breed and suck away at the spirit, leaving countless empty shells wandering the streets, desperate to find wholeness again.

**REALITY CHECK  The College v. Prison Myth**

Even President Obama got this figure wrong: Young black men between the ages of 18 and 24 attending college outnumbered those incarcerated by 4 to 1 in 2005.[1]

Still, more than 10% of young black men in that age group are in prison or jail—far too many—particularly since black men are sent to prison on drug charges at 13 times the rate of white men.[2]

_____

1. Dobbs, Michael. "What Obama Got Wrong." *Washington Post.* December 14, 2007.
2. Human Rights Watch. "Targeting Blacks." http://www.hrw.org/reports/2008/05/04/targeting-blacks.

Although we know the oft-quoted "statistic" that there are more black men in prison than in college is untrue (see Reality Check above for the facts), far too many young men of color are roped early and often into a corrections system that sacrifices their health and well being. Instead of being guided along the track of health and wellness, they are allowed to sink into the clutches of early, preventable death. Having been told this is the best they can expect, many begin to behave accordingly, leaving women and families stunned by the echo of emptiness around them, where once had been the deep peals of laughter, hard-working support, and the loving arms that build a home.

## Fractured Homes

In the African American community, the number of fractured homes is shooting up at a rate that would make any suburban developer jealous. Ongoing studies continue to report the sharp and continued decline in marriage opportunities for African American women. With the lowest interracial marriage rate of any group, African American women are most sharply affected by the disappearance of healthy, available African American men with whom to partner. In 2011, according to data from the Centers for Disease Control and Prevention (CDC), 72% of black children are born outside of wedlock.[1] Reasons for this situation are based on education, economics, and incarceration of the black male.[2] Shockingly, Andrew J. Cherlin, a sociologist at Johns Hopkins University and specialist in early-20th-century African American marriage and families, has noted that black children were more likely to grow up living with both parents *during slavery* than today.[3]

Although marriage rates have been dipping for every group since the 1960s, African Americans currently have the lowest marriage rate of any racial group in the country. Between 1970 and 2001, according to U.S. Census counts, although the average marriage rate declined by 17%, African Americans saw a drop of twice that—34%—leaving 43.3% of black men and 41.9% of black women in the "never married" category. Marriage rates are not only declining in black households. Among Latinos, census data shows a 5-15% drop in marriage rates when comparing U.S. and foreign-born Latino/a men and women, suggesting that, after generations of exposure to systemic racism American-style, Latinos/as, whose marriage rates are generally lower than whites, yet higher than blacks, begin slipping closer to the rates of African Americans.[4]

Throughout my career, I have been singularly focused on ensuring that everyone has a good shot at a healthy life. What has emerged through my work, and the work of so many others who are sounding the alarm, are the gaping holes in which critical data on communities of color should have been. When I first began researching men's health disparities, I was alarmed at what I saw, yet I could not even tell my colleagues everything that was wrong because nobody had bothered to collect the information. What I did have in abundance was a heartbreaking mountain of anecdotal data and the testimonies of others who had been witnessing the disappearance of men and boys from the community. I was not alone in hearing that slow, sucking sound. Even if I could not yet offer my colleagues in the field of public health hard data to back it up, I could still tell them what I saw.

What I saw were poor families headed by women who worked extremely hard just to keep their families and themselves intact, while wading through the deepest marshes of poverty. I saw married couples who had struggled hard to "make it" only to find themselves having to fight even harder to keep their own children from being sucked away by the vacuum created by a poor and discriminating educational system, an indifferent and often abusive media environment, and a criminal justice system stacked against them at odds far greater than three strikes. I saw grandparents desperate for help to raise their grandchildren, having already lost their own children to the violence, substance abuse, disease, and incarceration that began sweeping the streets of young men and women with renewed vigor in the 1980s.

With few exceptions, the policy framework that struggling men and their families encounter is not one that was established for or is engaged in their best interests. Instead, there is a whole lot of finger-wagging and

**REALITY CHECK** *Money Matters*

African American men are struggling to support themselves and their families:

- African American men earn less than 75% percent of the salaries earned by white men.[1]

- 27% of African Americans live below the poverty line—*3 times* the number of poor whites.[2]

- African Americans, in the 2 years prior to incarceration, tended to earn less than whites. After incarceration, the gap between black and white hourly wages not only still existed, but it increased over time.[3]

1. Bureau of Labor Statistics. "Usual Weekly Earnings of Wage and Salary Workers: First Quarter 2012." http://www.bls.gov/news.release/pdf/wkyeng.pdf.
2. Desmond-Harris, Jenée. "27 Percent of Blacks Below Poverty Line." The Root. September 15, 2011. http://www.theroot.com/buzz/27-million-blacks-under-poverty-line.
3. Criminological Highlights. "The Gap Between the Earnings of Black and White Americans Increases after Imprisonment." http://www.criminology.utoronto.ca/lib/CrimHighlightsV12N3.pdf.

an overwhelming attitude of punitive responses in the guise of solutions for what is seen not as a community in crisis and in need of positive, healthful interventions, but as a community of poorly bred, out of control, bad actors in need of correction.

## Unfair Drug Policies

The 1980s brought us a "war on drugs" that could more aptly be described as a war on the African American community. Disproportionate mandatory sentencing laws and predatory policing procedures led to prison cells swollen past capacity with small-time drug offenders who had been swept off the streets of poor communities. The little fish filled the jails, while the big sharks roamed free under now-infamous—and still active—policies that brought about a sharp spike in disproportionate numbers of African Americans being sent to prison for first-time and/or minor offenses.

For instance, in 1986, U.S. Congress passed federal guidelines enforcing a 100-to-1 sentencing disparity between crack and powder cocaine, which are simply different forms of the same drug and have similar effects on the body. A person would have to possess 500 grams (more than a pound) of powder cocaine—which only the very wealthy could afford to do—to obtain the same mandatory 5-year sentence handed down for just 5 grams of crack cocaine, an amount that sizes up to about one-half of your thumb. To further the discriminatory effect, actual sentences handed down have little to do with actual rates of drug use and sales and seem to depend more on the color of the person standing before the judge.

Civil rights advocate and lawyer Michelle Alexander, in her best-selling book, *The New Jim Crow: Mass Incarceration in the Age of Colorblindness*, connects the dots between unequal enforcement, the drug war, and how that reinforces poverty, asserting that the crackdown was less a response to the actual explosion of violent crime than a deliberate effort to push back the gains of the civil rights movement. She writes:

> What has changed since the collapse of Jim Crow has less to do with the basic structure of our society than with the language we use to justify it. In the era of colorblindness, it is no longer socially permissible to use race, explicitly, as a justification for discrimination, exclusion, and social contempt. So we don't. Rather than rely on race, we use our criminal justice system to label people of color "criminals" and then engage in practices we supposedly left behind.[5]

The war on drugs had devastating, innumerable consequences on the black community, far beyond the reality of incarceration and substance abuse, but it was not alone. Once someone is ensnared in the criminal justice system, it becomes increasingly impossible to get free. The Wisconsin Racial Disparities Project reported that the sharp increase in rates

 **REALITY CHECK** **Crack Cocaine Arrests v. Users**

Proportion of those sentenced under federal crack cocaine laws in 2006:

Black: 82%

White: 8.8%

This is despite the fact that more than two-thirds of people who use crack cocaine are white.[1]

1. The Sentencing Project. "Criminal Justice Primer: Policy Priorities for the 111th Congress. 2009." http://www.sentencingproject.org/doc/publications/cjprimer2009.pdf.

HISTORY OF CHANGE   **SANDRA BARNHILL, ATTORNEY**

Sandra Barnhill's work as a public interest attorney brought her in contact with women who had been sentenced to prison, as well as their children and families. While working with incarcerated mothers, Barnhill became so frustrated by the lack of support given to mothers sentenced to prison—as well as the families left behind—that she left her job in 1987 and founded an organization dedicated to providing the information and support that families sorely needed.

The organization was originally known as Aid to Imprisoned Mothers (AIM), but the more Barnhill and her colleagues worked with mothers, the more they heard, "If you want to help me, help my children." Taking the cue of the women they were dedicated to serving, AIM expanded its focus to include meeting the unique needs of the children of incarcerated parents.

Twenty years after founding the organization, it expanded its work even further to include working with imprisoned fathers and their children. The expanded organization, Foreverfamily, provides families with transportation for parental visitations, counseling for children, after-school programs, teen leadership programs, advocacy, and more.

Barnhill is a dedicated, soft-spoken woman who saw injustice and resolved to do something about it. She does not get a lot of attention or publicity. Instead, she focuses on getting results. Studies have shown that children of incarcerated parents are more than 7 times more likely to go to prison themselves—97% of the children involved in Foreverfamily programs avoid this fate.

of African Americans incarcerated was tied to repeated revocation of probation and parole for minor offenses, such as unemployment, vagrancy, and traffic violations. With everything stacked up against men and boys re-entering society after incarceration, once they reach the outside of the prison gates, they must immediately balance themselves on a slippery slope that, if they fail to find secure footing, leads directly back to prison.

## Welfare Reform

The 1990s brought us welfare reform, which was long celebrated as a massive success. Banners were flown, and public housing projects were raised, while millions cheered the booting of so-called lazy black "welfare queens" from public assistance. Just as the facts proved that far more whites used crack cocaine than blacks, the numbers overwhelmingly showed that whites received more welfare than blacks. Still, black women—and their "deadbeat dad" partners—became the face of welfare and the recipients of public outrage.

The success of policies stripping aid from those who needed it most were celebrated with much touted stories of black women getting back to work, but the question few dared to ask was "what happened to their children once they were gone and could not care for them?" The millions who simply vanished from the only communities they had to support them were also not up for discussion. More than a decade later, we have yet to fully examine the correlating effect of a family's inability to thrive when it meets the removal of the last rung of support, the forced removal of one of the primary breadwinners, and any hopes of moving up and out being swept away from yet another new generation. We are living with the results every day, and our recent economic recession has only made the situation more urgent.

## Power Failure

It is clear that we did not arrive at this place by grace alone. Instead, a complex set of public policy decisions and a grotesque failure to act on the part of community, public policy, and public health leadership has left a trail of destroyed families, lives, and communities in its wake. It is long past time to stand up and do something about it.

The 21st century has presented us with innumerable opportunities to create real change and daunting challenges to halt our progress. Although there are those who would linger in the 19th and 20th centuries and their antediluvian policies and practices, most of us who are in contact with the communities suffering most realize there is little to gain by dwelling in the past with its strictures and marginalization. I originally coined the term "power failure," alongside my friend and Kellogg Foundation colleague, Barbara Sabol, to describe our concern about a lack of leadership on critical public health issues as related to our most vulnerable groups of people. The face of the nation is changing, and, along with that change, we are long overdue for a revision in our priorities to align with the hopes, dreams and needs of emerging majorities, many of whom, despite years of national prosperity, have been left to cling to the margins.

Our work with men and boys of color, far too many of whom remain at the bottom of the ladder in terms of chronic and continuing health inequities and crushing denials of real life opportunities, forced Barbara and me to echo over and again, in meetings and roundtables around the country, the numerous facets to this problem. One of the first was that, in most of those very meetings, there were very few people of color represented. Of those people of color, fewer still were men.

It became quickly apparent that one reason this crisis was allowed to continue unaddressed was that those who could speak most eloquently for men and boys on the margins—men of color themselves—were either not present, kept silent, or had chosen to assert their power elsewhere. This is another fact of how power failure works: we fail to identify and develop new leaders and create opportunities for emerging leaders to work with mentors and supporters who can identify most closely with them.

This was not always the case. As we see in examples throughout this book, communities of color in this country have a long history of inspirational leadership that reaches down to lift a new generation into place. This is how we have survived despite the numerous forces that fought to deny our humanity, our existence, and our human and civil rights.

I have been fortunate to see a great shift happening over the past few decades: a shift in leadership and a shift in opportunity. Our country has once again entered into a heated debate about reforming our outdated, ineffective health care system. Some congressional leaders wish to pretend that everyone in the nation has access to health care, but their statements are directly contradicted by the evidence of scores of millions going without.

Others would have us believe that most of those who do not have insurance could get it if they just got a job or if they were responsible enough to pay for it. These discussions are often cloaked in lofty statements about what "the American people think" or what "the American people want." Where this conversation succeeds most is in making the millions of people, including the poorest among us, and, disproportionately, men of color who have *never* had health coverage disappear. Millions of the working poor have never had access to employer-provided insurance. Government-sponsored programs, such as Medicaid, which cover mothers and children, deliberately exclude men older than 18 years of age, while numbers continue to show the devastating effects of medical costs on their ability to work and provide for a family.

In Georgia alone, one in three people were uninsured in 2007 and 2008.[6] That number, nearly 3 million, doubled since 2005—just 2 years before. This was before the economic recession took hold. Here in Georgia, as in most of the country, minorities, men, young and low-income adults are disproportionately concentrated among the uninsured. Nonelderly Latinos—including children—were more than twice as likely as African Americans, and more than 3 times as likely as whites to be uninsured. Despite the rhetoric, low-income adults have few, if any, realistic options for private health coverage. The high-deductible options available have prohibitively high premiums, often far exceeding even the minimum wage, while offering minimal coverage options.

Leadership potentiates change at every level. Although our current leadership, those who are commissioners, mayors, principals of schools, and bureaucrats wielding the power of the budget and the purse in public administration, are arguably the most diverse in our nation's history, there are many left sitting, reverberating in the echo of a deafening silence around the realities faced by millions of Americans stuck in a dead end cycle of poverty, incarceration, chronic disease, and early death. Men and boys of color, in general, and African American men and boys, especially, are decades behind white men and boys and both white and black women in achieving the realities of improved health that our current medical and technological advances should endow.

Although the U.S. population has grown by more than 75 million since 1980, the most telling shift has been in the numbers behind the numbers. Although Black, Asian, and "other" categories have shown steady growth, the numbers of Hispanic and Latino Americans have more than doubled. The numbers for working class whites are estimated to drop between 1980 and 2020 from 82 to 63%.[7] The demographics of the country have changed community by community, state by state, and so has the face of leadership.

On the national level, the numbers are still rather abysmal: only one African American U.S. Senator and only two Latinos, two Asian Americans, and no Native Americans in the Senate. In the U.S. House of Representatives, the numbers come just a bit closer to representing the demographics, but not by much. Although we have the first African American U.S. President and Attorney General and the first Latina in the Supreme Court, among actual lawmakers at the federal levels, we still have quite a way to go. African Americans currently represent 10% of the elected officials in the House of Representatives. Latinos represent 5%, and Asian Americans and Native Americans together represent just over 1% by lumping together the single Native American and five Asian American congressional representatives.[8]

The truth, however, is that national leadership is only a small part of the story. Much of the public policy that actually affects the health and wellness of men of color is made at the local and state levels, where an explosion of people of color in leadership, both public officials and public servants, continues to take place. However, despite the growing representation of racial diversity in local leadership, nearly every region of the country— North, South, East, West, and off-shore island—is facing growing disparities between social and medical progress and marginalized communities who see none of the benefits of that progress. In communities across the

## TAKE A GOOD LOOK  Parents

Are you a parent? If not, can you imagine what it is like to be a parent? Look in the mirror and ask yourself:

- When you see a single black woman raising her children, what do you assume about her life? If she is clearly struggling, what is your response?

- What are you doing to help her or her children? What would you like for someone to do to help, if it were you?

- What skill do you have that you would use to engage children whose parents are struggling and their families?

- Does your job or career offer you opportunities to improve the lives of those who are struggling? If not, why not? If so, what can you do?

- What do you fear from your peers, if you reach out to help those that are barely surviving at the margins?

- Write one thing you are willing to do to support families in crisis in your community—then get busy: _____

_____

country, the vacuum continues to sweep men out of their families, out of schools, off the streets, and far away from their dreams.

These boys and men are not only vanishing from their neighborhoods and communities, they are vanishing from the conversation. These men are not clueless. They know they are being erased from the conversation. As it becomes simply one more kitchen table conversation to which he is clearly not invited, the African American man begins to tune out, to focus his attention on the pressing needs, including his own lack of care and how to address it. Our leaders must begin to think about the real cost— not only to the communities themselves, but to all of us—of continuing to ignore a large and growing segment of our population.

## The Potential to Lead

I have an unwavering belief in the people and communities with whom I work, and I am committed to providing a guiding light to develop new leaders at every level. I have continued to expand my own work in this area not only out of self-interest—I am the mother of sons and daughters, and they have their own children to raise healthy and strong too. The issue reaches farther than my own, or any of our own families. Whether or not we come from or live within a community of color, whether or not our families have ever been touched by the sting of the correctional system, whether or not we have health insurance or chronic disease, this crisis affects us all. And the numbers continue to climb.

One of the things I was taught since I was a child myself is that each of us has the potential to lead. Not only are millions suffering, but they are drowning in a sea of isolation and invisibility, cloaked in the fog of no-way-out. As a health professional, I recognize this as a public health crisis of the highest order, yet it is also much larger. This is a civil rights crisis, it is a spiritual crisis, and it is a cultural crisis that everyone in this country has ownership of. Our brothers and sons, potential husbands, doctors, engineers, and schoolteachers, are not simply disappearing from the health care roles—they are vanishing from the entire community at an alarming rate. It has been happening for decades, and it is currently going from bad to worse.

We have to tell the stories of people like Martin and Jamal, and we have to do the empirical research that continues to produce the data that will drive our leaders to act. But just as we could not wait for the data to get to work, if we wish to have a real impact on the healthy lives of men and boys of color, then we cannot approach it simply from a health perspective. We have to begin to take into account the whole life of a person.

Men and women are not simply their cardiovascular system, their brain, or the muscles in their legs. Our health is impacted by the entirety of our lives, and vice versa. For men and boys of color, this simple fact— understood and practiced since the dawn of medicine—opens up a can of worms that few have yet been willing to address. That "can" has many labels with nice names like *disparities* and *disproportionate representation* and even *discrimination*. The reality at the root of the unequal health and life opportunities for men and boys of color, however, can sadly still be boiled down, in most instances, to one unpleasant word: racism.

---

LEADERS AND HEROES

## DEBORAH KOENIGSBERGER, PARENT, FASHION INDUSTRY STYLIST, AND FOUNDER OF HEARTS OF GOLD

Deborah Koenigsberger spends a great deal of her time and energy helping dramatically and permanently improve the lives of hundreds of homeless women and children. The nonprofit organization she founded supports existing programs at various

New York City shelters and creates new programs based on the needs of each individual shelter. Dollars go directly to those in need, helping them get through the day and beyond. Once families move out of shelters and are on their own, moms are eligible to join the Alumni Support Group at which they get continued support with the essentials needed to sustain productive lives.

It was not always this way. Deborah Koenigsberger "worked extensively as a stylist in the fashion industry before founding Noir et Blanc, a women's clothing boutique in Manhattan featuring fashion forward yet classic European collections." Her accomplishments have been recognized on NBC News and in the press. As she tells us, there is more to life than fashion and accolades.

"I would walk down the street from my home to my store, and I used to see a mom and her children living in a cardboard box," recalls Koenigsberger. The sight of them sleeping in boxes on a cold winter's night with no food, medical attention, or companionship became increasingly distressing, but, she says, "I didn't think that I could do anything except give her food. I did not know that I could affect change. These were struggling people who were no longer just on the margins; they had fallen off of the edge. I began to wonder what I could do to help them."

In 1996, she founded Hearts of Gold (HoG), whose mission is "to foster sustainable change in lifestyle and levels of self-sufficiency for homeless mothers and their children." Utilizing her contacts in the fashion industry, Koenigsberger has "successfully organized the donation of hundreds of thousands of dollars worth of merchandise and financial support to various New York City shelters." Funding comes through an annual fundraising event and through the Hearts of Gold Thrift Store just two doors down from Koenigsberger's regular boutique. Fundraising dollars go "toward a variety of programs that assist in the progression from homeless to transformational housing resident, and ultimately, self-sufficient member of society."

"Many of these women and children have been victims of domestic violence. Some mothers have additional children living away from them either in the foster care system or with other family members." The husbands, the fathers, have gone missing. Koenigsberger and her organization seek to halt the downward spiral and family conditions that set African American boys and men on the road to incarceration.

Koenigsberger believes that if "the playing field is really level, everyone will achieve. Equal opportunity creates self-confident people who go out into the workforce and do something significant for themselves and for our world." But, in the community in which she works, people do not get the opportunity. She also notes that those who succeed have had someone in their lives who said, "You can do this." Although her parents did not have an advanced education, they pushed her to "reach for a star."

(continued)

LEADERS AND HEROES

## DEBORAH KOENIGSBERGER, PARENT, FASHION INDUSTRY STYLIST, AND FOUNDER OF HEARTS OF GOLD (*continued*)

One thing HoG will do this year is take some children up to Yale University; one of Koenigsberger's children attends Yale, and she wants her "other children" to see the campus, to begin to dream, to see themselves at that institution. She hopes it will motivate them to study, to stay the course even on difficult days. "Community colleges are very important," Koenigsberger says, "but, IF you can go to Yale, go there!"

She offers sane advice to parents and ordinary citizens: "You think because you can't fix a problem, then you should just do nothing. Take a small bite of the problem. Volunteer. This country could run on volunteerism. Ask your kids who seem to be struggling, who needs help. Sometimes the problems that families face are huge! But you can work on just that little bit. Get some kids together, and start a book club. Teach a child to crochet, if that is all you know how to do. Everybody knows how to do something: teach that, share that!"

"People are out there in communities looking for a vehicle to do something. People are glad to jump on a happy bandwagon. The bottom line is that we must all share either 'time or treasure,' but what people desperately need is human touch. There is a celebratory aspect to life that matters. When someone is doing something for you, it feels good."

In conclusion, Koenigsberger says, "I have grown. I have learned. I could not look the other way and live with myself as mother, wife, and member of our global community. I have raised two amazing boys who are good citizens, because they have learned by simply reaching and sharing their time and their treasure with others who have less but who want and even deserve much, much more."[1]

---

1. Hearts of Gold. Available at http://www.heartsofgold.org.

---

## Notes

1. National Center for Health Statistics. "Health, United States, 2011: With Special Feature on Socioeconomic Status and Health." Hyattsville, MD. 2012. http://www.cdc.gov/nchs/data/hus/hus11 .pdf#007.
2. Perry, Imani. "Blacks, Whites and the Wedding Gap." *New York Times*, September 16, 2011. http://www.nytimes.com/.

3. Cherlin, Andrew. *Marriage, Divorce, Remarriage*. Cambridge: Harvard University Press, 1981.
4. Copen, Casey E., Kimberly Daniels, Jonathan Vespa, and William D. Mosher. "First Marriages in the United States: Data From the 2006–2010 National Survey of Family Growth." *National Health Statistics Report* No. 49, March 22, 2012.
5. Alexander, Michelle. *The New Jim Crow: Mass Incarceration in the Age of Colorblindness*. New York: The New Press, 2010.
6. Families USA. "New Report Finds 2.9 Million Georgians Were Uninsured at Some Point in 2007–2008." http://www.familiesusa.org/.
7. The National Center for Public Policy and Higher Education. "Per Capita Income of U.S. Workforce Projected to Decline IF Education Doesn't Improve." http://www2.ed.gov/about/bdscomm/list/hiedfuture/reports/equity.pdf.
8. ThisNation.com. "The United States Congress Quick Facts." http://thisnation.com/congress-facts.html.

# Sick and Tired

## The Killer Disease of Racism

*"Equity means that no group has poorer health due to reasons outside its control, but within society's control."*
— *Meizhu Lui, Director, Closing the Racial Wealth Gap Initiative at the Insight Center for Community Economic Development, Oakland*

*Martin, feeling a bit better than this morning since having coffee and snacks from the hospital vending machines, is still a bit shaky. He is seen first. Doctors tell Martin his fainting spells are a result of severe drops in his glucose levels— his diabetes is speaking loudly and clearly and insisting that he keep his "sugar" in check.*

*A nurse walks him through monitoring his blood sugar levels. She gives him a handful of papers explaining the importance of good diet, nutrition, and exercise for managing diabetes, and once again he is sent on his way. There will be no follow-up visit. He is instructed to check online for more information, but after informing the technicians that he does not own a computer, he is told to read the paperwork and "eat right."*

*Two hours later, having been bumped down the list several times by more critical cases, Jamal is escorted into an examination room. His back still aches, but the spasms have been slightly minimized by taking the maximum daily allowance of over-the-counter pain medication. Jamal's examination by the emergency room doctor on rotation is quick and to the point. He is given some samples of additional painkillers and told to "take it easy."*

*Yet Jamal will not let the doctor walk briskly back through the door. Unfortunately, the doctor says, there is no more he could do for him tonight. Before he leaves, a kind nurse hands him the address of a community health clinic at which*

29

*she and a friend occasionally volunteer their time. She tells Jamal that one of the doctors who came into the clinic on Saturdays may be able to help him. Jamal takes the slip of paper and heads out into the night, feeling no better than he had when he first walked through the doors 2 hours ago.*

U.S. census data shows that young men of color represent more than 40% of American males younger than 25 years of age. In the United States, African American men and boys have the lowest life expectancy and highest mortality rate among men and women among all other racial or ethnic groups. In fact, the mortality rates of African American men who live in urban areas are in the range of men living in developing countries.[1]

---

 HISTORY OF CHANGE  **MIDIAN O. BOUSFIELD, PHYSICIAN**

In 1933, Dr. Midian O. Bousfield (1885–1948) became the first African American to address the American Public Health Association in its 60-year history. A 1909 graduate of Northwestern University Medical School and president of the National Medical Association, Bousfield fought tirelessly for both whites and blacks to take up the mantel of addressing black health issues in America and told whites they must not only do the work, but do it while showing respect for the black community for whom they were charged to work.

---

As shameful as these facts are, we did not get to this place in history with astounding health disparities by chance. This progressive move toward sustained crisis has not been random. A steady hand has been on the tiller—the hand of racism.

## The Reality of Racism

Harvard University health researcher Nancy Krieger stated it plainly while speaking for the "Unnatural Causes" documentary project. "To understand the legacies of the different aspects and time periods of racism in this country," she said, "you have to understand that it's about power; it's about property; it's about privilege; it's about control; it's about whether people are restricted to living under conditions that are inadequate for living a healthy, dignified life."[2]

The reality is that people of color suffer the real and lasting effects of racism at every turn and in every arena of their lives. Not only are there personal effects, but also the combined effects of social and institutional racism as felt through their friends, families, and communities. Because actual racial discrimination is so widely underreported, studying the ramifications of racism on health has been a complicated enterprise; however, many tenacious researchers are doing just that, and their findings are fascinating.

For instance, studies show that, among immigrants of color, the longer they live in the United States, the more deeply they and their children understand the realities of U.S. racism. What was originally thought to be a situation of simple interpersonal prejudice is understood, through experience, to be a much more deeply seated institutional system of ingrained discrimination that impacts children and adults at every stage of their lives.

Racism is a multi-faceted, complex, historical and contemporary phenomenon that adversely affects health in many ways. Whether it is physical exposures to dangerous environments and neighborhoods through violence or toxic chemicals, or sustained exposure to hazardous workplaces, or lack of access to appropriate medical and dental care, the impact of racism is immediate, sustained, and long lasting. The environmental and institutional impacts are *in addition* to the psychological impact of interpersonal prejudice and discrimination.

Ongoing research continues to show that the effects, rather than being less than we previously thought, are even more devastating. "It's many things: job exposures, neighborhood exposures, the exposures that your parents had that then get passed on to subsequent generations." Krieger continued, "*racism* may be a relatively short word but it encompasses a whole lot, and it can't be understood as simply about interpersonal reactions."[3]

Unfortunately, attempts to wash away the realities of racism on the bodies of men, women, and children too often include floating, underexplored and unproven theories about innate genetic differences between the bodies of people of color and those of whites. We have all seen the news reports: Hispanic and Latina women are supposed to be genetically more liable to suffer from obesity; black men are said to be genetically more likely to suffer from heart disease or hypertension; Native Americans suffer from a genetic pre-disposition to diabetes; and so on.

These types of genetically-based excuses to sweep environmental influences—including the effects of racism—under the rug often do more harm than good. Although the medical establishment rushes to excuse racism and discrimination by searching for biological explanations for continuing health inequality, the research that refutes many of these claims is growing. Still, a significant problem with this circular process is that, in some instances, the need to refute bogus claims serves as a serious distraction from being able to help people live more healthy lives. Just using the examples provided, we can see from history that, in fact,

**REALITY CHECK   Racism or Discrimination?**

Do you know the difference between "racism" and "discrimination"? We often use the terms interchangeably, but they are not the same.

**Racism** stems from the belief that one or more races of people are superior to one or more others and is often expressed through institutional and social segregation and/or barriers to the health, wellness, freedom, and life opportunities for those thought to be of an inferior race.

**Discrimination** generally involves interpersonal and/or institutional actions that stem from racist (or sexist, etc.) beliefs about one group's superiority over another's.

diabetes was relatively unheard of among Native Americans until well into the last century and hypertension among African American men has been shown to have strong ties to racism-related stress.

Although the genetic and biological claims often get prime-time news coverage, which serves to soothe the conscience of those who may feel uncomfortable with the idea that racism continues to negatively impact the lives of so many millions of our friends and neighbors, the ongoing and sustained studies that show just the opposite get little to no coverage. What we are left with is a society that continues to be absolved of any responsibility to take action and institute real change that makes a difference in the health and wellness of men of color, as well as others who remain marginalized and without care.

## Only the Faces Change

What we are seeing when we watch those evening news reports speaks to an underlying pattern of resistance to African American advancement at every level—this pattern continues to exist today, despite the election of our first black president. It continues, despite the existence of leadership of color at nearly every other level of society as well, and is able to function as such, because, although the face of the leaders may be changing, the institutions they are leading have not changed at the same level. This is a critical component of power failure—when our leaders, and far too many of them can be seen doing just this, find themselves contented to be figureheads of institutions that continue to play an integral part in keeping in place the status quo of inequality. The stereotypes are firmly in place that give those unwilling to lead the "courage" to do nothing.

Certainly, when we look around and see the progress we have made, we can feel proud that the situation for African Americans—men and women—has generally improved for the group as a whole, as well as for many individuals in particular. But, for far too many others, the situation has not gotten any better; in fact, it has gotten much worse.

 **REALITY CHECK   Teenage Pregnancy**

Speaking with a Latina woman about the effects of teenage pregnancy on communities of color, I was stopped short. She replied with a sharp denial that what we were seeing in African American communities had no connection to Latino communities. "We are not like you," she said without malice, but with a clear determination that we were indeed talking about a difference more like apples and oranges than anything akin to future indicators.

Sadly, the facts do not hold up to her denial.

Although teen pregnancy rates declined steadily in the United States from "1991 to 2005—from 60 out of 1000 teenagers in 1991 to 40.5 out of 1000 in 2005—the teen pregnancy rate increased for two years in a row in 2006 and 2007 to more than 42 out of 1000. Currently, the highest teen birth rate occurs in Hispanic women (83 out of 1000 in 2006)." The most dramatic reduction in teen pregnancy, a 23% drop, has occurred among African American teenagers.[1]

These numbers are stark but only begin to tell the story of how severely teen pregnancy affects the health, wellness, and life opportunities of both parents and their children. Teen parenthood is associated with lower annual income for the mothers, an 80% chance that the family will have to rely on welfare at some point and a higher likelihood of dropping out of school to support the family.[2] Teenage pregnancies are also "associated with increased rates of alcohol and substance abuse, lower educational level, and reduced earning potential in teen fathers."[3]

1. Hamilton, Brady E. E., and Stephanie J. Ventura. "Birth Rates for U.S. Teenagers Reach Historic Lows for All Age and Ethnic Groups." NCHS data brief, no 89. Hyattsville, MD: National Center for Health Statistics. 2012.

2. HealthCommunities.com. "Teen Pregnancies." http://www.healthcommunities.com/teen-pregnancy/children/overview-of-teen-pregnancy.shtml.

3. HealthCareveda.com. "What Are the Causes of Teenage Pregnancy?" http://www.healthcareveda.com/post/Causes-of-Teenage-Pregnancy.aspx.

Even as we celebrate our success, it is important for all of us—whether we are leaders on the job, leaders in our schools or communities, or leaders of our own families—to remind each other that, although we went through a civil rights revolution that brought us a great deal of progress, we did it not just so we could have a better house, but so all of us could have a better world.

As communities of color have continued to move up in society and leadership, many of us looked around and saw a situation in which there was a lot of give and not much get. Today, there are people of color sitting at the highest level of nearly every prominent institution in our society.

We are represented among both the very rich and the very powerful. Any drive through the streets of Atlanta shows people of color living in the finest houses in town, driving the nicest cars, and exchanging business cards emblazoned with the most exclusive titles. Certainly this type of progress has been very hard-won and is a key indicator of the fruits of our labor.

Still, on those same streets, we see people of color—and most especially men of color—representing the very poorest among us, suffering from the most basic to the most critical health care needs from chronic disease, to substance addiction, to poor mental health. The sharp parallel between those who have risen higher than many could have imagined 50 years ago and those who have slipped so deeply into cracks that would also have been unimaginable 50 years ago resonates strongly with the work my colleagues and I are struggling through Community Voices to complete. It also begs the question: At what point did we trade our commitment to community uplift for the personal benefits of quid pro quo?

"Many young men of color are less likely to simply *live*, to fulfill their potential, enrich their communities, and be a part of the progress of our nation," said Dr. Gail C. Christopher, writing for the Dellums Report,[4] which set out to explore a central question: *What must we do now so that young men of color may have life?* "Over the course of the last quarter of a century," she continued, "the lives and fortunes of young men of color have been caught in a tail-spin. By nearly every comparative measure—income, education, incarceration, health—the reality is stark."[3]

A huge gap exists between the life expectancies of both African Americans and whites, and the chasm has widened dramatically over the past 40 years, despite our progress. The reasons for the growing gap are quite sinister, because they are not those things that get the most ink, such as HIV/AIDS or homicide. The rates of HIV/AIDS infection among African Americans are indeed alarming and continue to climb—as of 2008, 42.6% of people living with HIV/AIDS were African American, as compared with 21.4% Hispanic or Latino and 33.3% white.[5] Yet, the reality is that chronic disease, such as heart disease, cancer, stroke, and chronic respiratory disease—things aggravated significantly by the specific types of stress faced by men of color—is what is killing African Americans faster than any other group.[6]

## Death by Zip Code

"Racism has subtle and not-so-subtle impacts," says former Alameda County Public Health Director, Dr. Tony Iton. Those impacts, whether subtle or not, are clear, measurable, and irrefutable. "Give me your zip code," he told me, "and I'll tell you how long you'll live." Iton has noted a 14-year "life expectancy difference between African Americans in West Oakland and white Americans in the Oakland Hills." His studies have also shown that the primary contributors are not the issues we see on the nightly news. In fact, "when you subtract out homicide as a contribution to that difference," he said, "it only reduces that 15-year difference by one year."[7]

Speaking for the "Unnatural Causes" project,[8] Iton explained the effects of racism on health, well being, and opportunity this way: "If I give you a tennis ball and I say, 'Juggle it,' most people can do it. If I give you two tennis balls, and say, 'Juggle them,' most people can probably do that too. But if I give you three, four, five balls, the number of people who can do this starts dropping off. Well, people in many under-resourced communities are juggling five, six balls all the time, and they don't have support; they're going to drop balls."

One of the key points to Dr. Iton's analogy is the fact that so many who are struggling to juggle too many balls are doing so with a significant lack of support. The juggling itself is not new, especially within communities of color. What does seem new is what seems to be a move from collectivism to individualism in the African American community, together with a decline in African American institutions that may have resulted in the loss of what were previously protective features of the African American community, which leave so many trying to juggle the balls all alone without help.

For men of color, especially, there is significant pressure to take on an extreme amount of pressure all alone and without complaint. When they cannot carry the super-human amount of weight on their own, our social concepts of masculinity—particularly as they are understood within the culture of communities of color—leave them open to judgment. In an attempt to avoid appearing weak or "soft," men often suffer in silence, hide their emotions, and deeply bury the pain they feel. These kinds of coping behaviors not only lead to physical health deterioration, but also have serious mental health consequences.

**REALITY CHECK  Pumping Irony**

If we all know that physical activity is good for health and can lower risk of a smorgasbord of diseases and illnesses, from heart disease to anxiety and poor academic and work performance, why is it so hard to come by in our poor neighborhoods and in our jails and prisons?

- A 2005 study found that "commercial physical activity-related facilities were less likely to be present in lower-income neighborhoods and in neighborhoods with higher proportions of African American residents, residents with Hispanic ethnicity, and residents of other racial minority backgrounds. In addition, these neighborhoods had fewer such facilities available."[1]

- A 2007 study found that "low income and people of color are less likely to have access to physical activity settings, including parks, bike trails, and public pools than whites and the more affluent."[2]

- A 1996 amendment "prohibited the Bureau of Prisons from purchasing training equipment for boxing, wrestling, judo, karate, or other martial art, or any bodybuilding or weightlifting equipment of any sort." Many states, including California, followed suit. Why? It is a "luxury" and makes the men intimidating and more dangerous on the inside and the outside.[3]

- Some research suggests that weight lifting actually decreases aggression among inmates. Wardens have noted that idleness is the biggest threat to order in a prison and weight lifting gives the convicts something to do. It may also help inmates protect themselves against prison rape.[4]

---

1. Powell, Lisa M., Sandy Slater, Frank J. Chaloupka, and Deborah Harper. "Availability of Physical Activity—Related Facilities and Neighborhood Demographic and Socioeconomic Characteristics: A National Study." *American Journal of Public Health* 2008;96:1676–1680.

2. Food and Research Action Center. "Why Low-Income and Food Insecure People are Vulnerable to Overweight and Obesity." http://frac.org.

3. Palmer, Brian. "Do Prisoners Really Spend All Their Time Lifting Weights?" http://www.slate.com.

4. Wagner, Matthew, Ron E. McBride, and Stephen F. Crouse. "The Effects of Weight-Training Exercise on Aggression Variables in Adult Male Inmates." *The Prison Journal* 1999;79:72–89.

Community Voices has found that racism affects mental health status in at least three ways: "First it can lead to reduced socioeconomic status, diminished access to desirable resources, and poor living conditions; compared to whites, African Americans are three times more likely to be poor. Second, it can lead to physiological and psychological reactions that bring about adverse changes in mental health status. Third the acceptance of negative stereotypes can cause negative self-evaluations that have damaging effects on psychological well-being."[9]

Doug Lomax, a former Substance Abuse Coordinator with the Boston Municipal Court and ex-offender himself, sees all three effects in his daily work. "You have people living life on an installment plan," he says. "Not only are you operating from racism from bigoted people, you're operating from racism from systems that try to break you psychologically and emotionally." [10]

Lomax began working with men in the criminal justice system after working through his own negative experiences with addiction and incarceration. Through his work, he encourages men to focus on who they are and where they are going, rather than the mistakes they have made and the price they have paid for them. In the 20 years he has been doing this work, Lomax has seen his approach change countless lives. "We're taking off these macho masks," he continued, "these territorial masks of being ashamed and of not wanting to include anyone, and we're at a place of saying, 'You know what? This is where I'm at. Where are you? Can we help each other?' You find men who can be sensitive and vulnerable. They have pain and can be hurt. We live in a society where everything we see in the media related to us is very negative. It's hard not to begin to believe the negative things about ourselves."[11]

Each of us plays a part—knowingly or not—in the continuing inequality throughout our society. Even when we are not personally practicing prejudice, our inaction in the face of discrimination can often be far more powerful than any personal prejudice we may refrain from exhibiting. Failure to act IS AN ACT! And that act HURTS!

The climb to leadership has certainly been both steep and rocky, and perhaps we have all been working hard to develop our own coping mechanisms for dealing with the stress of the many barriers that stand in the way of our success—no matter who we are. Of course, we could also have simply fallen into the trap of self-absorption that permeates our culture. Where do you fall in this continuum? What can you commit to doing to contribute to making a change?

The unrelenting effects of this type of self-defeat are the poisonous snake coiled in the bosom of our collective failure to lead our communities out of the cycle of crime, disease, and early death. So long as our

**TAKE A GOOD LOOK**  **Public Health Professionals**

Are you a public health professional? If not, can you imagine what it is like to be in public health? Look in the mirror and ask yourself:

- Leaving aside blaming the victim ideology, what do you think is the reason for the marginalization of African American boys and men in your community?

- How can and could you encourage health care organizations to make room in their services for affirmative inclusion of men without health care insurance, given their morbidity and mortality figures are so high?

- Can there be programs that engage African Americans (and other poor men of color) in relationship building that improves their health? Is there a role you can play in fostering these programs?

- Should there be "community benefit" programs required by those receiving tax credits to target programs for those whose health status is poor? If so, how can YOU make certain these programs are developed?

- Have you found yourself in a position in which you were trying to exercise innovative leadership, only to have others in authority pull the plug on your attempt?

- Why do you think they got in the way of your success? Perhaps it was simple politics. Maybe you were seen as competition by those in authority. Were you stumped by others who did not share your vision and refused to give you the support needed to carry it out?

- What strategies can you employ to get past the hurdles thrown up by those who would pull the plug on your work, reach out for help, and begin to set those strategies in motion?

- Once you've done your best to identify the reasons you were stymied, it is time to get busy moving past them. Write one thing you are willing to do to improve public health in your community: _____

_____

leaders fail to acknowledge the long-term effects of generation after generation being beaten down by oppression, the psychic injury of seeing one's parents rise up only to see their children beaten down again, then our piecemeal attempts at intervention continue to fail. In his Pulitzer Prize-winning book, *Slavery by Another Name*, Douglas A. Blackmon,

LEADERS AND HEROES

## Michael Ferrer, Director of Programs and Special Services Lorain County Urban League

At one point in his career, Michael Ferrer agreed to a pay cut, but he says he has learned something important along the way: "You are never paid enough. If you wait for more pay before you act to make a difference, you will do nothing for anyone. I wanted to work with young people. My young people were African American and Hispanic and had been kicked out of schools, social programs, and jobs because of their behavior. My work was to lead intervention programs with the courts and police to move young men away from crime, incarceration."[1] With that degree of commitment, it is no wonder that, in 2008, Michael Ferrer was selected to manage a project named "Save Our Sons." This was to be a national diabetes health pilot targeting African American males ages 19–74.

What made Community Voices declare that the project and Michael "had hit a home run"? What made us recommend that Save Our Sons be replicated in other cities across the United States? What made the funder provide $1 million to replicate the Save Our Sons project in two additional cities? And why are people calling them from around the country, asking them to share what they know?

"African American men get sicker sooner and die earlier than any other group of men in America," points out Ferrer, who is Director of Programs and Special Services for the Lorain County Urban League. "This situation is not being properly addressed by any system." When Ohio state did a research study of men's health among white and Hispanic males but none for African American males because they were harder to reach, "we decided that we had to act, as failure to do anything made us complicit in the neglect. We did not have a choice once we began to see the data from across the nation and knew that ours would be the same. Our grant was not large, but it showed the power of what a modest investment can do to address obesity and diabetes and connect men to a primary health care home plus other services."[2]

Save Our Sons has worked with nearly 350 men who collectively have lost nearly 600 pounds—a part of their measure of success. But they are more interested in reduced blood pressure, gaining control of diabetes or diabetic tendencies, managing blood cholesterol, and preventing illness and managing lifestyles. "We introduced new things: swimming, tennis, bicycling, and we even now have the men playing golf," says Ferrer. "We are working together, opening doors and windows to possibilities. MetroParks that gave us access to their fitness center, pools, walking

(continued)

**Michael Ferrer, Director of Programs and Special Services Lorain County Urban League (continued)**

tracks. Gathering Hope House, which offers mental health and substance abuse treatment, gave us unlimited access to their services that included a fitness facility. We saved six lives through PSA screenings."[3]

It did not stop there. Out of Save Our Sons grew "Save Our Families"—the men started bringing their wives and children; they were taking the nutrition lessons home, teaching their families and neighbors. Since, Save Our Families has worked with 400 family members.

Ferrer discovered that the people in his community do not like the word "grant," because they are used to people coming into the community, using them for data, and leaving when the money runs out. The community also feels that the people with the grants do not factor in the historical neglect. But, Ferrer states, when we implement the program together, then it works. "In order to overcome the concerns, we needed to 'be' the people who were being helped. So, if we are the Director of Programs at the Urban League, which I am, or if I am one of the community outreach workers, and we have four of them, we stand in the line and get our blood pressure, get our blood drawn for cholesterol tests, get diabetes checks, PSA screens, oral health cleanings and checks, and any other screening that the men are going through. We work in a way that does not separate us from the people we enroll. We get down off of our high horse and become one of the people we serve. When we have a program, we need to be at the front of the line to get our health fixed thereby demonstrating to the other men that we believe in, are committed to the program and take direct part in the program."[4]

But this is not just a story of weight loss or even general physical health—or even connecting these largely uninsured men to a primary health care home. As Ferrer explains, "We are saving lives, but we also gave some participants a reason to live."[5] Some of the older men lost their wives and give testimony whenever they can that they do not know what they would have done without Save Our Sons. The essence of Save Our Sons has become the establishment and formation of strong bonds between the men. Some of the men were terrified of the pool as they had never been swimming. But they worked together, each one teach one . . . so that everyone became comfortable. They do not recruit anymore, they rely on word of mouth—and they have a waiting list. The men come to the classes, because they want to come. They look forward to coming to be with other men, to work on their health together, to meet new friends, and reaffirm the value of relationships.

Ferrer is rightly proud of what he and the community have accomplished. "There were some in the community who questioned whether or not I, a Puerto Rican man, should be in charge of the program. But once our outcome data from our pilot program was presented to the community at large by our evaluator, everyone saw our tremendous achievements and we heard no more about whether or not this Puerto Rican man could provide effective leadership for this African American program. And we have put to rest the myth that black men won't seek health care. We have learned that they have not had an opportunity because they do not have the funds and often, with limited funds, they are not treated with respect."[6]

At the end of the day, Ferrer would tell others who want to do something: "If you believe, others will believe. If others believe, more and more people will believe and a movement will start that cannot be stopped. Believe, in the face of whatever negativity arises. . . . Some will always try to bring down your confidence, to make you fail. Believe against all odds!"[7]

For more information, visit: http://www.lcul.org/programs/health/.

---

1. Author interview with Michael Ferrer, October 2009.
2. Ibid.
3. Ibld.
4. Ibid.
5. Ibid.
6. Ibid.
7. Ibid.

---

Atlanta Bureau Chief of the *Wall Street Journal*, rightly identifies this as a continuing virus of "improved more subtle forms of discrimination," and millions of men are dying both quickly and slowly from the infection.

## Notes

1. Geronimus, Arline T. "The Health of Urban African American Men: Excess Mortality and Causes of Death." http://www.aspeninstitute.org/sites/default/files/content/upload/19Geronimus.pdf.
2. Krieger, Nancy. "Unnatural Causes: Is Inequality Making Us Sick?" Edited interview transcript. 2008. http://www.unnaturalcauses.org/assets/uploads/file/krieger_interview.pdf.
3. Ibid.
4. Joint Center for Political and Economic Studies Health Policy Institute. "Dellums Report: Meeting the Health Needs of Youth Involved

in the Juvenile Justice System." http://www.jointcenter.org/research/search/results?keys=dellums+report&edit-submit.x=18&edit-submit.y=9&edit-submit=Submit.

5. Avert.org. "HIV & AIDS Statistics Summary." http://www.avert.org/usa-statistics.htm.

6. Xanthos, Clare. "Feeling the Strain: The Impact of Stress on the Health of African-American Men." http://www.communityvoices.org/.

7. Author interview with Dr. Tony Iton, October, 2009.

8. "Unnatural Causes: Is Inequality Making Us Sick?" (2007 PBS documentary). http://www.unnaturalcauses.org/.

9. Phinney, Jean S. "Ethnic Identify and Self-Esteem: A Review and Integration." *Hispanic Journal of Behavioral Sciences* 1991;13:193–208.

10. Author interview with Doug Lomax, October, 2009.

11. Ibid.

# CHAPTER 4

# Lost in Translation

## "Access to Care" for Men of Color

*"As a society we're not set up that way. You pay for service in our country. If you can afford to pay for it, you get it."*
—*Rev. William Brown, CEO, William Brown Ministries, Atlanta and Director, First Step Transitional Academy*

*When he was growing up, Martin saw a black doctor who knew and was known by everyone in the neighborhood. He never went to the hospital; he either went to the doctor's office, or the doctor came to him. These days, he sees a different set of doctors and nurses every time he goes to the hospital. They do not know him, they do not know anything about his life, and each visit requires him to start from scratch. His medical records are on file, but, for the most part, what is recorded in them is just data—nothing about the man himself. As a young man, Martin did not know his neighborhood doctor very well, but he always had the feeling that the doctor cared about his well-being. The doctor wanted Martin to feel well and to live well.*

*These days, whenever Martin leaves the hospital, he feels more like a lab mouse, given this set of pills, then that set. He is given a sheaf of papers to read, understand, and apply on his own, with little explanation of what all the information means and how he can actually put the information to use in his daily life. Yes, he should be eating more fruits and vegetables, the papers say—when he has time to read them. But where is he supposed to find this bounty of fresh fruit? It is not available in any of the stores where he lives. Even if he could find the time to go outside his neighborhood to shop for food, how is he supposed to find fruit and vegetables he can afford and where will he find the time to eat them before they spoil? Martin knows that, if he has the extra money to buy these extravagances, then it means he is on the job for 10 or more hours a day.*

*This is why most of the papers the nurses and medical technicians give him on his way out of the hospital sit gathering dust on a small corner table. It is not that Martin does not want to feel better or take care of himself. But he lives alone. On what he makes, he just has not figured out how to do the things the papers tell him to do and still manage the day-to-day needs he must meet to survive.*

Focus groups that Community Voices conducted in 2008 found that stress is a major influence for African American men's decisions to see a primary care physician—when they have the opportunity to do so. Many men saw visiting the doctor as an unnecessary hassle in a life that was already excessively stressful. They do not bother to see the doctor because the cost is stressful, the time they wait is stressful, and, if they have a problem that requires a specialist, they will not get to see one.[1] So, ignorance is bliss. What you do not know you do not have to worry about . . . until the pain becomes so bad you just have to get on down to the clinic or the Emergency Room.

"Even in these free clinics, the attitude of the staff has a lot to do with turning men away," says Rev. William Brown, executive director of the First Step Transitional Academy, a re-entry and educational program for formerly incarcerated men in Georgia that emphasizes "responsible fatherhood" for the reunification of fathers to the family unit. Rev. Brown is also the faith-based liaison for the Imani Project of the Department of Pediatrics, Morehouse School of Medicine. "As soon as they come in, they're not treated the same as everyone else. They're treated inhumanely in many circumstances and say to themselves 'I've already suffered enough. I'm not going to suffer through that indignity too.'"[2] One could say they are turning themselves away. But the reality is that the clinics do not want them there as they cannot pay, so the subtle and not so subtle message is "you are not welcome here." I have had providers say to me, "Why would I want these men in my clinic? They can't pay!" It is just one more indignity.

Speaking at the 2009 Community Voices Freedom's Voice Conference, Democratic political strategist Donna Brazile said, "We can't prioritize some and not others. When we talk about health care, we talk about how we're going to become a better country, we better not start picking and choosing."[3] Yet, our studies into the reality of the health care environment continue to show that picking and choosing is exactly what we have been doing.

At nearly every level, especially when it comes to families living at or below the poverty line, our public policy works against the health of the entire family unit. Prohibitive public housing rules ensure that many fathers cannot go home to read to and care for their children. The predatory "deadbeat dad" legislation that has been sweeping the country also threatens these same men, who are struggling with untreated health and nutrition issues, to provide for their children at often-unreachable levels assigned by the state or lose their freedom and ability to work and provide anything at all. In many cases, these men are not "deadbeat," they are simply "dead broke," and the current punitive policies are not helping. Instead of helping support families and bring them closer together, what these policies really promote is keeping families apart, pitted against each other and tied to the criminal court system.

When 46 million Americans—18% of the population younger than 65 years of age—do not have the insurance needed to access health care, we are in a crisis that affects every part of our society. Uninsured and underinsured families do not just suffer physically; they suffer culturally, socially, and economically. This crisis is not just about basic medical

 **REALITY CHECK   Health (un)Insurance throughout Life**

Overall, nearly 25% of African Americans are uninsured compared with 16% of the U.S. population.

On average, Americans are expected to "spend about 12 years without health insurance coverage over their lifetime." Throughout life, African Americans fare worse than whites, except in their youth (probably because public health insurance coverage for children in low-income families was expanded in the 1990s). Disparities are widest between 50 and 60 years of age, when individuals "are more likely to need medical attention than any other age group not covered by Medicare."

- African Americans 20 years of age and older spend a higher proportion of time without insurance than any other age group.

- African Americans 20–24 years of age "live 43 percent of the time without insurance, as compared with whites in the same age group, who are uninsured for 36 percent of the time."

- Among the near-elderly 50–60 years of age, racial disparities between African Americans and whites are the widest regarding health insurance.[1]

1. Population Reference Bureau; Fustos, Kata. "Racial Differences in Health Status and Health Insurance Coverage in the United States." http://www.prb.org/.

needs. There are mental health and substance abuse issues that need to be treated. Without adequate care, many of those suffering would rather hide than face the perceived shame of seeking help and being turned away.

This is where leadership can and must step in. "We have the responsibility to protect the most vulnerable of our citizens," said Brazile, "including our children and our elders."[4] Insuring that everyone has health coverage is an important step, but certainly not the only one we need to take. Men and boys of color learn from an early age that when it comes to medical care and treatment they are less than welcome. But the influence comes both from the outside and from within the family.

## "John Henryism"

One reason men of color, and particularly African American men, have a hard time accessing the tools and resources needed to manage stress is contained in a concept developed by Duke University social epidemiologist Sherman James called "John Henryism." John Henryism gets its name from the legend of John Henry, an African American man who competed successfully against a mechanical steam drill in a famous steel-driving contest. Although John Henry succeeded in his goal, he fell to his death from physical and mental exhaustion immediately after the contest ended. As such, John Henryism is a useful synonym.

The California Center for Social Epidemiology defines John Henryism as "a synonym for prolonged, high-effort coping with difficult psychological stressors." James' research has shown that the effect may help to explain disproportionately higher rates of cardiovascular disease among both African Americans and other people of color. Doug Lomax says he sees the effects of John Henryism every day in his work. He believes that the way we socialize boys into health care has as much of an effect on their attitudes toward the system when they grow up as the compound influences of their negative experiences with it. "As young boys," he says, "especially if we don't have any money, we don't really start going to the doctor unless we have a broken arm, or some sort of sports injury. That's the kind of relationship we develop with the medical profession."[5]

This type of early-onset John Henryism couples with the fact that, especially among those with the fewest resources, public options for care, including Medicaid and SCHIP, primarily exist to cover mothers and children but exclude the fathers who are also responsible for their care. We, as a society, continue to create an unwinnable situation when we are unwilling to ensure the health of the entire family by discounting the health of the men we expect to lead that family. We insist that these men are poor fathers if they cannot read to their children at night or provide them with enough creative outlets to stir their intelligent minds. Yet, far too few leaders are willing to thoroughly investigate the health and nutritional barriers faced by those same men. And it is unreasonable to expect a father to teach a son or daughter how to take care of his or her health when he himself is not allowed to do so by the policies that leadership has put in place. Invisible again!

## The Stresses of Microaggressions

In his landmark 1970 essay, "Offensive mechanisms," published in *The Black Seventies*, psychiatrist Chester Pierce developed the concept of microaggressions to illustrate how the cumulative effect of every day instances of subtle discrimination could cause psychological distress. Stress has long been understood as a critical pathway that links low socio-economic status to poor health outcomes. Understanding how stressors, both large and small, uniquely affect men of color offers a window into why these men suffer such elevated rates of chronic disease. An examination of the role of microaggressions helps further by highlighting some of the barriers that stand in the way of men and boys of color who are not accessing the health care they need.

Microaggressions are subtle insults, whether verbal or nonverbal, directed toward people of color, often automatically or unconsciously. These microaggressions may seem harmless at first, but Pierce's studies have shown how their cumulative effect, over the course of a lifetime, can contribute to everything from lower levels of self-confidence and self-esteem to greater severity of disease suffered and even lower life spans.

Microaggressions are an integral part of the life experience of men of color. Men of color are also the most likely group to lack health insurance among all gender and racial categories in the United States, with various estimates ranging from 20 to 40% having no coverage at all. Accessing medical care can be daunting for the most privileged, but it becomes a steep mountain to climb when you have no way to pay for services. Couple that reality with the types of microaggressions faced by men of color from the moment they walk through the door, and many choose instead to take their chances with poor health until they wind up in need of critical care.

"The subtle, cumulative mini-assault is the substance of today's racism," wrote Pierce in a 1974 follow-up essay.[6] These mini-assaults result in reduced employment prospects, reduced promotion prospects, poor quality education, substandard housing, environmental pollution, and absent social support. These same conditions, in turn, create crumbling neighborhoods in which crime, crowding, and lack of access to nutritious

**REALITY CHECK  Employer Insurance Failure**

Conventional wisdom would have us believe that our current employer-provided insurance system is the best way to provide health care access for our neighbors and ourselves. The facts tell a much different story for the vast majority of working families living from paycheck to paycheck—which is more of us every day.

- "Rates of employer-based health coverage are just over 50 percent for employed African Americans, compared to over 70 percent for employed non-Hispanic whites."[1]

- 70% of uninsured families have one or more full-time worker.[2]

- Only 24% of low-income people have insurance through their employer.[3]

- Not all low-income people qualify for Medicaid and/or CHIP.[4]

- 34% of Latinos and 21% of African Americans 19–64 years of age are uninsured.[5]

- People with mental illness and/or substance abuse issues are more likely to be incarcerated than to receive medical care.[6]

A significant indicator of whether or not one will return to jail or prison is a lack of health insurance.[7]

---

1. Gallup Wellbeing; Mendes, Elizabeth. "In U.S., Employer-Based Health Insurance Declines Further." http://www.gallup.com.

2. Kaiser Family Foundation. "Medicaid and the Uninsured: The Uninsured and the Difference Health Insurance Makes." http://www.kff.org.

3. Benefits Pro; Mayer, Kathryn. "Employer-Offered Health Insurance Drops to Record Low." http://www.benefitspro.com.

4. State Health Facts. "Income Eligibility Limits for Working Adults at Application as a Percent of the Federal Poverty Level (FPL) by Scope of Benefit Package, January 2012." http://www.satehealthfacts.org/.

5. Commonwealth Fund; Mahon, Mary. "Hispanic and African American Adults Are Uninsured at Rates One-and-a Half to Three Times Higher than White Adults." http://www.commonwealthfund.org/.

6. Urban Institute; Mallik-Kane, Kamala and Christy Visher. "How Physical, Mental, and Substance Abuse Conditions Shape the Process of Reintegration." http://www.urban.org/.

7. Community Oriented Correctional Health Services; McDonnell, Maureen, Laura Brookes, Arthur Lurigio, and Daphne Baille. "Realizing the Potential of National Health Care Reform to Reduce Criminal Justice Expenditures and Recidivism Among Jail Populations." http://www.cochs.org/.

food or safe outlets for exercise, increased isolation, and disproportionate rates of incarceration.

Psychological stress has long been linked both to exposure to violence and crime and to fear of violence and victimization. For young African American men, who suffer from the highest rate of homicide death, living with this type of stress can become both chronic and debilitating.

Imagine how it feels to be an African American boy between 15 and 17 years of age, for whom the homicide rate is more than 14 times higher than for white males the same age. In addition, outlets for managing stress, both social and clinical, remain out of reach for many men, compounding the issue so that getting sicker, sooner, mixes with access issues to create a toxic cocktail.

"The stress inherent in living in a race-conscious society that stigmatizes and disadvantages African Americans may cause disproportionate physiological deterioration, such that an African American individuals may show the morbidity and mortality typical of a White individual who is significantly older," reported Dr. Arline Geronimus, a professor and health researcher at the University of Michigan School of Public Health.[7] Geronimus has focused decades of research on the effects of racism on individual and community health. Her findings have sometimes generated a great deal of controversy, but, as research in the field continues to add up, so do her conclusions. "Not only do African Americans experience poor health at earlier stages than do Whites," she continued, "but this deterioration in health accumulates, producing ever-greater racial inequality in health with age through middle adulthood."

## Cycles of Stress

"Culturally, if you come from a place where you do not trust a system because you've been caught up in systems that have used, abused, oppressed you, people have serious trust issues with the healthcare system," said Doug Lomax, a substance abuse coordinator in Boston.[8]

Historical wounds, such as the Tuskegee Experiment, leave lasting impressions. For 40 years between 1932 and 1972, the U.S. Public Health Service, working with the Tuskegee Institute, endangered the lives of 600 Black men—without their consent—to study the effects of untreated syphilis. The men were not informed that they had the disease, and treatment was withheld. Hundreds died unaware before the Associated Press broke the story and public anger ended the study. Memory of this study, and numerous other historical medical slights, survives within the oral tradition in the African American community in which trust of the medical system has never been fully regained.

"Families and parents have had a bad experience and have passed that on," says Lomax. "It's very hard to get people motivated for healthcare, especially men because men operate from a space of 'I'm not dealing with them until something is wrong with me.'" The more men continue their attempts to "shake it off," Lomax says, the more we see related increases in street crime, in broken families, and in children living in extreme distress. When you have an individual "shaking off" his pain—whether it is physical, mental, or emotional—you have an individual who is continuing to get sicker every day. Yet, when that individual is a part of an entire community that is steadily "shaking off" its pain and suffering in isolation, then the problem does not just get worse—it spreads.

Because stress diverts energy and resources away from the work our bodies need to do to ensure long-term health, when stress is chronic or cumulative, people become far more vulnerable to a number of health problems and diseases, including infections, diabetes, high blood pressure, heart attack, stroke, and cancer as each of these researchers has shown. What is more, stress encourages people to engage in unhealthy behaviors, such as comfort eating and smoking to cope with their stress. Unfortunately, this vicious cycle leads to health problems, including obesity, lung cancer, and even higher rates of the same chronic diseases elevated by the original stressors. The cycle only continues when the need to address the resulting poor health creates even more added stress.

African Americans, in particular, must manage this stress while also navigating the heightened vulnerability of being a clearly visible, and highly stereotyped, minority. In addition to race, poverty is a critical component exacerbating the problem. The Children's Defense Fund reports that nearly 40% of black children are poor.[9] Poor children often grow up to be poor adults with few resources to learn positive health behaviors or access care when needed. As Lomax said, and the studies conducted by the researchers noted back him up, these problems are passed down from family to family. Although our current leadership sits wringing their hands, there continues to be no end in sight to the cycle.

When hope has been destroyed, life—my life, your life—has little meaning. Our failed "war on poverty" affects the problem on many fronts. A report, "Understanding Neighborhood Effects of Concentrated Poverty" by the U.S. Department of Housing and Urban Development, shows that crime and violence, major stressors, tend to be higher in areas in which 20% of the residents are living below the poverty line.[10] These same neighborhoods are often characterized by high unemployment, high levels of residential instability, family disruption, overcrowded housing, drug distribution networks, and low measures of community participation, as well as high rates of high school dropouts, teenage pregnancy,

## Stress and Disease: The Cortisol Connection

In 2012, Michael P. O'Donnell, the editor of the influential *Journal of Health Promotion*, re-examined his core beliefs about how we can help "those less fortunate, more disadvantaged, more oppressed than me." He came to realize the importance of stress and poverty. He writes that one way the stress of poverty and inequality increases the risk of many diseases is through the increased and sustained production of body chemicals, including cortisol and proinflammatory cytokines. One type of stress occurs when disadvantaged people judge themselves negatively relative to other people. This phenomenon, known as "social evaluative threat," has been shown to trigger release of both types of these biochemicals. "Cortisol impedes immune functions, increases the risk of heart disease, and threatens other physiological systems," wrote O'Donnell. Cytokines lead to chronic inflammation, which has been linked to increased rates of autoimmune disorders, asthma, ulcerative colitis and Crohn's disease, cardiovascular disease, bacterial endocarditis, cancer, urinary infections, and cystitis.

When people are victims of discrimination because of their race, regardless of Income, in addition to increased threats of violence and exclusion from many opportunities, the same type of stress is created as that caused by social evaluative threat. "For people with low income, it increases the stress they already endure from poverty and income inequality," he concludes.

In addition, pregnant women suffering from the elevated stress caused by inequality also have elevated cortisol and other stress related hormones and toxins. A fetus bathed in these damaging chemicals is at higher risk of low birth weight, premature birth, or other congenital defects. Combined with the damage to the fetus caused by malnutrition, one can begin to understand why poor black children have such a hard time catching up to their better-off counterparts. Children who are less bright than their classmates often have lower social status, which produces more stress, stress chemicals, such as cortisol, and the physical problems caused by stress. And so on.[1]

---

1. O'Donnell, Michael P. "Erosion of Our Moral Compass, Social Trust, and the Fiscal Strength of the United States: Income Inequality, Tax Policy, and Well-Being." *American Journal of Health Promotion*. 2012;26:iv–xi.

and a disproportionate number of households headed by women. African Americans and Hispanics are also more likely by a wide margin, especially if they are poor, to face time in prison, with all of the negative health consequences that are associated with incarceration.

Family poverty also has a direct connection to depression and poor mental and physical health among teens. Simple issues, such as a lack of quality food, clothing, and recreational activities must be added to the already significant impact that the stress faced by their parents and families has on the health of poor adolescents. Community Voices has reported that distressed parents are more irritable, authoritarian, and rejecting toward their children, all of which add to the weight of stress carried around by the developing bodies and minds of these children.

## Is Money the Answer?

Even the success of pulling oneself out of poverty does not solve the problem. Although poverty is a major determinant of poor mental and physical health, for men of color, attaining wealth does not necessarily offer the protection from poor health status that it does for whites. Studies show that wealth has less of an affect on health than specific factors often associated with wealth, such as occupational status, security, power, and control. However, African American men who attain wealth and status often do so without having the opportunity to leave behind the high levels of stress brought on by living with racism, which is often added to by the struggle to achieve despite it.

In their groundbreaking report,[11] Alabama researchers Leigh A. Willis and colleagues found that, rather than their wealth and class status offering protection, adolescent African American males of higher socioeconomic status may be particularly vulnerable to minority status stress, as they are more likely to attend schools in majority white environments. In fact, young men and boys of color who come from middle and upper-class families have been found to have a higher risk of suicide now than in the past because of their lack of an accessible reference group during their maturation process.

Here too, young men and boys must wage a unique battle for health and survival. Adolescence is already a time of significant transition, full of physical, mental, and emotional changes. During this time, young men and boys of color are particularly vulnerable to mental health problems, including depression, anxiety disorders, and suicide, especially when a family history of mental illness is present.

In this way, the failure of leadership in this area continues to multiply. Because we are not speaking of a simple problem, limited to an easily contained community, the fact that too many of those in charge continue to offer interventions of limited scope and scale will never add up to a real solution. What we need is a multiplicity of approaches that deal with men and boys of color from a variety of backgrounds and at every age level. It is too simple to say, "Let's deal with the behavior issues of poor kids in the schools" without also looking at their homes, their neighborhoods, the reasons behind their poverty and the intersecting challenges faced by their larger community.

We must also widen our vision to begin dealing with boys at their earliest ages, while also understanding that, although poverty is a significant indicator of poor health, the unique circumstances brought on by race—both within and outside of the scope of poverty—remain its own contributor. Interventions and programs must be designed to target boys and men of color in every community, including educating wealthier families of color who, like their poorer counterparts, often do not realize there is a significant problem with their children until it is too late.

"Here's the rub," says Dr. Robert Ross, president and chief executive officer for The California Endowment, a health foundation working to address the health needs of millions of Californians. "When you start talking about the health of men and boys of color, you can't authentically get into the issue without starting with race and poverty. The trouble is, while that is authentic and true, if that's the starting place, what is the policy and grant-making strategy to end poverty and racism before we can get to addressing health inequities?"[12]

Dr. Ross is one in a growing circle of leaders working within philanthropy circles to identify a set of approaches that can begin to make a lasting difference. The California Endowment has made a 10-year commitment to address health inequities among men and boys of color. From the beginning, it has not been an easy road, and, as Dr. Ross has said on many occasions, it is one that requires more than just writing a check. Successfully addressing the crisis requires a dedication to finding ways to think anew completely.

Not only do we have to demand leadership that is accountable, consistent, and connected to the work, it is important that we challenge ourselves to become that leadership. "The issue is too thorny, too complex, too deep, and it's going to take an approach that is some balance of being targeted and focused but also comprehensive," says Ross. "If you're not interested in a serious minimum of 5- to 7-, and even 10-year run at it, then I don't think you can expect meaningful progress forward."[13]

One definition of leadership that I heard from Rev. Ivory Varner, who works with the Houston Food Bank and serves as pastor of the Bible Way Fellowship Baptist Church and mentor to men re-entering the community after incarceration, is that it must "meet standards of quality that you would expect internally, not externally."[14] Rev. Varner insists that leaders must be prospective, not just reflective. They must be willing to invest over the long haul, and they must be consistent in their approach. Too many blacks, according to Rev. Varner, "are afraid of losing position, power, and prestige." Rev. Varner is one of many leaders I spoke with who has seen men of color in leadership that she perceived as too afraid to step into issues that concern communities of color until they see the issues have already garnered white support.

 **TAKE A GOOD LOOK  Physicians or Other Health Care Providers**

Are you a health care provider? If not, can you imagine what it is like to be a health care provider? Look in the mirror and ask yourself:

- What could you do to bring greater attention to the country of the plight of poor men? What "narrative" would you initiate to draw attention to the issue? What WOULD you do?

- What action would you take, despite any oppositional odds, to make certain that poor men of color receive their health care in the community, as opposed to only in prison where there is some Constitutional guarantee?

- Do dentists, doctors, nurses, and other health care providers have any responsibility to lead community health improvement activities? If not, why not? If so, what is reasonable and how would you go about engaging them in providing care?

- How can you educate yourself and others about the lack of equal access to health care and the consequences of this lack of access? Do your local newspaper, television, or radio offer adequate education? If not, how would you change this?

- Demand that your local transportation systems work for the public—if they are not adequate, then get a coalition of friends, neighbors, social groups, advocates, and others to get them working.

- Write one thing you are willing to do to improve health care in your community—then get busy: _____

_____

Dr. Ross also highlighted the challenge of reaching across traditional barriers to secure buy-in to address the crisis. "Philanthropy isn't going to lead a movement here," continued Dr. Ross. "Philanthropy doesn't lead movements. If we're lamenting action, then we've got to start from an action place. If people say we've got to start with 400 years of racism and deal with that first, then, as an African American man, I want to throw up my hands—and that's *me*, so never mind the head of the Chamber of Commerce who might want to play a role in addressing these health issues but doesn't know where to get involved."[15]

Still, the kind of principled leadership shown by Ross and others highlights the ability of each of us to find ways to use our own avenues of leadership to make a difference. If we think we can escape the implications of this crisis, we are sadly mistaken. When was the last time you checked the locks on your front door or avoided driving through a neighborhood you did not feel safe in? These are the mechanisms by which those of us who feel we can comfortably pretend this crisis does not touch us are allowed to fool ourselves with. If we think back, however, anyone Martin's age—and many of us much younger—can remember a time when we did not have to think about locking our doors. We remember a time long before home security was one of the fastest growing industries in the nation, when security alarms were a thing for museums or the U.S. Mint.

It is fruitless to wait for *someone* to do *something* when this crisis—whether we think it touches us or not—continues to grow. Speaking to the Second Annual Freedom's Voice Conference, organized by Community Voices Civil Rights veteran and U.S. Congressman John Lewis said, "We can not wait for someone else to do it. We have to do it, and we must do it." Rather than wonder when or from where today's civil rights heroes will arise to take up the mantle, the better question might be to ask ourselves: *Where is the hero in me?* Each one of us has a bully pulpit, whether we currently serve in leadership positions of large-scale power or not. Now is the time to use it.

---

## LEADERS AND HEROES

### Charles E. Moore, MD; Founder of Health, Education, Assessment and Leadership, HEALing Community Center

Dr. Charles Moore had an "AHA moment" as he looked out into the community from the surgical suites at Grady Hospital, at which he is a head and neck surgeon. He recalls, "I woke up one day to the fact that I was seeing primarily men who looked

(continued)

LEADERS AND HEROES

## Charles E. Moore, MD; Founder of Health, Education, Assessment and Leadership, HEALing Community Center (*continued*)

like me coming in with head and neck cancer and who had no options. I even saw one man with cancer that I could not treat anymore because he had no insurance. The man told me, 'Just wait a bit, doc; I will be back.' The man had himself arrested and as a result he was able to come back to me to complete his treatment. His only option for access to care was going to prison."[1]

As a result of that epiphany, northwest Atlanta now has a free clinic that serves 600 people a month. Its motto is "Healing Our Community One Person at a Time."

The HEALing Community Center is dedicated to providing free specialty medical care to low-income children, women, and men. It is located in one of Atlanta's poorest neighborhoods, where having no medical insurance is commonplace. The people living in this community must overcome tremendous barriers to receive even the most basic medical care. When complex medical issues arise, specialty medical care is often simply not available. Health conditions that are curable and preventable are killing the community members, because simple screenings and care are beyond their reach.

"In hindsight, my path into the community was not dimly lit," says Moore, the founder of the clinic. "Grady Hospital has high patient volume, and I kept seeing the same thing over and over. Day after day, month after month, and year after year, I saw patients with cancers that could have been treated easily if the cancer had been identified early. And each time I would say to myself that someone should do something about this travesty. One day, I finally realized that maybe the person that was supposed to do something about this travesty was me."[2]

Moore decided there was more that he could do—and more that he should do—to help increase awareness on head and neck cancer. He knew that relatively simple things could be done. So, he focused on the three zip codes that represented the areas that had the highest percentage of head and neck cancers that he saw in his clinic at Grady. All three zip codes represented medically underserved areas. All of the convenience stores in poor neighborhoods sold tobacco and alcohol and displayed them prominently, even though these were the main causes of the cancer that he was seeing.

"I just got in my car and started going out to the community to meet people to see what their concerns were," Moore says. "Once people began to trust me, they began to call me to tell me about their needs. They had been 'burned' so often by people coming in and making promises. I went to homeless shelters, community and faith-based organizations to meet the leaders and the people of those organizations and communities. I gradually started giving cancer prevention talks, focusing on head and neck cancer. Through this process, I began to see all of the medical problems that were not being addressed. I also began to realize that, in many cases, people were just not aware of other options that could be taken that would improve their health. I began to see, with the community's help, all of the medical needs that were not being addressed and decided that comprehensive care was needed."[3]

Everything that happened was not positive, but Moore persevered. At one point, he and the individuals working with him to establish the center that they would name formally the HEALING Community Center thought that they had found a community partner and a space that would meet their needs. Things did not work out, and they had to find a new space. Grady Hospital has been very helpful to them, and their new space will allow them to provide even more health services, high-tech gardening, a grocery, and more. It will function like a community revitalization center when they really achieve their vision. Ninety percent of the head and neck cancer he saw came from this community. "With time and re-emergence of a strong community, we can change this," Moore believes. "And we actually grew stronger, thrived as a result of the adversity we experienced. We were not deterred. We will not miss a beat."[4]

Numerous community and academic institutions are now their partners. And they have had "wonderful support" from the Zeist Foundation, the United Way of Greater Atlanta, the Jessie Carson Williams Foundation, and Kaiser. Individuals have helped them develop a program that has authentic and workable wraparound services.

"There is a certain level of despair that touches something in all of us, and feeling that despair in those that I talked to is what compelled me to act," Moore recalls. "I came to understand that sometimes it is not the size of the act—big or small—but it is the act itself that can put things into motion. That action can open the door to provide not only access through barriers allowing patients to get healthcare, but also provide a conduit for healthcare professionals to do what we went into medicine for originally—to provide care for those most in need."[5]

"My chairman at Emory asked me what made me decide to establish the clinic. My response: 'How could I NOT?' These people looked like me, but that is where the similarity ended."[6]

For more information about the HEALing Community Center, visit http://www.healingourcommunities.org/index.html.

---

1. Author interview with Charles Moore, March 2011.
2. Ibid.
3. Ibid.
4. Ibid.
5. Ibid.
6. Ibid.

## Notes

1. Xanthos, Clare. "Feeling the Strain: The Impact of Stress on the Health of African-American Men." http://www.communityvoices .org/.
2. Author interview with Rev. William Brown, October 2009.
3. Brazile, D. Community Voices Freedom's Voice Conference, Atlanta, Georgia, 2009.
4. Ibid.
5. Author interview with Doug Lomax, October 2009.
6. Pierce, Chester M. "Psychiatric Problems of the Black Minority." In S. Arieti, ed. *American Handbook of Psychiatry*. New York: Basic Books. Vol. 2, 1974, pp. 512–523.
7. Geronimus, Arline T., et al. " 'Weathering' and Age Patterns of Allostatic Load Scores Among Blacks and Whites in the United States." *American Journal of Public Health* 2006;96:826–833.
8. Author interview with Doug Lomax, October 2009.
9. The Children's Defense Fund. http://www.childrensdefense.org.
10. HUD.GOV. "Understanding Neighborhood Effects of Concentrated Poverty." http://www.huduser.org/portal/periodicals/em/winter11/ highlight2.html.
11. Willis, Leigh A., David W. Coombs, William C. Cockerham, and Sonja L. Frison. "Ready to Die: A Postmodern Interpretation of the Increase of African-American Adolescent Male Suicide." *Social Science and Medicine* 2002;55:907–20.
12. Author interview with Robert Ross, November 2009.
13. Ibid.
14. Author interview with Ivory Varner, November 2009.
15. Author interview with Robert Ross, November 2009.

# CHAPTER 5

# A Deafening Silence

*"We must have unselfish, far-seeing leadership or we fail."*
—*W.E.B. Du Bois*

*After seeing doctors about his ongoing back pain, and receiving a short-term prescription for pain relievers that seemed to help somewhat but were quickly running out, Jamal hit the streets to begin looking for work. He had few leads, but knew he was interested in construction work. It seemed to be one of the few areas in which a man could become successful without having had a lot of schooling, and it was a skill he could take with him anywhere. It was a skill, however, that he had yet to possess. But Jamal was willing to start at the bottom, if only someone would give him a chance.*

*He visited site after site, some on the suggestion of friends and neighbors. Others he found by walking the streets and reading in the paper where new developments were being built. Again and again, his lack of experience was a problem, but one compounded by the time he had served incarcerated. Because he had, thus far, spent nearly his entire adulthood in prison, Jamal had no opportunity for job experience of any kind. He had occasionally worked in assembling products, or telemarketing, or washing dishes while in prison, but none of those experiences helped him find work on the outside.*

*It was becoming increasingly difficult to not just give up, but Jamal knew that giving up was not an option. Even if he wanted to revert back to an old life of crime to make money, which many of those he had served time with had done after finding it impossible to live a "straight life," his criminal background was nothing but petty juvenile nonsense that had gone from bad to worse. Jamal was no drug kingpin and did not even want to be one. He just wanted to find work, eventually have a family, and live a quiet, comfortable life. That was his dream, but, day after day, as he hit the streets, he felt that dream was slipping away.*

59

Through Community Voices, we regularly convene meetings with the community to ask its members how we can make a difference. I have long understood that you have to trust the people you serve to understand their needs better than anyone else. Far too many leaders forget that these are people we work for and with, not simply data sets. More often than not, the people living with the problems we are charged to solve can offer the most creative solutions to those problems—solutions that those working on policy and research may take twice as long, if ever, to get to.

Ask someone in trouble how he got there, and he will probably have a pretty good idea. He may not be honest about it with you if he does not believe you can be trusted to take responsible action, but, deep down, he knows how he got there. He is also most likely to be able to offer at least one way to save someone else from falling through the same cracks.

## Hope for Another Way

In one Community Voices meeting, a young black man said to me something so simple and clear that it continues to ring in my ear. He said, "You gotta give these folks some hope out here." Hope. It is precisely what is needed. Yet, although the word gets tossed around in leadership circles, the real concept has yet to elevate itself beyond the realm of talking point into multi-level policy recommendations.

We can offer people hope by addressing unfair housing policies. We can offer hope by working to repeal or reform unfair and unequal child support laws by reframing them not through punitive public policy, but through opportunity. We can offer people hope by developing pathways to help people start their own businesses if they cannot find a job.

These are not new ideas. People living in marginalized communities have been fighting an uphill battle to try to get leaders to listen to them for years. So how then do we explain the deafening silence of leadership to passionate ideas for solution? This silence continues even in the face of a continuing explosion of public policy that works against the poor, the near poor, the middle class, and the communities of color.

Hope is the most important window a community can have to help break through the terror. Even without the tangible available, people need hope. Sadly, for men and boys of color, today's statistics speak to anything but an opportunity for hope. Rather than investing in the hopes and dreams of developing minds, it becomes somehow acceptable to live in a nation in which one in three African American men can expect to spend some time in a jail cell at some point in his life. Even as we celebrate the increased numbers of African Americans in positional leadership in

**REALITY CHECK  How Do Your Beliefs Compare?**

In 2009, Community Voices commissioned a survey that included the statements in the chart below. These are the percentages of people who agree with the statements in the first column, nationally and in the state of Georgia. How about you?

| | National (%) | Georgia (%) | You: yes or no? |
|---|---|---|---|
| I personally know a prisoner. | 52 | 49 | |
| I am very concerned about crime in community. | 32 | 50 | |
| The prison experience reinforces criminal behavior. | 50 | 48 | |
| Prisoners re-entering society experience too many obstacles to living a crime-free life. | 57 | 48 | |
| Access to job training is very important for re-integration. | 85 | 84 | |
| Someone who has committed a felony should have access to medical services. | 88 | 84 | |
| Someone who has committed a felony should be allowed to vote. | 64 | 64 | |
| Inmates should be tested for communicable diseases when released. | 89 | 88 | |
| Additional state money should go toward treatment and services for ex-offenders over the building of prisons. | 70 | 69 | |

Wittman, Rebecca. "Attitudes Toward and Support for Services to Successfully Reintegrate People with Felony Convictions Back into Society: A Survey of Residents of the United States with an Oversample of Georgia Residents." Zogby International, 2009.

critical areas, we must ask: Where is the leadership that says there must be another way?

"People get into powerful positions," said Doug Lomax, a Substance Abuse Coordinator with the Boston Municipal Court, "and this becomes a non-priority for them. It's not a priority, because it's not something glamorous. We have leaders who are about moving something forward for us all as a people, but then we have those leaders who take from us to move forward their own agenda."[1]

People in leadership positions have the opportunity to give suffering men and boys hope by letting them know they are there to serve them not just in name and title, but through their commitment to action. When people are suffering, they need to know someone will look at their situation and respond. What men and boys of color too often see, however, is a society that has been judgmental instead of exploratory, knee-jerked into punitive responses instead of investigative of the cause of the problems people face.

Because we live in an era of increased African American leadership representation, we finally have the opportunity to have the discussion in an environment open to taking action. This is not an opportunity that comes along regularly, and it is the responsibility of each and every one of us to not squander it. We must, instead, work diligently to make the most out of this moment, and we must do it not only for those living on the margins, but for all of us who can and will benefit from a society led by the health and wellness of all of its people fully engaged in our collective growth.

Our current crisis requires that we each take responsibility for where we are as a community and as a nation and that we act responsibly and plan comprehensively for systems and policy change to reduce health inequities. One thing each of us can do right now is ensure that, as we move individuals of diverse backgrounds into leadership positions, our goal is not simply to have leadership that *looks* different, but leadership that *thinks* and *behaves* differently.

Right now, we are in a time when many feel we can consider doing things that never seemed possible before. The recent presidential election showed people from different communities coming together to do things differently. We saw people speaking out in support of their desire to become a better, more inclusive nation within which all voices matter. The pundits and the people, for a moment in time at least, seemed to agree: we could not keep going in the same direction. But that huge injection of hope can only be sustained if each of us continues to apply pressure to make the changes so many of us agreed were needed, real and present, in our lives.

## The Aging Prison Population

Human Rights Watch released a report in 2012 highlighting the soaring number of aging prisoners, as well as the impact that it is having on their health and, hence, our society.[2] The number of American men and women in prison who are 55 years of age or older is growing at a faster rate than the group's share of the general population. They are suffering;

**REALITY CHECK   Our Prisons Are Full of Old People**

Who thinks of old people when they think of the incarcerated? No one. Yet, the general population of the United Sates is getting older, and it should be no surprise that the prison population is not staying forever young either. This is having an enormous impact on the health and health care of prisoners, as well as on what it costs to keep people in prison long after they are a danger to society, as documented in a 2012 Human Rights Watch Report.[1] For example:

- The number of US state and federal prisoners 65 years of age or older grew at 94 times the rate of the total prison population between 2007 and 2010.

- The number of prisoners 65 years of age or older increased by 63%. There are now 26,200 prisoners 65 years of age or older.

- There are now 124,400 prisoners 55 years of age or older.

- 14% of federal prisoners are 51 years of age or older.

## Impact on Health Expenditures

- Chronic diseases, including dementia; high blood pressure; diabetes; incontinence; frailness; and mobility, hearing, and vision impairments are skyrocketing.

- Medical expenditures for older prisoners are 3–9 times as high as for other prisoners (varies from state to state).

- In Florida, 16% percent of the prison population is 50 years of age or older; yet they account for 40.1% of overall medical care and 47.9% of hospital days.

- In Georgia, prisoners 65 years of age or older averaged medical costs of $8,565 per year; compare this with the average medical cost for those younger than 65 years of age, which is $961 per year.

- Michigan estimates that its average annual health care cost for each of its prison inmates is $5,801; as prisoners age, the cost goes up—from $11,000 for those between the 55 and 59 years of age to $40,000 for those 80 years of age or older.[2]

---

1. Human Rights Watch. "Old Behind Bars: The Aging Prison Population in the United States." 2012. http://www.hrw.org/reports/2012/01/27/old-behind-bars-0
2. Ibid.

to provide needed health care, it can cost as much as 9 times more than for younger inmates. It seems no one planned for this, and the problem is compounded by strained budgets, non-accessible prison architecture, limited medical staff and facilities, and a lack of support from elected officials.

> "Prisons were never designed to be geriatric facilities. Yet U.S. corrections officials now operate old age homes behind bars."
>
> —Jamie Fellner, Senior Adviser to the U.S. Program at Human Rights Watch

In its report, Human Rights Watch recommended that "state and federal officials review sentencing and release policies to determine which could be modified to reduce the growing population of older prisoners without risking public safety; develop comprehensive plans for housing, medical care, and programs for the current and projected populations of older prisoners; and modify prison rules that impose unnecessary hardship on older inmates."[3] In the meantime, California has only three hospitals for prisoners with about 120 beds that must contract with private operators for inpatient care—for $850,000 a year. Their solution is to build a $750 million medical center for inmates. It will be located in Stockton and have 1,772 beds, a pharmacy, and a dialysis clinic.[4]

In Milledgeville, Georgia, the former Bostick State Prison (closed in 2009) will become a geriatric facility for parolees. These individuals have served their sentences and have nowhere to go, as extended sentences or broken relationships with families over the years of separation have left them homeless and without family support. The state will provide $6 million for the conversion if the legislature approves the expenditure. The facility will create 250 jobs for this rural community and provide 150 beds for elderly sex offenders and other prisoners with health problems. The facility will be operated by a private company paid for with federal Medicaid dollars, not state funds, for the care of the parolees. This type of care is not available to those who have served their sentences but do not qualify for SSI and Medicaid, even though they, too, may have nowhere to go.[5]

## Collectivism vs. Individualism

For too long, we have been moving from collectivism to individualism in the African American community. This move, merging as it has with the decline in African American institutions, has resulted in the loss of what were previously protective and insulating features of black communities. African Americans have lost many leaders who were fighting to realize a dream of equality. Walk through our remaining institutions, and you will find monuments erected to honor their memory; there are ways, however, to honor their sacrifices that are even more lasting—realize the dream for everyone.

Because so many of those in leadership do not see themselves in the faces of those living at the margins, the sense of urgency to address these problems, even as they grow in scope and size, evaporates.

The reality is that the young black men who are imprisoned today are the same young black men of yesterday who marched for civil rights. These are the same young black men who were once the doctors, dentists, artists, poets, teachers, and lawyers of yesterday. When we look around and wonder where all the men have gone or why colleges and universities are now seeing a 10:1 ratio of black women to black men, it is certainly not because all black men suddenly became unintelligent. They did not suddenly lose their capacity to dream.

What has happened is that they have been systematically disappeared into criminal justice facilities. It is my hope that, rather than continue the deafening silence, every one of us looks into the mirror to face the fact that millions have been lost because we have not been doing our jobs. Whether our job is mother or mentor, school principal or governor, philanthropic leader or fraternity brother, employer or employee, each of us can step up and take responsibility for our role in continuing the silence that accompanies the vanishing of one after another after another young black man from his ability to contribute to the building of a better world for us all.

Until we do this, the silence will continue, despite the fact that there are fewer and fewer spaces left in which young men of color are simply not represented, including, despite increases in public leadership, at the leadership tables at which they are needed to ensure that their interests are met. I am sad to note that the seats at many of the meetings I attend to address the health inequities of men of color are still filled by a white majority. Each of us, despite our race or gender, has a role and a responsibility to address this crisis, but we also have a responsibility to ensure that access to the arenas in which consensus is made on strategies for solution is available to those who are suffering most directly from the crisis at hand.

The future of the African American community rests firmly on the shoulders of the African American community. There is not one bit of progress we have ever made for which we have not had to work long and hard. That has not changed. The question is: When did *we* change?

When did our chants of "*we* shall overcome" change to "*me* shall overcome?" Despite changes in leadership at the top, we cannot forget there is no one person who can come to save us. We all have a stake in our collective survival.

None of us, no matter our position, got to where we are solely because we were just good at what we did. Whether we are in the halls of leadership or we are struggling to make a way out of no way, we stand on the shoulders of many who have died for us all to live better, healthier, more fulfilling lives. For centuries, people of color have been good at building this country. We owe a great deal of our success to those who came before us and took up the mantle of leadership to pave the way for us. We did not just climb the ladder on our own. Someone had to build each one of those rungs so we could step up.

When we look through the history of African American community, we can look as far back as the depths of slavery and still identify clear heroes who stepped forward with passion to say, "This is not right." Frederick Douglass used his pen. Harriet Tubman risked her safety time and again to return south and lead people to freedom. In the 20th century, we watched leader after leader sacrifice his or her very life to ensure our nation's progress.

Today, although so many have moved into powerful and prestigious positions in every sector of society, we have yet to finish the job of releasing people from the ravages of slavery and segregation. Everyone everywhere has a place in this story of change. Those working in middle and upper management, whether in a corporation, a small business, or a nonprofit or a government agency, have a special responsibility. That responsibility, however, is not limited to those who have made it to the top—at every level we can make a difference.

The very fabric of our community is being destroyed, yet, when my colleagues and I look around, we see far too many leaders blind to the sense of alarm leaking from the community. The public health community has worked hard to create space for improving the health status of women and children, but a major part of that effort necessitates the support networks inherent in a whole family, a whole community.

We need those in powerful positions within the institutions charged with ensuring an equal shot at a healthy life to be determined to think tactically and strategically. Some of our leadership may already come into such work feeling disempowered, and those feelings must be both addressed and put to the side in the name of real progress. Too often we are socialized, particularly when we come from marginalized communities, to believe we must ask permission for every step we take. The continuing crisis demands we move resources from bloated and ineffective

**TAKE A GOOD LOOK** **Business Owners**

Are you a business owner or human resources professional? If not, can you imagine what it is like to be in the position of hiring employees? Look in the mirror and ask yourself:

- Would you hire someone who had previously been incarcerated if he or she were black? What if he or she were white—would that make a difference?

- What can you do to ensure hiring practices at your place of employment offer a fair shot to *all* qualified applicants?

- Is your company willing to remove questions about felony convictions from the first round of job applications in an attempt to level the playing field, using those questions only when needed for security clearance for those who are being offered positions?

- What could local businesses and others do to not just give people a job, but also help them from their own business as entrepreneurs?

- Does your local federal Job Corps program offer training to those with a felony conviction? If not, why?

- Does your local Small Business Association offer funds to those who have completed a felony conviction access to capital so they can start their own businesses since others do not hire them? If not, who provides access to capital? If so, to what degree are ex-offenders taking advantage of these programs?

- What role can you play in keeping tabs on local hiring policies and practices and in changing these?

- Write one thing you are willing to do to level the playing field for job seekers—then get busy: _____

_____

programs to those in which need is most critical. The communities, and a select group of emerging leaders, have been identifying those needs even in the face of that deafening silence. It is up to those in positions of power to push to know when they really need permission to act versus when it might be more expedient to take necessary action and inform those they might otherwise ask permission later.

## Reentry: Getting Down to Business

Once many prisoners are released, having lost a significant amount of workforce years to incarceration, they are discriminated against in their search for honest employment.

Often the problem is misinformation about the rights of the formerly incarcerated. To counteract this widespread situation, the Federal Interagency Reentry Council has created a series of "Reentry MythBusters"— no-nonsense fact sheets clarifying existing federal policies that affect formerly incarcerated individuals and their families. (Sample myths and facts are provided in the box following.) The sheets cover access to benefits, public housing, employer incentives, parental rights, Medicaid suspension/termination, and more. Some federal laws and policies are, in fact, narrower than is commonly perceived, such as in public housing and food assistance benefits. States and localities often have broad discretion in determining how policies are applied, and states have various opt-out provisions. Many people are surprised to learn that certain statutory barriers do not exist at all or are very limited, as is the case with federal hiring. If you are an employer, you may not be aware that some federal policies and practices even contain incentives for assisting the formerly convicted population!

According to the Society for Human Resource Management, "more than 80 percent of U.S. employers perform criminal background checks on prospective employees. More than one in four U.S. adults—roughly 65 million people—have an arrest or conviction that shows up in a routine criminal background check." [6] Pepsi Beverages is a recent example. According to a Web site for people working in the Human Resources field, an EEOC investigation "revealed that more than 300 African Americans were adversely affected when Pepsi Beverages applied a criminal background check policy that disproportionately excluded black applicants from permanent employment. Under Pepsi's policy, job applicants who had been merely arrested pending prosecution were not hired for a permanent job even if they had never been convicted of any offense. Pepsi's policy also denied employment to applicants from employment who had been arrested or convicted of certain minor offenses. The use of arrest and conviction records to deny employment can be illegal when it is not relevant for the job, because it can limit the employment opportunities of applicants or workers based on their race or ethnicity. Pepsi Beverages has agreed to pay $3.13 million and provide job offers and training" to resolve the charge, and it has changed its background check policy. [7]

The Reentry Council urges people in the following positions to refer to their fact sheets[8] when making decisions about formerly incarcerated individuals:

- Prison, jail, probation, community corrections, and parole officials: Do you want to ensure that individuals can access federal benefits, as appropriate, immediately upon release to help stabilize the critical first days and weeks after incarceration?

- Reentry service providers and faith-based organizations: Do you want to know how to access the laws and policies related to public housing, SNAP benefits, federal student financial aid, and Veterans, Social Security, and TANF benefits?

- Employers and workforce development specialists: Are you interested in the incentives and protections involved in hiring formerly convicted individuals? Do you want to better understand the appropriate use of a criminal record in making hiring decisions?

---

 **REALITY CHECK Reentry Myths**

The following three examples from the Reentry MythBusters fact sheets[1] may surprise you:

**Myth:** Individuals who have been convicted of a crime are "banned" from public housing.

**FACT:** Public Housing Authorities [PHAs] have great discretion in determining their admissions and occupancy policies for ex-offenders. While PHAs can choose to ban ex-offenders from participating in public housing and Section 8 programs, it is not [U.S. Department of Housing and Urban Development] HUD policy to do so.

**Myth:** Employers have no federal income tax advantage by hiring an ex-felon.

**FACT:** Employers can save money on their federal income taxes in the form of a tax credit incentive through the Work Opportunity Tax Credit (WOTC) program by hiring ex-felons.

**Myth:** People with criminal records are automatically barred from employment.

**FACT:** An arrest or conviction record will NOT automatically bar individuals from employment.

---

1. Federal Interagency Reentry Council. "Reentry MythBusters." http://www.national reentryresourcecenter.org/documents/0000/1090/REENTRY_MYTHBUSTERS.pdf.

- States and local agencies: Do you want to understand, modify, or eliminate certain bans on benefits (TANF [Transitional Assistance to Needy Families], SNAP [Supplemental Nutrition Assistance Program]) for people who have been convicted of drug felonies?"[9]

As blogger Sharon Zaleski advised, "Based on what's happened at Pepsi, it's probably a very good idea for businesses to revisit or examine their hiring and background check policies to be in compliance with the EEOC [Equal Employment Opportunity Commission] and avoid against problems in the future."[10]

Aside from the risk of a lawsuit, it is the right thing to do. A 2009 study by Carnegie Mellon researchers shows that people who stay clean reach a point—in some cases as soon as 3 or 4 years—when their prior arrest is of no value in predicting future arrests. Eventually, those who stay out of trouble are largely indistinguishable from the general population in terms of their odds of another arrest. The researchers write, "People performing criminal background checks would find it valuable to know when an ex-offender has been clean long enough that he presents the same risk as other people in the general population. Employers also might be more likely to use this type of analysis if there were state statutes protecting them against due diligence liability claims when they adhered to reasonable risk-analysis findings."[11]

## Our Ongoing Task: Growing Champions

As Doug Lomax said, addressing the crisis of continuing health inequalities may not be the most glamorous work, but ignoring it is no longer an option. We have run out of time for responses like the one I heard in a recent meeting of public health leaders when the subject was broached. Instead of exploring the options put on the table, this leader expressed his frustration with being asked to continue discussion of the topic by saying to the entire group, "We talked about disparities yesterday!"

Some will argue that the crop of leaders may not be made of the same grit that built the rungs of the ladder they climbed to get into power. Although it is true that it may sometimes seem as if the second and third waves of leaders are not sufficiently immersed in the issues that brought us to this place, that fact may actually be both hopeful and helpful, because it removes a great deal of baggage. It falls on the shoulders of those who have been working far longer to ensure what we do not lose is our historical memory—something that will help us not only push past the barriers, but understand the nature of those barriers and why they persist.

LEADERS AND HEROES

## Darrell Ellison, Business Owner; Executive Director, Jails to Nails, Inc.

Darrell Ellison has been in the contractor business for about 20 years; for the past 4 years, he has also been in the business of helping released prisoners rebuild their lives. He knows about the obstacles the people face first hand: his brother has been in prison for 18 years. Ellison's brother's incarceration and the incarceration of many friends opened his eyes: he says, "You do not see it unless it hits you at home." He now knows that getting employment is very difficult for those coming home from incarceration. "No one gives them a chance. I felt that I had to do something."

According to the Jails to Nails Web site, that "something" turned out to be Jails To Nails, Inc., "which was conceived, organized and implemented with the main goal of providing employment, training, education, and housing for non-violent ex-offenders that would otherwise not have the opportunity nor the resources." Ellison's vision for Jails to Nails began with a conversation with a key employee that suggested using non-violent ex-offenders in existing and future projects from halfway houses and other federal and state programs.

As Chairman of the Board, President and Chief Executive of Jails to Nails, today Ellison is "responsible for the overall performance of the organization. He relies upon a diverse board of directors, advisory board and a strategic business development model to sustain and maintain its mission."[1]

According to Ellison, Jails to Nails fills the void created by the reality that former inmates often face numerous barriers to successful employment. These include hesitancy on the part of employers to hire ex-offenders and a lack of skills on the part of ex-offenders to market themselves effectively to potential employers. In addition, ex-offenders often lack the social supports needed to allow them to enter and remain in the workplace and there may be substance abuse and lack of permanent housing. As a result, employers in need of qualified workers are more likely to hire ex-offenders who are supervised by a structured re-entry program than those who are not.

The Jails to Nails ex-offender re-entry process provides initial services to program clients during the prison pre-release phase and expanded services during the community transition in a halfway house or work release program sponsored by the Federal Bureau of Prisons or the State Department of Corrections. The organization's unique business model solution is wrapped around this 270-day critical period in an ex-offender's life as it draws from a limitless supply of newly-released state and federal inmates.

The business model provides daily, weekly, or sustained employment. As their Web site explains, The Job-Training Program provides "onsite physical training and offsite classroom training during the course of the ex-offender's Jails to Nails contract. The

*(continued)*

**Darrell Ellison, Business Owner; Executive Director, Jails to Nails, Inc. (*continued*)**

job-training program offers all of the phases of residential and commercial construction including site preparation & labor, foundation, concrete, framing, roofing, exterior siding, gutters, landscaping, electrical, Heating, Venting & Air Conditioning, plumbing, drywall, painting, flooring and inspection. Working in conjunction with the job-training program, the Continuing Education Program will provide GED studies, computer literacy skills, internet access and job placement services to include resume preparation and job interviewing techniques."[2]

Ellison says, "85% of the people we hire come from jail or county or state prison. Jails to Nails works insofar as giving an individual coming home a job and some income. But much more is needed as the person coming home probably has housing, healthcare and other needs and they cannot generally solve all of these problems by themselves particularly if their family support is limited." Jails to Nails does try to get those that are working with them involved in some faith-based activities as a way of getting some support.

Jails to Nails is located in Grayson, Georgia. It is, in Ellison's words, a "mom and pop" organization. They would like to grow. They would like to specialize in housing development that his workers could afford to rent or buy, but he also wants to continue to use his crews to do the seemingly small jobs like repairing a bathroom in the home of an elderly individual who could not afford the repair without the economies of scale that Jails to Nails brings to them. "The smile on their face means a lot to me."

Ellison states, "We need more partners and greater investment. We would like to franchise." Communities like Virginia Beach, Cincinnati, and Detroit have asked him to bring Jails to Nails to their cities. They do not have the funds to franchise at the moment, but there are some strong supporters, Ellison points out, such as Home Depot, who "has been wonderful in that they provide a great deal of construction material without charge." Ellison's goals are both lofty and down to earth: "Our hope and vision is to make a difference in the lives of individuals that desire the opportunity for a second chance. With the help and support of our partners and alliances we will achieve our goals . . . to successfully transform prior convicted offenders into productive citizens with the desire to help others."[3]

For more information about Jails to Nails, visit: http://www.jailstonails.org/.

1. Jails to Nails web site. http://www.velozi.com/websites/jailstonails/about.html.
2. Jails to Nails web site. http://www.velozi.com/websites/jailstonails/programs.html.
3. Author interview with Darrell Ellison, March 2012.

"We have to be better equipped ourselves as people of color," said Joe Brooks, Vice President for Civic Engagement at Policy Link. "We have to grow our own champions, and grow them with an analysis and connection to community who are accountable and who are transparent and whose articulation of concerns is connected to community—not to remain silent."[12]

## Notes

1. Author interview with Doug Lomax, October 2009.
2. Human Rights Watch. "Old Behind Bars: The Aging Prison Population in the United States." 2012. http://www.hrw.org/reports/2012/01/27/old-behind-bars-0
3. Human Rights Watch. "Old Behind Bars" The Aging Prison Population in the United States." 2012. http://www.hrw.org/reports/2012/01/27/old-behind-bars-0
4. Williams, Timothy. "Number of Older Inmates Grows, Stressing Prisons." *New York Times.* http://www.nyt.com.
5. Savage, Randall. "Former Prison Becoming a Parolee Nursing Home." *13WMAZ.* January 18, 2012. http://www.13wmaz.com/.
6. Burke, M.E., 2004 Reference and Background Checking Survey Report: A Study by the Society for Human Resource Management, Alexandria, VA: Society for Human Resource Management, 2006.
7. HR and Employment Law News. "Pepsi Agrees to Pay $3 Million After Investigation into Background Check Policy." http://hr.blr.com/.
8. Federal Interagency Reentry Council. Reentry MythBusters. http://www.nationalreentryresourcecenter.org/documents/0000/1090/REENTRY_MYTHBUSTERS.pdf.
9. Federal Interagency Reentry Council. Reentry Mythbusters. http://www.nationalreentryresourcecenter.org/documents/0000/1090/REENTRY_MYTHBUSTERS.pdf.
10. Zaleski, Sharon. "Pepsi Reaches $3.1 Million Settlement with EEOC Due To Racial Discrimination." http://www.intellicorp.net.
11. Blumstein, Alfred and Kiminori Nakamura. "'Redemption' in an Era of Widespread Criminal Background Checks." *National Institute of Justice Journal* 2009;263:10–17.
12. Author Interview with Joe Brooks, November 2009.

# CHAPTER 6

# The Marginalization of Voices for Change

*"We all must find a way to get in the way.*
*You must do your part and encourage others."*
                                        —*U.S. Congressman John Lewis*

*Early one morning, palming a steaming hot cup of coffee at the roadside with a group of eager men in search of day work, Jamal met Benjamin. Benjamin is in his mid-30s and is struggling to feed his children, make enormous court-mandated child support payments to his ex-girlfriend, and find a path to stability so he can get a place of his own where he and his children can stay so he can finally fight for shared custody. Benjamin, a veteran, is easily irritated, is nervous all the time, and has had trouble holding a regular job. He needs eye care and dental care, but could not get it, because his problems were not "war related." Like so many of the men teetering on the edge of homelessness and mental problems, he fought in a war and could get care on the battlefield if injured, but cannot get it at home. Fortunately, he has avoided incarceration, unlike many other veterans sliding down the slippery slope of home. Benjamin walks with a slight limp from an old work injury, which he hides whenever a pickup truck pulls up with a potential employer. Of course, this injury has not been properly treated either.*

*Jamal and Benjamin finished their coffee and huddled under a tree for shade. As the day got hotter and the hours grew later, the sense of hopelessness over losing another workday was climbing both of their bodies like a choking vine. Benjamin eventually suggested they give up and go get something to eat; he knew of another site at which he has had luck, and they could walk there together. Jamal had no money for food and was begging off, suggesting he would stay here to wait it out, when Benjamin told him they did not need any money. They could go down to a church he knew of at which they could get food, clothes, even shelter if they wanted to get on the long list.*

*Jamal had not had a decent meal in days and jumped at the chance. When he walked through the church's front door with Benjamin, a jovial, older man greeted them as he struggled beneath the weight of a heavy box he was trying to get downstairs. Jamal quickly jumped in and took the box from the man, Benjamin grabbed another, and the two men helped the man, who introduced himself as Pastor Hobson, move the heavy boxes of canned goods down to the basement storage room. Before Jamal had a chance to get self-conscious about why they had come, Pastor Hobson put a friendly hand on their shoulders and asked if the men were hungry. A relieved smile crossed their faces, and Jamal and Benjamin allowed themselves to be led to the rectory, where they were given a plate full of steaming hot, home made food.*

*Pastor Hobson sat with the men for a moment, and they told him about their failure to get picked up for work after standing in the growing heat for hours. They thanked him for helping them get up and go out to the next site to try again for the afternoon. Pastor Hobson thought for a moment about all of the boxes of donated cans yet to be moved and organized and suggested the church could hire them for the day to help him get the job done. "Now, I can't do this all the time, or for everyone," he said. "But you two came at just the right time. You'd both get a full day's wage, and you can stick around for supper when you're through."*

*With full bellies and hearts bursting with hope and gratitude for the first time in days, the men got up and got busy working. The work was easy, if a little aggravating on Jamal's sensitive back and Benjamin's bad leg. The church had just completed a very successful neighborhood canned-food drive and needed to move and organize the supplies so they could be inventoried for use in their hot food program. At the end of the day, Pastor Hobson paid them both and told them not to be strangers. "This house is God's house," he said, "and you are always welcome here."*

To have a lasting impact on the healthy lives of young men and boys, effective leadership must be engaged with a steadfast commitment to educational and social change. As Dr. Robert Ross, director of the California Endowment, said to me, the time for quick-fix thinking has long passed.[1] When we reflect on the kind of leadership that has succeeded in improving the lives of African Americans in the past, we cannot escape the important role of African American institutions like churches and historically black colleges and universities (HBCUs) in driving social change. Today, however, these institutions generally seem to be stuck on "pause" and are not leading to change in the same way they used to. It is my hope that they rethink their level of activism and advocacy in a truly visionary way. It is my conviction that, if the churches would just stand up, the rest of us could stand down, or sit down. Faith in Action! It also seems to me that much of the church has become a place to save MY soul versus saving the heart and soul of ALL of humanity. When did the scriptures, of all faiths, become so SELF-centered?

Fortunately, things are beginning to change in our faith communities, which often remain the best first stop for triage to help people in crisis. I have spoken about the current "power failure" to faith leaders who are dedicated to stitching the wounds that are bleeding black men from their families. Many have shared their thoughts with me about this book, and what recurs is that, although many institutions understand there is a crisis unfolding right outside of their door, many are struggling—much like Martin and Jamal—simply to keep their doors open and stay in business

 **REALITY CHECK   Brokenhearted**

Left unchecked, chronic stress can wreak havoc on physical, psychological, and emotional health. In fact, there is a name for the effects on the cardiovascular system: broken heart syndrome. Stress can increase risk of cardiovascular disease in a variety of ways, such as affecting the sympathetic nervous system and hemostasis and triggering unhealthy behaviors, such as smoking and overeating. Considering the stresses they face, is it not surprising that:

- African American men are 30% more likely than white men to die from heart disease.

- African American men (and women) in the United States have the highest rates of hypertension in the world.

- African American men, 30-39 years of age, are 14 times more likely to develop kidney failure due to hypertension than white men in the same age group.

- African American men in the United States have the highest rates of prostate cancer in the world.

- African Americans are 1.5-2.5 times more likely to suffer from lower limb amputations than other diabetes patients.[1]

1. Department of Health and Human Services Office of Minority Health. "Data Statistics: African American Profile." http://minorityhealth.hhs.gov/templates/content .aspx?lvl=2&lvlID=51&ID=3017.

from day to day. Our institutions are financially fragile and many are balancing precariously on the brink of economic disaster. Without a wider investment of public and private resources, many of our best minds look to those suffering with a growing sense of helplessness.

By finding new ways to work together, we can untie the hands of our leadership. Although it is true that many HBCUs are struggling with tiny endowments that barely allow them to keep the lights on, there are others that have more latitude to engage in creative thinking. Because the crisis is not confined by state, region, or community, working together is not an option; it is a necessity. Bringing those with resources together with those without, we can also work to build a strong firewall so every institution is in a secure enough position to take on the difficult dialogue needed without scaring off potential funders.

## Mentors—Leading from the Middle

And where are our mentors? In an interview, I once said, "Those who assume powerful positions must have a full understanding of their very solemn responsibility to reach out a hand to up-and-comers. Nobody can say truthfully that they made it on his or her own. All of us have had a mentor, an ancestor, or a family member, such as my Aunt Modjeska who you will meet in this chapter, or a cheerleader somewhere along the path to success. It is important not to forget them, and it is equally important to be a mentor or cheerleader for others working in the same direction, regardless of your field."[2]

"Without mentorship, I would not be who I am today," said Pastor Donna Hubbard.[3] Hubbard is a tireless advocate for the formerly incarcerated. Having been incarcerated herself, Pastor Hubbard looked up from her prison bunk and saw a life stretched out before her that held no hope for anything but the continued cycle of desperation, degradation, and hopelessness. With the help of her mentor, the evangelist Margaret Reynolds who founded Revelation Seed, Pastor Hubbard resolved to take control of her life so that, once she was released, the only time she would see the inside of a prison again would be when she came to help others.

"There are plenty who come out of prison every day that do not find themselves in my place," she said. "I'm here because of the mentors who have taken on my struggle and believed in me. The greatest words you can say to another human being are, 'I believe in you,' and the greatest attribute of mentorship is that it empowers the people who are helped to turn around and mentor someone else."[4]

Being a woman and being outspoken is a huge leap of faith that comes with its own critics. The mothers of the millions of African American

HISTORY OF CHANGE **MODJESKA MONTEITH SIMKINS, CIVIL RIGHTS ADVOCATE (1899–1992)**

Modjeska Monteith Simkins was a "leader of African American public health reform, social reform and the civil rights movement in South Carolina."[1] She received her Bachelor of Arts degree in 1921 and taught at Booker T. Washington High School until she was forced to resign after marrying Andrew Simkins in 1929.

"In 1931, Simkins entered the field of public health as the Director of Negro Work for the South Carolina Anti-Tuberculosis Association, and became the state's only full-time, statewide African-American public health worker."[2]

"I couldn't divorce my interest in civil rights from my dedication to trying to solve these health problems," said Simkins in an interview about how she persevered in her work toward health equality despite the many odds stacked against her.

By creating alliances with influential white and African American groups and raising funds, Simkins made a substantial impact on the health of black South Carolinians. She lost her position with the Anti-Tuberculosis Association in 1942, owing, in part, to her work with the National Association for the Advancement of Colored People (NAACP).

"My boss sensed it, and she said that I would have to leave off some of these activities. My answer was I'd rather see a person die and go to hell with tuberculosis than to be treated how some of my people were treated. Although I was not fired, my position became untenable and we parted ways."[3]

---

1. Modjeska Monteith Simkins House. NPS.gov. http://www.cr.nps.gov/nr/travel/civil rights/sc3.htm.
2. Modjeska Monteith Simkins House. NPS.gov. http://www.cr.nps.gov/nr/travel/civil rights/sc3.htm.
3. Author interview with Modjeska Monteith Simkins, January 1982.

---

men who are incarcerated are all women, and as the crisis continues to affect the life opportunities of men of color, more women than ever are ascending into leadership positions with the determination to take action. Given the current power failure, expressed at every level by a lack of sustained action and commitment, we all have to realize that the stage of leadership is wide open to all of us and auditions are being held for men and women who are prepared to lead. There are men in leadership positions who want to own this issue—let them step up. But all of us, men and women, who are committed to ending the crisis know that what we do not have room for is more of the leadership of self-aggrandizement without much substance.

This crisis is one played out in the bodies and minds of men, but those bodies and minds have been grown and nurtured and loved by women, and we have an enormous stake in their health and survival. Our families—or even our hopes to someday have families—are being threatened. If the women who are leading are willing to do so with more facts and a greater passion for change, then let us all step up and lead. There is still plenty of room for some women—famous and not, wealthy and resource poor—to lead us out of this challenge. Our historical role as conductors of the proverbial underground railroad is still very much in need. What each of us needs to remember is that we do not have to be at the front of the pack to lead. In these times, we are better served by those committed to helping to drive a movement lead from the middle.

Throughout our history, there have been African American doctors, nurses, mothers, fathers, and teachers who walked with a sense of justice that related directly to health justice and who connected through a deep belief in civil rights. My aunt, Modjeska Monteith Simkins, was one of those people. She worked tirelessly for the health, education, and welfare of African Americans at a time when open and often violent hostility made the work especially dangerous. Serving in leadership positions traditionally unavailable to women in the civil rights movement, her outspoken activism was considered controversial, her life and home became targets. While active with the NAACP, she had her house shot at by unknown assailants and was accused of subversive activities and investigated by the Federal Bureau of Investigation and the House Un-American Activities Committee. None of this deterred her from continuing to press forward and doing the work she knew was right and important.

I learned a great deal about how to be truly dedicated to the healthy lives of the people who may not have been able to speak for themselves from my aunt. In the 1940s and 1950s, intimidation was a serious force. To a different degree, intimidation is still at work, but, just like my Aunt Modjeska, we do not have to let it stop our work.

## Being "Difficult"

One barrier to leaders taking unpopular positions is threats—or perceived threats—to career or funding. People do not want to be perceived as being "difficult," an accusation particularly used against women in leadership. I have heard it myself many times, but, as I tell myself, my staff, and my colleagues, these difficult times call for difficult dialogues. Until we get honest about the problems we are facing, we will never make a difference. To be truly effective, men and women in leadership positions cannot be intimidated into losing focus. Engaging in an active support system and having a clear vision are the best tools to fight anyone who would tell us to step down, step back, or stand silent.

Too many leaders do not draw the line in the sand needed and say "Here I stand." If you do not make that statement to yourself, then how will anyone be able to follow you? Despite threats to life and livelihood, people like my aunt spoke up and acted out on behalf of the larger community, black and white, rich and poor. These people did not ask for permission to act. They knew the risks to life, limb, and career, but they did what they knew was right anyway and made significant strides. Hospitals were opened. Through her efforts, and those of the many in the network of activists supporting a sound vision, the American Medical Association finally abandoned the bankrupt policies of discrimination that allowed them to throw their hands up and say they "wished" that doctors would treat poor people, and black people, but there was "nothing we can do."

There is always something we can do. Failure to act is an act that embraces discrimination and propels health inequities. Our ideology should be based on what *is* versus what we think should to be. Unless we are working in the context of realism—not nihilism— but dealing with the situation as it is and guiding our work with a profound optimism for what it *can* be, then we are destined not only to failure, but to burnout and giving up on our goals.

There once was a time, when discrimination was rampant and publicly accepted, when people were explicit in saying who they would not serve. These days, those same people are not being served, but people are quiet about it and say nothing. It is a quiet affront, a silent omission that allows the same type of discrimination to exist, although we are allowed to pretend that those days are behind us. In reality, there is a power failure of leadership at the local and national levels, leaders who create health care policy and continue to act as if there are not large segments of the population not being served in our health care system.

## Moving beyond Our Own Limitations

Even beyond outside forces that erect barriers to our success, power failure exhibits itself when we are the ones who limit our own success or find success in personal aggrandizement rather than community uplift. An effective leader moves beyond public censure to insist that their hospital system and school or public health program reach out to the most vulnerable individuals, and he or she does it not for personal publicity, but out of a firm commitment to healthy communities and a healthy society.

Philosopher, activist, and Princeton University professor Cornel West has called too many of today's leaders "too hungry for status to be angry, too eager for acceptance to be bold, too self-invested in advancement to be defiant."[5] This is one of the most insidious manifestations of power failure. It creeps up not only when leaders hold themselves back from difficult action, but also when they hold back others in their network.

Power failure can feed on itself in this way and spread to infect entire agencies, organizations, and communities. "Not only do I have power failure," an honest leader might say to him- or herself, "but I want you to fail too." Such leaders pull the plug on innovative work, shut down opportunities for creative thinking, and push back those who might step up to offer the kind of leadership that is lacking.

Barack Obama won the election, in large part, because people were attracted to his impulse for reconciliation and compromise. At the beginning of the 2008 election season, all four of the candidates had an equal shot at my vote—Clinton, McCain, Romney, and Obama. In the end, like millions of my fellow citizens, I voted not just for hope, not only for change, but also for compromise, for working together toward the common good. Obama's victory showed that many voters needed to see a charismatic leader not just in their president, but also in themselves. We are now in danger of losing yet another opportunity to keep the focus on what we can each do as leaders to create a culture that values the lives of every person.

---

 **TAKE A GOOD LOOK** **Patrons or Producers of the Arts**

Are you an arts patron or producer? If not, can you imagine what it is like to be a patron or producer? Look in the mirror and ask yourself:

- Is *STAINS* a film that individuals in your community would view? If so, would you be able to host a viewing? (see page 83)

- If your community would not have an interest, why is this case?

- How would or could you work to have a dialogue in your community about finding ways to help the families of those left behind?

- What could you do personally to help?

- How do you feel about those who have gone to prison and those who were left behind? Do your feelings help you move to do something positive?

Today, we have one of the best opportunities in a generation to crawl outside of the grip of power failure and build strong networks that can withstand efforts to marginalize voices for change. We have run out of time to keep supporting leaders who are reluctant to take the risk of working on a certain issue if it is unpopular with their colleagues, constituency, or administration. Working together we can leverage resources, energy, and talent to force the spotlight on the plight of men and boys of color.

---

LEADERS AND HEROES

## Doris Mangrum, Book Author, Activist, and Executive Producer of *STAINS*

Doris Mangrum has been a parenting professional for more than 25 years. For the last 20 years she has focused, in particular, on incarcerated parents and the plight of their families, including the pangs of long separation and the reunification process. She says, "Once we throw away the offender we do nothing else. There are 3–5 other people that are connected to that person—parents, relatives—this is a forgotten population. It's time to stop rationalizing our inhumanity. It's time to stop wondering why so many people keep going back to prison when we do so little to help them transition back into society. It's time to stop treating families affected by incarceration as if they committed crime. They have not."

Born and raised in Georgia, of parents who "reared me to help," she has become a "sought-after expert on program and intervention design by correctional facilities, an advisor in high profile criminal cases, and an expert panelist" in academic forum discussions on incarceration. She is the author of *After the Bungy Jump, There's Still a Lot of Jerking Goin' On*, which provides us with a unique look at a mother's 8 years of incarceration and the challenges it presents, as well as the concerns of her family during the same period. She is also the Executive Producer and screenwriter of the feature-length documentary film, *STAINS: Changing Lives after Incarceration*, which premiered at Tribeca Cinemas in 2011. *STAINS* deals with the challenges of the formerly incarcerated and their families. It introduces us to programs throughout the United States that support easing the transition from incarceration to society and that help families deal with the challenges of separation.

In trying to get her message across, Mangrun believes that "The film was the way to go. . . . I wrote the book to show what the mom and the family went through and what role they might have played. But not everyone reads and the visual can bring things home to people. If people 'see it' they may be moved and they can move others."

(continued)

LEADERS AND HEROES

## Doris Mangrum, Book Author, Activist, and Executive Producer of *STAINS* (*continued*)

Mangrum is the founder of Saidiana Productions, which produced *STAINS* and "whose mission is to develop books, arts and media productions that call attention to the plight of families affected by incarceration. Mangrum also runs Saidiana Works, Incorporated, a non-profit dedicated to supporting resource linking, training and helping families navigate through separation by incarceration, military deployment, study abroad and any other reasons causing long periods of separation."[1] Saidiana means "help each other" in Swahili. Mangrum intends to make Saidiana a movement—a call to action for America to move forward beyond its general lack of interest about the formerly incarcerated and their families.

As Mangrum reminds us, America is the prison superpower of the world. She sees this disconcerting distinction as causing a stain on our nation. The stain of incarceration on the offender is indelible because of our action or inaction. However, there is an unintended consequence: the stain bleeds out and touches the lives of those connected to the incarcerated individual, "leaving a deep discoloration of shame on families and children left behind who have committed no crime. Society must step up and help to remove that stigma."[2] Mangrum says, "These are the multiple millions of these family members who sit next to us in our workplace, our schools and our places of worship—often in silence." Mangrum and the members of the movement are "making a call to action for America to change its mindset, stop the rhetoric, and roll up its sleeves on behalf of this population."

"I want volunteers (for example the Rotary Club) so when a person is incarcerated we can ask 'Who did you leave behind? What is the gap/hole that you are leaving? Money? Childcare? What is now missing that your family needs?' If the family runs out of food by the end of the month the volunteers can help; or the child can get to basketball; or whatever. Current programs do not work well together, so we need to partner to give us the greatest return on investment. The longer we let people stay behind bars with no contact, the more difficult it is to get them back together. The people come back feeling like aliens," she observes, echoing the words of Fred Anderson, who appears in Chapter 7. "I see people for a minimum of 2 months. People bring their children, and the children are happier—fewer problems in school, less acting out. Relations that were on the verge of breaking up are somehow problem-solved," says Mangrum. She says that 35% had significant changes.

"In neighborhoods where scores of men and women are removed on a regular basis, there can be another unintended consequence: destabilized communities. Not only are the families affected by the crisis—the neighborhood economic activity is weakened, the high rates of crime produce more crime, depressed property values, reduction in social cohesion and trust, and there is often a general cynicism and alienation between law enforcement and the citizens." Mangrum feels that this is not an isolated dilemma but a national emergency that must be attacked by society at large: "Individuals who are currently not a part of helping to solve this crisis and ultimate destruction caused by the finger pointing, isolation, stigmatization and general lack of public interest must become engaged. That need to connect society is the driving force behind the Saidiana Movement and the production of STAINS."[3]

"While all segments of this nation are beginning to feel the effects, our urban neighborhoods are most dramatically upset. All communities need support to help improve overall public safety and are looking for an answer. The Saidiana Movement is part of the answer, as it looks beyond the problem to the unit that is best equipped to help solve it—family."[4]

Mangrun offers these parting, passionate words: "The Saidiana Movement is about change—but not the change that looks to others to make it happen. This change will come about when we—all of us—look at ourselves and start to move forward on behalf of this population who are being stifled out of the basic necessities of life—decent wages, adequate housing, and basic assistance. A silk garment allowed to unravel over time will be destroyed. If reworked . . . it can be reinforced and strengthened. Families are like silk—the making of which is a lengthy process demanding constant close attention."[5]

For additional information about the Saidiana Movement, please visit http://www.stainsthemovie.com/

---

1. Saidiana Web site. http://www.jumpingnow.com/.
2. STAINS: Changing Lives after Incarceration. http://stainsthemovie.com/.
3. Saidiana Web site. http://www.jumpingnow.com/
4. STAINS: Changing Lives after Incarceration. http://stainsthemovie.com/.
5. Author interview with Doris Mangrum, March 2011.

---

## Notes

1. Author interview with Robert Ross, October 2009.
2. Kathleen M. Nelson. "On Inspiration and Leadership: A Conversation with Barbara Sabol, MA, RN, and Henrie M. Treadwell, PhD." American Journal of Public Health 2008;98:1553–1555.
3. Author interview with Donna Hubbard, December 2009.
4. Ibid.
5. West, Cornell. "Race Matters." In: The Crisis of Black Leadership. Boston: Beacon Press Books, 2001, p. 38.

# PART TWO

# Beyond Blaming the Victim

# CHAPTER 7

# Brownian Motion and Dynamic Equilibrium

*"Too many Americans living behind bars and too many children, especially children of color, living without their parents because they are incarcerated. This level of incarceration is endangering our families and our children in so many ways, most especially in the area of health care."*
—*John Lewis, U.S. Congressman, Georgia*

*Finally feeling like his old self again, Martin was rushing on his way to a job site one sunny morning a few weeks after his hospital visit when he was stopped on the street by a bright young woman with a fist full of flyers. Her friendly smile caught him off guard among the crowd of people surrounding the bus stop, and he said good morning and accepted her flyer. Emblazoned across the top were the boldfaced words "Fresh Food, Grown Right Here!" along with large photographs of lettuce, collard greens, peppers, peaches, tomatoes, and cucumbers.*

*Seeing him looking over the sheet, the woman introduced herself and began explaining the flyer. "My name is Dorothea," she said, "and I am an organizer of one of the community gardens we've been building in the neighborhood."*

*"There is a garden here?" asked Martin. He had never seen a garden in his neighborhood; only block after block of buildings, some abandoned, most in a state of disrepair, bordered at the major thoroughfares by run-down liquor stores, convenience stores, dollar stores, and the occasional nail shop. Despite his doctor's orders, he had not been very successful in filling his diet with fresh fruits and vegetables. For the first week, when he had been working at the Croft's place over in Buckhead, he had stopped by the grocery store there a few times on the way home. Since he began working long hours on a job closer to home, he had been forced to choose between the greasy spoon chains and whatever was dusting the shelves of the corner stores.*

*"Absolutely," said Dorothea. Her perkiness suited the bright morning, even if it did feel a bit out of place among all the other morning-commuter-women, huddled over their thermoses and leaning a bit with the weight of purses that carried everything they might need for the 12+ hours they would be away from home. Dorothea told him that she and her group were working with some community health workers, school children, and other volunteers to grow fresh food in the vacant lots and sell the produce cheaply to people in the neighborhood. She wondered if he might like to come down and volunteer some time. "We even have free cooking classes," she said, "so you can learn new exciting ways to cook the food you buy!"*

*Martin politely declined her offer. He was intrigued by the woman and what she was doing, but he barely had time to get home, feed himself, and get to sleep before it was time to head back out for the next day's work. He did, however, promise to come by the vegetable stand she and the volunteers were operating that weekend to see if he could pick up some groceries. As he got on the bus, he remembered how much better he had begun to feel that first week after he got back to work, when he was eating the good, cheap food from the Buckhead neighborhood grocery store. Not only did they have much better food, but it also cost so much less than the processed food he could get nearby. Martin resolved to stop by and see if he could get some good food to fill his lunch pail for the week and continue to feel stronger on his feet and sharper on the job. Maybe he would even take one of those classes some day. If everyone was as friendly as Dorothea, perhaps it would not be an inconvenience at all.*

Once we recognize the genuine need for an injection of real and sustained hope for a fulfilling life into the hearts and minds of boys and men of color, it is time to begin building the ladder to success. We cannot build that ladder alone, but need to do so in conjunction with the people and communities we hope to serve. Just like you cannot build a house without clear blueprints and a clear understanding of structure and foundation, plumbing, and electricity, and the basic laws of gravity, making a positive impact requires an understanding of both the challenges faced and the environment in which those challenges operate.

Fortunately, positive interventions do not require us to figure it all out alone or to re-invent the wheel. The people in the communities we wish to serve are great teachers. These are the people who do not need to be told how to walk a mile in the shoes of those facing these daunting challenges—they wear them every day and can tell you exactly what it feels like. More importantly, they can utilize the benefit of the experiences they have had and skills they have learned to navigate often-treacherous waters to help outline any real blueprint for success.

Today, we are living in a unique time in history when we have an opportunity to engage each other, and our struggling communities, in the dialogue needed to develop that blueprint in an environment that is more politically open than we have seen in decades. At Community Voices sites across the country, we took advantage of this opportunity to gather young men together for small-group conversations, town hall meetings, and even larger conventions to identify not only the issues faced, but also real paths to success. (See the Appendix for Community Voices sites.)

## Two Principles

One of the greatest obstacles to success is a widespread belief in the central culpability of those who are suffering most. Time and time again, we hear that it is the fault of the poor that they are poor, the fault of the uneducated that they are uneducated, and that people living in crisis have only themselves to blame. This kind of "blame the victim" thinking is a key player in our ongoing power failure. It stands directly at odds with the available research, anecdotal evidence, and the realities of our own public policy that leaves millions of young boys and men of color drowning at the bottom of the well and offers few avenues to rise above the water line and reach dry land. Two scientific principles might inform our analysis of why we are experiencing the difficulties we see when our young people take the path to adulthood. The principles are Brownian Motion and dynamic equilibrium.

Brownian Motion occurs when small atomic particles randomly collide and bounce off of each other. In this instance, substitute particles for people and you get the picture. How many times can young people hear that it is up to them to pull themselves up by their bootstraps when they do not even have any boots? And we ignore the fact that even those with boots live in a complex neighborhood diaspora in which the web of violence "reaches out and touches" their lives even when they want to do the right thing. Here is how the principle of Brownian Motion applies: if we drop a small amount of red dye in a jar of clear water and leave it there unattended, the red dye ultimately spreads throughout the water without any help from an external hand, just because the molecules and atoms bounce against each other and push each other around until the jar is full of red water. Everything is colored red. So too will violence—bred of poverty and loss of the hope—spread, unless someone comes along to remove the offending dye and reinvigorate the faith in the future and the will to achieve. We in leadership positions have to take a long, hard view at the realistic choices faced by men and boys of color today with an eye not toward blame, but toward solution. Still, a thorough understanding of the forces at play against men and boys of color, from the moment they are born until the moment they die, is a crucial tool toward understanding not only why "blame the victim" tactics do not work, but why they are completely unwarranted and, in fact, serve only to further exacerbate the problem.

In dynamic equilibrium, the parts of a system are in continuous motion, but they move in opposing directions at equal rates so the system as a whole does not change. In other words, although a lot seems to be happening, we are taking two steps forward, two steps back. A lake, for instance, is said to be in a state of dynamic equilibrium when the rainfall or runoff water that enters it is equaled by the water that is evaporating out of it. In this state, the level and amount of the water in the lake remains unchanging, even though new gallons of water may be added every day. Dynamic equilibrium also applies to the crisis of men and boys of color in what is both an era of hope and a time of power failure: we are living in a system locked in a steady, unchanging state in which any attempts at injecting change are nullified by an equal and ongoing change in the environment into which those attempts at change are injected.

The health and wellness crisis among men and boys of color is not new. Years of public policy decisions have led us to where we are today. The attempts at intervention are also not new. Public and private organizations and agencies, as well as countless individuals, have been pouring resources into efforts to improve the lives of those suffering most for decades, but they have not focused on the boys and men, except in a negative manner. For example, we see economic development to aid rural communities has consisted principally of building prisons to house boys and men of color and hiring a few people from the community to guard the prisoners. Much of the aid has been misguided economic development with no humane thought for the lives destroyed. The injury continues as the elderly remain in these areas in geriatric facilities and, therefore, bring nothing they have learned of value back to their community to build a positive rung on the ladder for the young people. Much like the men in Douglas Blackmon's novel, *Another Form of Slavery*, who were spirited off to live and die in the steel mills or other industries "up North," these men went off to work in the prisons and were lost forever to their families. The funds might have been put toward the development of jobs and housing so people could stay at home and not become victims of a not level playing field that propels too many into prison.

And, if we have thought at all about the pain and suffering that result from poverty and the physical and mental illness visited on the poor, regardless of gender, witness the lack of ANY public policy that targets the poor man and protects his health. NO public policy has been formulated for Jamal's and Martin's ancestors or for them, other than the constitutional amendment that guarantees access to health care ONLY if they are incarcerated. Given the lack of humane and universal vision, it is not surprising that much of that effort has had very little lasting impact and the crisis continues to grow.

## Interventions in Isolation

One of the problems with many of the interventions that have taken place is that they focus on the individual, rather than the community. Targeting intervention strategies at the level of "at-risk" persons allows the myth of blame to continue unchecked. It also does not work. To date, there has been extremely limited, and short-lived, success shown by attempts to change the devastating levels of violence, crime, or drug abuse that were focused solely on individual behavior. Strategies that work to affect change at the community level, focused on the physical and social environments in which unhealthy behaviors are occurring, are needed.

As leaders, dreamers, and people with a stake in our communities—whether we are members of "at risk" communities or not—we need a more comprehensive understanding of how multiple stressors affect behavior. Dr. Tony Iton's juggling analogy, discussed in Chapter 3, is critical to understanding how this works. The effect of stressors that come from living in communities deprived of basic services, and filled with real and perceived danger, increase the likelihood for a wide range of unhealthy behavioral responses, including agitation, aggression and anxiety, poor school performance, social withdrawal, depression, and suicide. Opening a community park, an after-school program, or healthy food programs to neighborhood families are all important. However, even with the best intentions, when these interventions are attempted in isolation, they simply cannot have the sustained impact that working on multiple fronts at once will.

It is important for families to have access to healthy foods and understand how to prepare them. If the heads of those families are chronically unemployed, however, then, even if there is a grocery store stocked with healthy food items, those foods will remain outside their reach. Similarly, helping young people learn better homework skills is critical, but, if we do not deal with issues of depression, discrimination, or lack of adequate medical care that impact their ability to concentrate and study, then our interventions continue to operate within the limits of dynamic equilibrium—every positive aspect we introduce continues counterbalanced with equally weighted negative aspects that keep the situation in crisis. And, given the vise that substance abuse has on far too many parents, should we not consider how to treat while we train people to be better parents? Many parents may just be too tired, too sick and compromised, and otherwise unable because of their own issues to do all that they might if they were well. What to do about them, leaders? Do we continue to preach "though shalt raise thy child within the values of my eyesight," while turning a blind eye to what too many parents face?

This is not to say that attempts to create a healthy environment are a waste of time. They certainly are not. Instead, we need to push past our attachment to individual projects to find ways to work together so each intervention can be strengthened by a complementary intervention in another area.

We must begin understanding that violence and drug use are not merely causes of poor health; they are symptoms. The real causes of violence, crime, poor educational outcomes, and drug and alcohol abuse include the sense of hopelessness, oppression, stress, and disenfranchisement that men and boys of color feel pressing down on them from the

 **REALITY CHECK  Homicide Rates**

African Americans, from adolescence to middle age, suffer from the highest homicide rate in the country. A quick look at the numbers, thanks to the Kaiser Foundation, when compared to whites in the same dge group, illuminates the scope of the crisis. Imagine how stressful it is for a black man to know the following homicide rates:

*Young African American Men*
84.6 out of every 100,000

*Young White Men*
5 out of every 100,000

*African American Men 25–44 Years of Age*
61 out of every 100,000

*White Men 25–44 Years of Age*
5.1 out of every 100,000[1]

1. The Henry J. Kaiser Family Foundation. "The Health Status of African American Men in the United States." http://www.kff.org/minorityhealth/upload/7630.pdf.

earliest ages. Until we begin treating violent death as the chronic illness it has become in our communities, we will remain unable to address it at its roots, where it festers and spreads. And these young men have their own fears. At a recent meeting of the Georgia Campaign for Adolescent Pregnancy Prevention, the young men in high school spoke of their fear of walking to school in the faint light of morning. Fears of violence, fears of being kidnapped for their organs, fears for how their single mothers can continue to support them given all of their problems: these same young men just say, "we do not have enough time to just talk, to each other, and to someone who can help us sort through our hopes and our fears."

And it is chronic. The CDC listed the ten leading causes of death for black males 18-24 year of age in 2004. At the top of the list were homicide, unintentional injury, and suicide. These represent the symptoms of living in a devastating environment in which boys are raised without the opportunity to simply relate to each other in the most basic human ways. When we can show our humanity to each other, outside of the threat of constant danger, then we can make healthier choices not only for ourselves, but for our families and neighbors.

## Taking the Longer View

Our interventions must not only be multivariable and comprehensive, but research continues to confirm they must also start early. It is not enough to simply backtrack and work to heal people after they have been broken down nearly beyond repair. "We don't take the long view in this society," agreed Joe Brooks, Vice President for Civic Engagement at Policy Link.[1] Indeed, the long view is exactly what is called for by a crisis of this magnitude. The best, easiest, and most efficient investment—not only in terms of resources, but in terms of the wellness of our neighbors and communities—is to work to make sure people's lives do not get broken in the first place.

Playing the blame game is one of the most pernicious aspects of power failure that gets in the way of our ability to address these symptoms as they devastate our communities. From neighbors to schoolteachers, from community and social organization heads to non-profit and government leaders, there is a persistent stubbornness of many in the very powerful positions that could make a difference to turn a blind eye to the problem and blame it on those who are suffering. Just as there is power in numbers when we band our interventions together to make an impact on multiple fronts, there is the same power in numbers when people sound the alarm of how men and boys in crisis should simply know better, act better, and take responsibility for changing their own circumstances.

### Come on, Bill!

Those who want to blame African American boys and men for their precarious plight have recently gained a powerful voice on their side in actor/comedian Bill Cosby, the author of the book *Come on, People*, who has recently put the full weight of his international fame behind the already loud cacophony rush to blame the victims. Although personal responsibility is an important issue, it must be weighed with the reality of how many tennis balls society is tossing their way, demanding they juggle. No one is born with the opportunity to choose the circumstances into which they are born or the challenges that their family must face.

"Equity," said Meizhu Lui, director of the Closing the Racial Wealth Gap Initiative at the Insight Center for Community Economic Development in Oakland, California, "means that no group has poorer health due to reasons outside *its* control, but within *society's* control."[2] We need to address the concept of personal responsibility head-on, but we need to do it with the understanding that many of the so-called "choices" do not feel like choices to the people themselves when made within a context that offers them few real options or opportunities.

Instead of empathy and understanding for the realities young people face, time and time again, our leaders, including Bill Cosby, who himself talks about growing up poor, wait for men and boys of color to stand up and accept all the blame for the situation in which they find themselves. "Yeah," goes the script, "I just made some bad choices." The truth is, people are making *poor* choices, but, more often than not, they are making those choices within the context of a range of options that goes from poor straight through to poorer and poorest. The reality lies far beyond the simple effect of choice. What is missing from this argument is the powerful effect of policies either designed without young men of color in mind or designed specifically to control their destinies—and not for the better.

We can no longer afford to press ahead with blinders on to the devastating choices that yet another generation is being asked to make. The death and disability toll is too high. We also cannot hope to simply turn the clock back to an imagined simpler time. Rather than lamenting the loss of traditional family, it is up to those who wish to lead to address the situation as it is. Simply shaming mothers for the absence of their children's fathers does not help those mothers or their children. In the meantime, while leaders are daydreaming of the nostalgic times of yesteryear, the lake is filling up and emptying at a steady rate. Dynamic equilibrium continues to be the victor, and our communities—as well as our children—continue to suffer.

What is needed to unearth and address the deep-seated problems destroying the health and devastating the lives of millions of men and boys—and the families who love them—is a complete systems fix, and accomplishing it will take each one of us with a stake in making our community and our society better—all of us. Again, Brownian Motion. Without it, even if we manage to wave a magic wand and fix every problem and blight we see today, magically awarded everyone the same income, the same education, and the same beautiful homes and cars without addressing the real forces—cultural and political—that force people into poverty, then, within a generation, we will find ourselves back in the same situation we see now. This is the essence of the effect of dynamic equilibrium on the crisis.

This is not mere conjecture; ongoing research proves the point. Harvard researcher, Nancy Krieger, recently published a study with a group of her colleagues that showed that the differences in the early death rates between blacks and whites actually narrowed during the period immediately following the Civil Rights Movement and the War on Poverty of the 1960s.[3] This was a time when systems fixes began to be put into place and great strides were made toward leveling the playing field for everyone. However, once that progress was halted by the onslaught of devastating public policy in the 1980s, those gaps once again expanded.

The prevailing thought process driving the helm of our current state of power failure is based in a very black-or-white way of thinking. In this view, you are either making good choices or bad choices; you are either lifting yourself up or holding yourself back—either way, your future is completely in your own hands. However, even when we look at those who have come out of poverty to become successful, very rarely have they been able to do it alone. The difference between those who "make it" and those who do not lies in some sort of intervention and support, whether from a teacher, mentor, parent, or entire community that invests itself in a young person's success.

It may be a very American notion—the Horatio Alger story of one man rising up solely on his own gumption, against all odds—but that story is actually a destructive fairy tale. Those who succeed do not succeed against the odds; they succeed because a number of forces have come together to reshuffle the odds in their favor. To argue, then, that the responsibility lies solely with personal responsibility is not only untrue, but it is harmful because it only further discourages those who find they can not possibly continue to juggle each new ball without stumbling or dropping one from even bothering to try.

We have failed young people in this country, particularly young people of color, and we continue to do so by relying on stories full of half-truths and no-truths that continue to disempower them and isolate them from the resources needed to fully realize their potential. Being born into poverty certainly does not mean you have to go down a destructive path, but, without sustained intervention, you might.

As Doug Lomax and Pastor Donna Hubbard know well, one group of people tend to shy away from is people in prison. Incarceration rates among young black males continue to soar past those of whites and Hispanics. The August 2003 Bureau of Justice Statistics analysis "shows that 32 percent of black males born in 2001 can expect to spend time in prison over the course of their lifetime. That is up from 13.4 percent in 1974 and 29.4 percent in 1991. By contrast, 17.2 percent of Hispanics and 5.9 percent of whites born in 2001 are likely to end up in prison."[4]

The route to prison is determined early and paved by the same symptoms of community violence that black men and boys are disproportionately exposed to when compared to their white and Hispanic counterparts—even those living below the poverty line. Studies have shown that, among those living in poverty, poor black children are far more likely to live in poor neighborhoods than poor white children. The additional environmental stressors they are exposed to in those neighborhoods place them at a much greater disadvantage than that of their white counterparts, who may have a similar family income but have access to the kinds of resources that make all the difference: schools, grocery stores, parks, and safe streets.

The prison population is among the most at-risk in the nation for nearly every imaginable health problem, from chronic to infectious disease to mental health issues. We need to pay attention to the health of incarcerated people not only because they represent an increasingly large percent of African American men and boys, but because they often serve as canaries in the coal mine: their health issues eventually become ours. Incarceration is a key indicator of premature death and poor health not only of incarcerated individuals, but also of their entire communities. Although many people in comfortable positions may think that what happens in prison does not affect their lives, in truth, what impacts the health and welfare of incarcerated and formerly-incarcerated people touches their families, their communities, and, eventually, us all.

Every year, more than 700 thousand people move between their communities and prison. According to the Pew Research Center, 1 out of 31 Americans (1 in 18 men) now lives under some form of correctional control— either in jail, in prison, on probation, or on parole. The report stated, "Black adults are four times as likely as whites and nearly 2.5 times as likely as Hispanics to be under correctional control. One in 11 black adults—9.2 percent—was under correctional supervision at year-end 2007." The report also pointed out gender disparities, stating, "[M]en of all races are under correctional control at a rate five times that of women."[5] In addition, "The percentage of young African American men in prison is nearly three times that of Hispanic men and nearly seven times that of white men. . . . While African American men represent 14% of the population of young men in the U.S., they represent over 40% of the prison population."[6]

African American men represent nearly 8% of the 18- to 24–year-olds in the United States, but, in 2004, they made up only 2.8% of the undergraduates at 50 public flagship universities across the nation. Twenty-eight percent of black males enter state or federal prison during their lifetime, compared with 16% of Hispanic males and only 4.4% of white males.[7,8] That is an astounding percentage of the community—any community.

Where were you, community leaders, when this was happening? Why could you not speak? Did you not see this happening? Or were you afraid? Or perhaps, and I must ask, "were you indifferent because it was not your son or brother?" We must have your answer to move forward quickly, as time is not our friend.

"Once you are incarcerated, the chances of you having any kind of productive community life upon return are becoming slimmer and slimmer," said Brooks, "because the institutions of incarceration seem to turn these men and boys out—harden them." This slamming of the doors on life opportunities for men and boys of color is only getting worse. Since 1991, the percentage of state prison inmates who were members of racial or ethnic minorities climbed 5%. Given the enormous growth of the prison population, those numbers mean hundreds of thousands of young men. As Brooks observed, "If we leave this population behind, we're all going to suffer in the future."[9]

## Sick and Getting Sicker

Over 30 years, the U.S. prison population grew from 204,211 prison inmates in 1973 to become the world's leader in per capita incarceration with 2.2 million inmates in 2003.[10] The numbers have grown so staggering that, no matter how fast we continue to rush to pump economic development dollars into rural districts to build prisons, we are running out of room to house prisoners even faster. During the summer of 2009, the *San Francisco Chronicle* reported that a "three-judge panel in California concluded that overcrowding at the prisons, jammed at twice their designed capacity, was chiefly responsible for poor health care. The panel has tentatively ordered the release of between 37,000 and 58,000 inmates to local custody, treatment programs or parole in order to ease the burden on the system, avoid constitutional violations for cruel and unusual punishment."[11]

We are one of the few nations in the world that incarcerates children. The mass institutionalization of young men of color has a direct and preventable effect on their health. As Gabrielle Prisco thoroughly and eloquently explains, "African American youth represent only seventeen percent of the overall youth population, yet they make up thirty percent of those arrested and sixty-two percent of those prosecuted in the adult criminal system. They are also nine times more likely than white youth to receive an adult prison sentence. This unequal racial breakdown of arrest, detention, and incarceration rates does not reflect the racial breakdown of crime rates." Further, Prisco argues that "Our nation's current youth justice system is iatrogenic" (meaning it worsens the very thing it is trying to cure). Her monograph also summarizes the ways in which our system too often leads to more violence and recidivism, exacerbates mental health symptoms, increases the likelihood of self-harm and suicide, and places youth in physical and mental danger. She documents that "Children in adult [prisons] are fifty percent more likely to face an armed attack from a fellow prisoner and twice as likely to face physical assault by prison staff than are incarcerated adults," and "are five times more likely to be sexually abused or raped than their counterparts in youth centers."[12] Further, nearly all of them lack adequate health insurance coverage and access to providers who accept the coverage they have (principally Medicaid).[13]

As far back as Martin's time, medical professionals were speaking out about the need to address the health needs of prisoners. Growing out of the Medical Committee for Civil Rights, the group that organized the medical contingent of the 1963 March on Washington, the Medical Committee for Human Rights was formed in June of 1964 to support Freedom Summer. One of their most popular causes was prison reform. They fought to end what they called "the selective use of prison medicine as a form of punishment."

That selective use and withholding of medical care as a form of punishment continues throughout the prison industry today—and it does so relatively unchecked. Attempts to quantify prison medical records often hit a brick wall. Records are often poorly kept and incomplete. With no universally accepted health care standards in place, it continues to become even more difficult to regulate the care and treatment of the people held within their walls—especially as the prison industry becomes more privatized. And many of us on the outside "say" we cannot do more for them than we do for people on the outside who do not have access to health care; however, if this is the case, why have we set up a system that has made it so those who are incarcerated will ONLY get some level of care if they are living inside the razorwire fence and NO guaranteed access to care if they are living free and working (or trying to work) in the community?

To make matters worse, prisoners are sicker on average than the rest of the population. The prevalence of tuberculosis, hepatitis C, and HIV is, on average, 4-10 times higher among prisoners, and the prevalence of chronic diseases, such as asthma, hypertension, diabetes, oral diseases, and substance abuse is even higher.

 **TAKE A GOOD LOOK** Returnees or Friends or Family of Returnee

Are you a formerly incarcerated person? Do you know any? If not, can you imagine what it is like to be or know a returnee? Look in the mirror and ask yourself:

- What do you see as the biggest obstacles to re-entry?

- Do you know of any organizations helping the formerly incarcerated re-establish their lives?

- Do you know of any organizations working to prevent incarceration? To break the cycle of poverty, absentee parents, and youthful offenders?

- How can we begin to "recognize" the children in our communities and classrooms on an individual, personal basis so you might help them and help their families divert them from trouble?

- What special activities can you, in your career and personal life, implement to help a child "fit in" in a setting he or she may otherwise feel out of place or be bullied?

- How important is the shirt with a logo or the pair of shoes by a certain maker to the child who feels on the outside? Do his or her feelings about what is important trump your feelings?

- Write one thing you are willing to do to support re-entry for those formerly incarcerated and their families in your community—then get busy:

_____

_____

Of the 2 million incarcerated persons, more than 1,600 return home to their families and communities each day. A 2007 study in Washington State found that, during the first 2 weeks after release, the risk of death among former inmates was 12.7 times than among other state residents. The leading causes of death among former inmates were cardiovascular disease, drug overdose, suicide, and homicide.[14] Without the necessary continuum of care needed to ensure that medication and treatment are consistent both inside and outside of the prison system, the physically and mentally ill continue to get worse, continue to exhibit symptoms, continue to engage in behaviors that lead them to trouble, and continue to move back and forth between homelessness, their communities, and the criminal justice system—often spreading unchecked illness all along the way.

Thirty years of get-tough policies have failed young men of color. "Rather than judging the people as victims," cautions Rev. Brown, "love them through it. These people, for whatever reasons, need help. That's the bottom line. When you see a fight, it's not about who threw the first punch, it's about human life. You've got to break it up."[15] The profound lack of action and the continued state of acute power failure should indicate to us all that the stage is open and auditions are being held for men and women who want to lead. Right now, it is not a question of when to lead, but how to lead. We do not need to be heads of organizations, public officials, or even parents to take on a leadership role. All we have to do is step up, pull together, and engage a network of like-minded people for support, to share resources, and to begin to lead from wherever we are.

---

## LEADERS AND HEROES

### Fred Anderson, Ex-offender; Founder of Felons Adjusting to Life Again (FALA)

"All they want is a better life," declares Fred Anderson, reflecting on the motivation behind the acts that young men and women take that get them into trouble. And, once in trouble, they tend to stay in trouble. "In today's world, when a person is sentenced to incarceration and has served their time, society tends to not accept nor grant these individuals a second chance," says Anderson. "It is hard to get employment, housing and family foundations structured with these individuals because of their crimes."

Anderson is in a strong place of reflection. An ex-offender himself, he has a story to tell, the story of the opportunity he's had to understand first-hand the obstacles that a man getting out of prison faces; however, he has gone beyond reflection and has literally and figuratively "escaped." He has taken action in his own life—and has gone on to help others do the same. Thanks to Felons Adjusting to Life Again (FALA), the nonprofit organization Anderson and his wife, Lisa, operate, people are getting that second chance.

FALA assists ex-offenders with getting re-adjusted back into society after serving time or being convicted of a crime. FALA holds training classes that educate ex-offenders on how to recreate themselves and their lives, even with a felony conviction. Anderson guides them through entrepreneurship and opportunities to not just survive, but to be successful.

It has been a long road for Anderson. "I grew up poor. My parents were uneducated. We, as a family, did not know how to set up our lives. When we, African Americans, were freed from slavery, there was no one there to educate the masses. And then these systems—jails and prisons—were put in place and were baited as a trap for us. And we took the bait . . . whatever it was. Far too many of us just did not know (and still do not know) how not to take the bait."

Anderson describes his school days: "In school, I was on the poorer side of my classmates. They wore Nike sneakers; and I wore Payless. I was teased, bullied. I felt like I was the lower side of humanity. Without the direction of a father, you begin to resort to the people around you that have those same feelings of isolation that you feel. So, I began to hang out with the outcasts, and we began to take our 'revenge' through fights. I was now trying to take the tennis shoes from the kids who were teasing us! As I went up in grade level, so did my negative behavior. I changed my friends and my behavior. I was introduced to drugs. I had an addiction. I became a predator. When you sell drugs, you have to form a protective network around you so you enter into criminal person-to-person bonding, destruction, for your protection. But it was all negative."

"My mother sent me to a home for troubled children. She was trying to do the right thing," he continues, "but it was inside this home that I really began to be exposed to criminals. I stopped caring. I formed my own gang. I was 17 years old when I went from selling drugs on the corner, a 'hit' or two, to selling kilos. Finally, the FBI came, and they arrested my entire gang. They waited until I was 18 to arrest me so that they could charge me and keep me in prison. I broke out of prison twice, once by tying over 160 sheets together so I could escape from my cell on the 16th floor of the facility."

"I was arrested again. I was sentenced, and we were charged, my gang and I, under RICO charges. Twenty-four of my gang members were with me in Louisburg Penitentiary, so we could just keep up our business. The criminal justice system often

(continued)

LEADERS AND HEROES

## Fred Anderson, Ex-offender; Founder of Felons Adjusting to Life Again (FALA) (*continued*)

places you in facilities where everyone you knew who was guilty of breaking the law is present. I learned a lot about serious criminal behavior. We kept on breaking the law behind bars." He alludes to the ever-present danger of sexual assault: "When you go into those showers, it is all around you. My brother happened to be in the same prison, so he helped me escape that. He was released but was later arrested on another charge and is now serving a life sentence."

Anderson left prison after serving his sentence. He lived in a halfway house while he held two jobs—one with UPS and one at a plastics factory. Today, Anderson is a well-known entrepreneur in Dekalb County, Georgia. He owns a few businesses, but his primary goal is to help ex-offenders. He is also a public speaker/motivational speaker, having spoken at colleges and been interviewed on radio and TV.

He has a unique take on things: "Now too many of us are left floating around with no place to land. It is as if we are the dinosaurs and people have to eliminate us, as they do not believe that we can be educated into being something different. Society teaches people to fear certain things. These young men and women feel like they are aliens and become so conditioned to feeling on the outside that they no longer have the fear that society instills. So they do things that get them in trouble with the law."

"My wife, Lisa, and I have a program that does not change the lives of those ex-offenders that have been in trouble; rather, we work to help them change their minds, the way they look at life. We can't help anyone until they are ready. The people who come to our program feel that their mind is changed. Once their mind has changed, then they can begin to rebuild their lives. They are sure that they do not want to go back to prison or jail. But the negativity in their lives that has sent them to prison has to be changed over generations. My son will be touched by the negativity in my life and past. It will take some time for all of it to go away."[1]

For more information about Felons Adjusting to Life Again, please visit http://www.falagroupinc.org.

---

1. Author interview with Fred Anderson, March 2012.

## Notes

1. Author interview with Joe Brooks, December 2009.
2. Author interview with Meizhu Lui, November 2009.
3. Krieger, Nancy, David H. Rehkopf, Jarvis T. Chen, Pamela D. Waterman, Enrico Marcelli, and Malinda Kennedy. "The Fall and Rise of US Inequities in Premature Mortality: 1960–2002." *PLoS Medicine* 2008 February;5(2):e46.
4. "Young Black Males Headed for Extinction?" *Washington Post*. http://blog.washingtonpost.com.
5. The Pew Research Center. "One in 31:The Long Reach of American Corrections." Pew Center on the States. http://www.pewstates.org/research/reports/one-in-31-85899371887.
6. Harrison, P.M., and Beck A.J. "Prisoners in 2004." Bureau of Justice Statistics Bulletin. October 2005.
7. Bonczar, Thomas P., and Allen J. Beck. "Lifetime Likelihood of Going to State or Federal Prison." Bureau of Justice. http://bjs.ojp.usdoj.gov/content/pub/press/LLGSFP.PR.
8. The Pew Research Center. "Collateral Costs: Incarceration's Effect on Economic Mobility." Pew Charitable Trust. http://www.pewtrusts.org/our_work_report_detail.aspx?id=60960.
9. Author interview with Joe Brooks, November 2009.
10. The Pew Research Center. "Collateral Costs: Incarceration's Effect on Economic Mobility." Pew Charitable Trust. http://www.pewtrusts.org/our_work_report_detail.aspx?id=60960.
11. "Tentative deal on state prison medical care." *San Francisco Chronicle*. http://www.sfgate.com/
12. Prisco, Gabrielle. "When the Cure Makes You Ill: Seven Core Principles to Change the Course of Youth Justice." *New York Law School Law Review* 2011/12;56:1433-1473.
13. Healthy Returns Initiative. "Connecting Youth and Families to Benefit and Resources." http://www.healthyreturnsinitiative.org/pdf/HRI_Benefits.pdf.
14. Binswanger, Ingrid A., Marc F. Stern, Richard A. Deyo, Patrick J. Heagerty, Allen Cheadle, Joann G. Elmore, and Thomas D. Koepsell. "Release from Prison—A High Risk of Death for Former Inmates." *New England Journal of Medicine* 2007;356:157–165.
15. Author interview with Rev. William Brown, October 2009.

# CHAPTER 8

# Feeding the Pipeline

*"Not everything that is faced can be changed, but nothing can be changed until it is faced."*

*—James Baldwin, Author*

In 2007, the Children's Defense Fund released a report on America's "Cradle to Prison Pipeline" as part of an ongoing campaign to improve the life opportunities, particularly for young boys of color. The report addressed the funneling of children into the criminal justice system and found that "poverty, racial disparities and a culture of punishment rather than prevention and early intervention are key forces driving the Pipeline."[1] Since the time the report was issued, further research has confirmed these characteristics of the Pipeline.

Despite the mounting evidence to the contrary, the same vacuum that sucks young men and boys of color out of their communities and into jail and prison is accompanied by the echo of misplaced blame. This, coupled with the culture of punishment identified by the Children's Defense Fund, tightens the chains that hold so many back from fulfilling their potential. Blaming the victim is a no-win strategy. To understand why it is a no-win strategy, it is important to first make clear why the approach is wrong, both morally and factually. We are blaming and punishing black boys and men for the fallout from policy decisions they had nothing to do with, except for the accident of being born black. We expect nothing from them and then are surprised if we get nothing.

## Images and Messages

This rush to blame the millions who suffer most from the policy decisions of a few is nothing new. Thirty years ago, despite evidence of the positive impact on children and families that the Johnson administration's anti-poverty programs were beginning to have, a new recession began to take hold and the backlash against the most vulnerable was in full swing. By the 1980s, the War on Poverty had exploded into a War against the Poor. At the same time, the public face of poverty shifted from the rural whites with whom middle-class whites could identify to urban blacks who were portrayed as frightening, dangerous, and alien.

This new image was trumpeted across every conceivable form of media. Television sitcoms, Hollywood films, and Madison Avenue advertising all served to promote the idea that urban poverty was an environment not only created by African Americans, but desirable by all but a special few. Like pigs rolling in the mud, the danger and filth of the city streets were where blacks thrived. Do not feel bad for poor, young black men, we were told. In the words of a popular young TV star whose character was barely surviving in the urban housing projects, everything in the inner city was "Dy-no-mite!"

Slowly, the images of poor rural whites starving in the hills without electricity, telephones, and modern conveniences began to vanish. Although *those* poor people were living hardscrabble lives, we were sold the idea that it was not their fault because they had no access to anything better. Poor blacks in the city, the messages countered, were mere steps away from the best our society had to offer. If they could not grasp the brass ring, it must be because they simply were not reaching hard enough.

Simultaneously, African Americans began to move into professional positions in larger numbers, and rich and poor city-dwellers were living closer to each other than ever. Blacks were suddenly more visible, no longer merely the clean-up crew that operated in silence during the day or out of sight at night. We were now colleagues at the office and class-mates at school. But for every "clean-cut" African American passed on the way to the water cooler, they were counterbalanced by the growing destitution of the inner-city neighborhoods that the growing middle class had to bypass on the way to work. Although conspicuous consumption and ribald displays of wealth became our cultural calling cards, the wealth gap grew wider than ever between the black upwardly mobile profession-als (Buppies) and those who were not.

By the 1990s, anyone watching television learned that the only poor children worth saving lived overseas: spend a penny a day to save a poor child in a third-world country, while turning a blind eye to the poor child down the street. This was the message on every network. The barely hidden side note: much like the rural whites in the hills, those children "over there" did not deserve their fate—but those living here in our urban ghettos brought it on themselves. In other words, if some urban blacks could climb out of poverty, they all should.

To reinforce this belief, a harmful brand of self-righteousness has taken root. It is reflected most sharply in the tone adopted by leadership at every level. Instead of challenging us all to dig deeper into our well of empathy and help our neighbors, our leaders have engaged in the kind of power failure that asks us to join the chorus of derision. Kicking people further down the ladder is even encouraged as good entertainment. Despite our long-cherished belief in freedom and "achieving the American dream" as basic cultural values, a crucial exception has been made when it comes to the poor.

And why is it that poor men and women are being held to a standard of behavior—despite battling extreme levels of stress without the resources to manage it—that leaders are allowed to freely skirt? In contrast to the rich and powerful, who have gotten increasing amounts of leeway from the public about their scandalous behavior, the poor must sit mute while the larger society tells them how to live. Clearly, this approach has failed. We have become ever more critical of the poor and blamed them for the situations they were struggling to juggle, yet their situation has steadily worsened.

## The Changing Labor Market

The labor market changed drastically in the 1980s with the Reagan administration, to the disadvantage of many African American men. Beginning with his famous 1981 firing of 13,000 air traffic controllers, Reagan worked throughout his presidency to weaken the labor laws and organizations that had, for the previous two decades, given African Americans opportunities to enter the middle class. Industrial and factory employment opportunities, once a standard route for advancement into the middle class, began to disappear. Poor black men, who had struggled with a wholesale dislocation from the labor market since the time of slavery, found themselves once again on the outs.

Reagan's work to lower the minimum wage, cut back job training programs for the unemployed, ease child labor and anti-sweatshop laws, and increase tax fringe benefits had a devastating impact on African American workers, especially men. Rather than address the absence of policies that would ensure access to the labor market, or the growth of Reagan-era policies that pulled the rug from beneath low-income workers, Americans were once again distracted from the realities of public policy and sold the idea that the poor brought it on themselves.

Soon, the image of the alien, dangerous black man was complimented by that of the lazy, black welfare queen. With limited education and skills to suit the changing economy, poor blacks of either gender could no longer find work. Yet, the media tagline was that they did not want to work. Black men did not want to support their families, the logic went, and black women were perfectly happy to take advantage of the situation so long as the government was there to support them.

## Predictive Zip Codes

As Dr. Anthony Iton, former Director of the Alameda County Health Department in California, pointed out in Chapter 3, your zip code can predict how long you will live. According to Iton, and numerous studies on the effects of race and poverty on health and life opportunities, these easy calculations are not possible simply because of the poor decisions of parents and their children. Instead, they are the result of a long legacy of geographically-embedded racism. The same legacies that have led to the much higher likelihood that poor black children will live in poverty-stricken neighborhoods than poor white children also ensure that the health of poor black children is compromised at every stage. Some factors that would have affected the childhoods of Martin and Jamal include restrictive racial covenants in neighborhoods, destructive public housing policies, lackadaisical zoning regulations, concentration of environmental pollutants near communities of color, food and physical activity "deserts," and uneven distribution of public resources meant to aid the poor. These are policy decisions, not behavioral decisions.

Some leaders would have us believe that the African American community is corrupting the system; the truth is that the system is corrupting the community. The myth of access remains a pervasive one, and the idea that poor city-dwellers have greater access to resources than the poor living in rural environments is as destructive as it is untrue. An increasing number of studies show how closely tied our health behaviors and outcomes are to the physical, social, and environmental resources—and lack of resources—of where we live. Chronic diseases like asthma, heart disease, and diabetes, and unhealthy behaviors, such as violence, drug and alcohol abuse, smoking, eating junk food, and dropping out of school, are all greatly impacted by our environments.

These realities offer a strong counter-argument for leaders who find themselves faced with the "blame the victim" mentality. Poor families have limited options as to where they make a home. Although they work hard to control the environmental elements about which they have decision-making power, it is the environmental realities about which they

**REALITY CHECK   Hazardous Waste**

The most significant factor in determining the location of commercial hazardous waste facilities in the United States is race, according to a 1987 report. In 40 out of the 44 states that house hazardous waste facilities, disproportionately high percentages of people of color live within 2 miles of those facilities.

In 2007, a follow-up study found that not only do communities of color still face the same problems as a result of this widespread environmental racism, but those problems have multiplied "because of government cutbacks in enforcement, weakening health protection, and dismantling the environmental justice regulatory apparatus."[1]

---

1. Bullard, Robert D., Paul Mohai, Robin Saha, and Beverly Wright. "Toxic Wastes and Race at Twenty: 1987–2007." The United Church of Christ. http://www.ucc.org/assets/pdfs/toxic20.pdf.

have little to no control that can have the most severe impact on the health of the family. "Mom didn't develop the landscape," agrees Iton. "She didn't site the diesel plant next to the house; she didn't site the crime and lack of community next to her home."

"To the extent that they are constantly being given more balls to juggle, the likelihood increases that they will become unsuccessful," Iton says, "and ultimately, they will give up. That's what we see in these communities. It's not an either-or, individual responsibility versus social responsibility. Social responsibility sets the context for individual choices." It is difficult enough to raise and feed children and make a life for a family. Punitive public policies that separate fathers from their families and site environmental hazards in poor communities along with cultural values that prioritize policing and punishing the poor more than helping everyone reach their potential serve to make a difficult task feel impossible.

"Some of us could get through that narrow road that they paved for us to get out of poverty," says Donna Brazile, a Democratic political strategist. "Many of us got caught and trapped. Some made it, some didn't, but there was no difference between me and those who got stuck or couldn't cross over."[2]

For many families, their situation is not simply a case of dreams destroyed but, as the poet and writer Langston Hughes wrote, of dreams deferred. As awful as it is to see someone's dreams destroyed, the finality of the act at least offers people the chance to rebuild. The process of dreams deferred, conversely, acts like a rabbit to a race hound, forcing people to run themselves, literally, to death without ever having had a real chance to grab that rabbit.

## Educational Barriers

What could be more emblematic of the failure of our communities than the state of education for poor black children? "For too many men and boys of color, it starts with concentrated poverty in too many communities," says Joe Brooks, Vice President for Civic Engagement at Policy Link. "Young boys of color go to school with circumstances that put them at a disadvantage such as coming from homes and communities with poor housing, without proper nutrition, and no balance in their diet, and then they are suspended too early from school."[3]

The Children's Defense Fund's Cradle to Prison Pipeline campaign places special focus on the educational barriers faced by African American boys—and with good reason. Educational outcomes are one of the most critical determinants for future life opportunities, for physical and mental health, and wellbeing into adulthood. Instead of a pathway to opportunity, inner-city schools offer African American boys a host of potentially deadly outcomes, including imprisonment and death.

Most of our public schools are funded by local property taxes. This process guarantees that poor communities are left with poorly-funded schools whose students are faced with poor educational opportunities, missing out on an important link to positive and expanded opportunities for life fulfillment. Over the past 30 years, this situation has gone from bad to worse. "It has a lot to do with residential development patterns over the past 20 years," says Brooks. "Policy connected to suburban sprawl has had a severe impact, resulting in a large-scale movement of the tax base which is tied to education."[4]

The public schools in impoverished communities are chronically under-resourced in every way. Textbooks are out of date and tattered; teachers are over-taxed and under-trained; buildings are crumbling; extra-curricular activities are all but non-existent; and the environment often feels more like a prisoner's training ground than a nurturing learning environment. It is no wonder that testing scores begin to fall during early education and slip further from there.

Punitive policies, including the "zero tolerance" policies that have exploded nationwide and reach all the way into kindergarten, have a disproportionately negative impact on boys of color. "Last year a record 15 percent of all 8th grade boys—roughly three times the rate for girls—were suspended or expelled from school." Although they represent

## ✔ REALITY CHECK   School Daze

Education is a major factor in how well a person does in life, so these facts, from the Southern Poverty Law Center, are sobering indeed:

- Suspension rates for K-12 students have "doubled since the early 1970s for all non-whites."

- There are "substantially different suspension rate increases for racial/ethnic groups and this gap has grown remarkably since 1973, especially for African-American students."

- "In the 1970s, Black students had a suspension rate of about 6%—twice the likelihood of suspension as White students (about 3%)."

- From 1973 to 2006, suspension rates for black children increased by 9 points, from 6% to 15%; white suspensions grew by less than 2 percentage points.

- From the 1970s to the 2000s, the gap between black and white suspensions "has grown from 3 percentage points to over 10 percentage points in the 2000s."

- Black students are now more than "three times more likely than to be suspended" than white students.[1]

The authors conclude "that minority students are being removed from the opportunity to learn at a much higher rate than their peers. . . . Educators and policymakers should be concerned about the harms that overuse of suspension can cause to students and their academic careers. Where the data suggest that certain racial/gender groups are at far greater risk, the potential harm from harsh discipline policies becomes a civil rights issue as well."[2]

So, is it any wonder that:

- "Researchers found that graduation rates vary by race, with 91.8 percent of Asian students, 82 percent of whites, 65.9 percent of Hispanics and 63.5 percent of blacks graduating on time."[3]

- And that the number of African Americans between the ages of 16 and 24 years of age with no high school credential is nearly double that of whites.[4]

---

1. Losen, Daniel J. and Russell J. Skiba "Suspended Education: Urban Middle Schools in Crisis." The Civil Rights Project at UCLA. http://civilrightsproject.ucla.edu.
2. Ibid.
3. America's Promise Alliance. "Building a Grad Nation Report: Progress and Challenge in Ending the High School Dropout Epidemic." America's Promise. http://www.americaspromise.org/.
4. "Black and Jobless in America." The Economist. http://www.economist.com/blogs.

only 7% of students, almost 35% of these actions were against African American boys.[5]

There is, as Brooks says, a pervasive "lack of sensitivity and training on the part of school administrators about young men of color who come to school acting out. It could be that these kids don't have anything to eat, or that they have a diet highly concentrated with sugar and are therefore on the edge. But the result of not understanding these circumstances and not understanding the temperament and behavior patterns of these kids, is that they are kicked out and turned to the street." And, more than 17% of black students in grades K-12 are retained at least one grade, compared to just more than 9% of white students.[6]

"We have data suggesting that these boys are being kicked out as early as elementary school," Brooks continues, or else they are immediately tracked into remedial or special education courses, leading to even more complications. Special education has become a dumping ground within which actual educational opportunities are slim and dropout rates are high. Black children represent only 17% of all students but 41% of special education placements. Widespread misdiagnosis of mental retardation and behavioral disorders among black children has been documented. This practice has a particularly destructive impact on black boys, who represent a whopping 85% of black children in special education.[7]

Black boys with physical disabilities are also more likely to land in special education classes. Although they represent only 17% of public school students, black students account for 32% of suspensions and 30% of expulsions. There is an enormous stigma associated with disability. Coupled with the lack of understanding, the knee-jerk punitive attitude toward black students is demoralizing and can have devastating effects on their self-image, state of mind, and level of academic achievement. [8,9]

But you do not have to be disabled to feel the detrimental effects of negative expectations. Stanford researcher Claude Steele has shown that, when given a test on which they are told blacks do poorly, African Americans, in fact, score worse than those African Americans who were simply asked to take the test.[10] The effect of social stereotyping on young minds is even more acute than on adults, particularly when reinforced by authority figures like teachers and school administrators. Whether students know they are being stereotyped or not, the lack of positive expectations quickly erodes their own belief in their abilities and their performance begins to reflect it.

Along with a lack of positive images of African American males both in education and in the media, exposure to school environments that are culturally insensitive leads African American boys to develop a mistrust of their environment and a deep uncertainty about their place in society.

The educational environment encourages a poor self-image: silence, timidity, and voicelessness among black boys who are taught it can be dangerous to speak out. With few outlets to access positive health and behavior information and limited models that are truly invested in their success, children and young men slip through the cracks, despite any positive leadership interventions.

Although it is true that, in 2008, only 47% of African American males graduated on time from high school, as compared with 78% of white males,[11] it does not have to be this way. Success is possible with the appropriate support systems. Black males who do well in college have parents who set high expectations of them, a teacher who took a personal interest in their future, ample financial aid, and programs that helped them make the transition from high school to college.[12] Although African American youth are overrepresented on revenue generating intercollegiate sports teams, have some of the lowest college completion rates among all students,[13] and endure racial stereotypes and microaggressions that undermine their achievement and sense of belonging,[14] the opportunity and responsibility is not to argue with the need for supports, but simply to provide them until the need diminishes or disappears as cohorts on campus grow.

## Truancy: A Category All Its Own

Truancy poses an array of issues and an additional potential step toward incarceration. Its cause and costs may not be what you think. In a 2009 *New York Times* Op-Ed piece,[15] Barbara Ehrenreich, author of *This Land Is Their Land, Reports from a Divided Nation*, discusses the enormous cost of truancy to children and their families. This cost is levied both in real dollars and in heightened mental anxiety it produces. Much like the vagrancy laws used for decades to unfairly incarcerate black men unable to produce paperwork proving their employment, truancy laws offer children a no-win situation.

If managing stress both at home and at school were not enough, traveling between the two can put enough strain on children and families to make them throw their hands up and surrender. Navigating violent streets and unreliable public transportation to get to school is dangerous and difficult on an average day; however, during the early morning rush hour, when there are not enough buses to serve the communities that rely on them most, buses are packed and getting space can be nearly impossible. According to Ehrenreich, the Los Angeles Bus Riders Union "estimates that 80 percent of the 'truants,' especially those who are black or Latino, are merely late for school, thanks to the way that over-filled buses whiz by them without stopping."[16]

The union estimated that 12,000 students were ticketed for truancy in 2008. "In Los Angeles," she writes, "the fine for truancy is $250; in Dallas, it can be as much as $500—crushing amounts for people living near the poverty level." Five hundred dollars. *Each time.* This can quickly ratchet up to an amount that is unfathomable for many families, even those of means. For a family of four living near the poverty line, this is more than one-quarter of its monthly pre-tax income. "I met people in Los Angeles who told me they keep their children home if there's the slightest chance of their being late," says Ehrenreich. "It's an ingenious anti-truancy policy that discourages parents from sending their youngsters to school."[17]

## Stress, Frustration, and Vanishing Hope

As frustrating as this may be to think about, these policies are even more frustrating to live through, especially for a developing mind. Once kept out of school, staying away becomes a habit. When speaking with young African American boys, which we do regularly through our work at Community Voices, their vanishing sense of hopefulness is palpable. You can almost see their yearning for learning and excitement about their future melting before you. As Iton says, "hope equals health." As their hope disappears, their health is not far behind. This is where the soil is cultivated for those symptomatic behaviors of hopelessness to take firm root. Young boys without this sense of hope become easy targets for the kinds of behaviors that numb their pain—alcohol and drug abuse, poor nutrition, aggression, and violence.

In addition, the vast majority of black boys are growing up in single parent homes; many are being raised by a guardian who is not a parent. Six out of every ten children living with a single mother are living at or below the poverty line. Children who grow up in fatherless homes are more likely to commit suicide, exhibit destructive behavioral disorders, drop out of school, and abuse drugs and alcohol. Young boys raised in fatherless households have significantly higher odds of incarceration than those in mother-father families. Never having a father in the household raises the odds even higher. Income disparity only partially explains the difference.[18]

The trials faced by black boys in the foster care system are even more devastating. Black children represent more than 30% of those in foster care—more than twice their representation in the general population.[19] In her synthesis paper, Delilah Bruskas writes, "Most children in foster care, if not all, experience feelings of confusion, fear, apprehension of the unknown, loss, sadness, anxiety, and stress. Such feelings and experiences must be addressed and treated early to prevent or decrease poor developmental and mental health outcomes that ultimately affect a child's educational experience and the quality of adulthood." She documents high rates of psychological and physical abuse as well.[20] We must begin to seriously address these mental health needs. It is up to our institutional leaders to place the much needed resources into the community and to begin to repair the damage that has been done.

## Incarceration

Whether innocent or guilty of offense, a majority of youth of color are arrested before 21 years of age. Once arrested, the door opens and closes on them, typically many times, and they are inside for longer periods of time. This "recidivism" is often the result of mandatory minimum sentencing policies for drug offenses, the charging of youth as adults, and re-incarceration for minor parole violations. In fact, 82% of the youth charged in adult court were youth of color.[21] As Ehrenreich points out, "the most reliable way to be criminalized by poverty is to have the wrong skin color."[22]

To add to the danger visited on these children, they are far more likely to be detained while awaiting trial, and two-thirds will be held in adult jails. One-third of those who are detained in adult prisons are held in the general population with adult inmates, including the most violent criminals. Conservative estimates show that at least 22% of male inmates are raped in prison. Rape has real life and death health consequences, along with emotional destruction. This is a devastating sentence for anyone, much less a minor who has yet to be convicted of a crime. The decision to try children as adults is not even made by the judges entrusted by the community to weigh the evidence fairly. Forty-five percent of the cases in which youth were tried as adults occur because prosecutors exercise their authority to file charges against youth directly in adult court. In an additional 40% of the cases, the decision is made by statewide policy mandates, not by the judges whose authority had been stripped by statute. Twenty-three states report overrepresentation of minority youth transferred to adult criminal court.[23] We need to begin making a real decision about the people we are upset with versus the people we are truly afraid of—the latter are the people who need to be behind bars

African American men and boys, incarcerated at rates alarmingly disproportionate to their percentage of the population, suffer equally disproportionately from the crisis in prison health, as do their children and families. As our rate of incarceration for nonviolent drug offenses has increased, prisons have become severely overcrowded, and the first thing on the chopping block of the prison budget is health care. This can allow chronic and infectious disease to spread nearly unchecked.

Among the incarcerated, rates of diabetes, hypertension, and asthma are much higher than in the average population. For communicable diseases, the numbers are even more sobering. The number of HIV/AIDS cases, for instance, is 5 times higher than in the general population. We do not even test for Hepatitis C because of the cost. Even if only sentenced to 1 or 2 years in prison, coming home with tuberculosis, hepatitis, or HIV can be a life sentence. Mental illness is also epidemic among the prison population. A recent Department of Justice study revealed that more than 60% of local jail inmates, nearly 60% of state prisoners, and 45% of federal prisoners have symptoms of serious mental illnesses. These figures are far worse than they were thought to be.[24] Since the closing of state-run mental health facilities, prisons have become the

 **REALITY CHECK  Four Strikes, You're In!**

If you want to determine someone's chances of incarceration, you need only measure for four factors:

- Who he or she is: What is his or her color and gender?

- How dark is his or her skin color?

- What is his or her level of education: Did he or she finish high school?

- How can he or she access resources: What is his or her family structure and wealth status?

As of 2005, if that person is poor, black (especially dark-skinned black), and male, then his chances became increasingly bleak:

- A black male born in 1991 has a "29% chance of spending time in prison at some point in his life. The figure for Hispanic males is 16 percent, for white males it is 4 percent."[1]

- In 2005, African American males were incarcerated 5 to 7 times more often than those white males.[2]

1. Beck, Allen J. and Thomas P. Bonczar. "Lifetime Likelihood of Going to State or Federal Prison." Bureau of Justice Statistics. http://bjs.ojp.usdoj.gov.

2. Mauer, Marc and Ryan S. King. "Uneven Justice: State Rates of Incarceration by Race and Ethnicity." The Sentencing Project. http://www.sentencingproject.org.

default housing facility for the severely mentally ill, which serves as a poor alternative to homelessness.

Increasingly, communities are calling for an emphasis on the justice end of criminal justice. A 2009 ZOGBY poll[25] shows public support for leaving behind our "punishment only" approach to correction, yet politicians and community leaders continue to ignore the public's pleas. Instead, our prison population has quadrupled in the last 25 years—2.2 million people were sentenced to prison in 2005, up from 204,211 in 1973. Forty percent of those imprisoned in 2005 were African American, and an additional 20% were Latino.[26] Unless there is change, Latinos may represent the replacement team for the prison beds in the prison-industrial complex as the demographic shift occurs.[27]

 **TAKE A GOOD LOOK** Teachers

A 1992 New Orleans study found that nearly 40% of the African American male students in grades 4 through 6 felt that teachers did not set high enough expectations for them. Nearly 60% wanted to be pushed harder by their teachers. Children will either live up to or down to the expectations of the adults around them.[1]

Are you a school teacher? If not, can you imagine what it is like to be a teacher? Look at yourself in a mirror as you ask yourself:

- What are the expectations I am sending to my students?

- What kinds of signals am I sending to my students?

- How would I respond to those same signals?

- How am I going to start expecting more of my students? What is "more"?

- How am I going to send more positive signals?

- How will I acknowledge my students' accomplishments?

- Write one thing you are willing to do to increase expectations for and of African American students: _____

_____

1. Garibaldi, Antoine M. "Educating and Motivating African American Males to Succeed." *Journal of Negro Education.* 1992;61:4–11.

The fact that the majority of the incarcerations for young men of color are for non-violent crimes—including minor parole violations—reflects the pathway from cradle to prison that can feel all but unavoidable. It is time for our leaders to stand up and demand accountability in the criminal justice system. Community leaders and family members should be empowered to insist on fairness in sentencing. There are certainly crimes that demand even young offenders be separated from society. If these are not the crimes for which the majority of children of color are first incarcerated, however, then it is in the best interest of the children, their families, and communities for alternative sentencing to be explored.

## Freedom?

Once released, the formerly incarcerated re-enter the community having been stripped of the ability to access public assistance, including the medical care they need. Thirteen percent of all black men have lost their right to vote because of state laws that strip that right after incarceration—affecting more than just the individual. This dislocation from the political process affects the entire community. With the high percentage of African American men having spent time in prison, immediate action is required from every level of our leadership to begin to dispel the stigma and restore this right.

Further, they are often unable even to return home, if their families live in public housing, driving a deeper wedge between them and their families. Those who suffer most are their children; without effective intervention, up to 70% of the children of incarcerated parents will themselves become involved with the criminal justice system.[28]

"There was a time you could come out of prison with a college degree," says Boston Municipal Court drug abuse counselor, Doug Lomax. "Those days are gone. Now when you come out you end up doing 'social time.'"[29] Once released, many formerly incarcerated people find they must add severe depression to any illness they may have brought home with them. They are depressed to find themselves with a criminal record, depressed from the torment they survived while incarcerated. Creating, or recreating, the kind of significant relationships necessary to help them deal with this depression is often made all the more difficult by acute post-traumatic stress symptoms.

Once out, daily life can be a constant battle just to stay out—a battle so difficult that many feel powerless to win and simply surrender. Because such a high percentage of those incarcerated enter jail or prison suffering from mental health, drug addiction, or both, a significant indicator of one's likelihood of returning to prison is a lack of health insurance. The stress and helplessness is so overwhelming that up to 12% of those coming home from prison die of a drug overdose within 2 weeks of release.[30] Prison health care may leave much to be desired, even on a good day, but it can seem miles ahead of no health care—particularly when that lack of health care is mixed with the additional nightmare of homelessness and rejection from family and friends.

Where is our calling to find and offer redemption to those who have paid for their mistakes? Our continued inaction means the gates to basic citizenship are closed forever to many of those who have been to prison. So far, we have not had sufficient political will to open the doors and help people rebuild their lives. But the stakes remain too high for black communities—we have lost too many men already and are losing more every day.

## Limited Jobs for Formerly Incarcerated

If formerly incarcerated men are unable to access public assistance for housing, food stamps, or health care, they are also largely unable to generate those resources for themselves because of the limited work possibilities for those reentering. The work of Princeton sociologist, Devah Pager,[31] offers disheartening evidence of just how high the barriers are stacked against African American men in the job market. In her research, Pager found that African American men were less than half as likely as white men to be considered for open positions. Even without criminal records, only 14% percent of black men were pursued for employment, versus 34% of white men without criminal records. According to Department of Labor statistics, African American men are more than twice as likely to be unemployed as white men.[32]

It gets worse. According to Pager,[33] African American men without criminal records are 3% less likely to be considered for employment than white men with criminal records. This information is no surprise within the African American community. At Community Voices sites across the country, we see men juggling as fast as they can to fight through the piercing sense of hopelessness these statistics reflect. When they can find work, they are disproportionately represented in lower-income jobs that offer limited job security and even more limited access to health care and other benefits.

African American boys are the first to be dismissed and tossed out by society. They have been neglected by our institutions, targeted by law enforcement, and often abandoned by families unable to care for them because of their own poor health behaviors. As children, it is impossible to expect them to juggle the weight without their physical and mental health taking a beating. Once people have paid their dues, the formerly incarcerated should be allowed to participate fully in society. We cannot penalize people forever. It benefits the entire community to find new ways to smooth the re-entry process, not just to reduce recidivism, but to grow human potential before it is lost forever.

"We don't have bad children," says Brazile. "We don't raise prisoners. We don't stigmatize people because they've fallen down. Even Scripture tells you to pick them up and bring them out."[34] We are in a state of emergency, and we have to do something about it—now. Education, health, family support and child welfare, economic and workforce development, juvenile and criminal justice, and the impact of the media are all matters of urgency for communities of color, especially young men, and are central to the prospects for America's future.

The fact that 30% of all African American men experience some time in the prison system is a sobering indicator of our nation's well being. Instead of blaming them and punishing them for eternity, our leaders, all of us, must be held accountable to the most vulnerable in our communities. The ongoing dispute about personal responsibility misses so many key pieces of the puzzle that it has served mostly as a distraction from the real issues. As Christopher Heredia, reporter for the *San Francisco Bay Chronicle*, writes, "The debate must fade in face of the cost that so many of America's young men have paid and that ultimately our society will pay. We have a duty to stop blaming the victims now and reverse course. We cannot give up on our young men. We must ask that they not give up on us."[35]

---

LEADERS AND HEROES

**Nat Turner, Teacher**

Meet Nat Turner, 39-year-old former teacher from Manhattan who, with $12, started a community gardening project and Our School at Blair Grocery in an abandoned grocery in the Lower Ninth Ward in New Orleans. During our conversation, "Turner," as he prefers to be called, spoke about his study at Emory University, his teaching of college students, and his ultimate determination that his greatest impact would be with adolescents as they form their dreams for a future.

His students are young men from backgrounds of entrenched poverty, crime, or dysfunctional family life who have essentially dropped out of school and are fast running out of options unless someone cares enough for them to stand in the gap. A school day sometimes consists of Mr. Turner or Mr. Qasim Davis, the Dean of Students, accompanying the young men to court. But every day consists of showing the students that they care and that they believe in them and of removing unrealistic expectations. In Turner's words, "Inconsistently applied inexplicable expectations will make you crazy."[1]

This small heroic effort has received support from the W.K. Kellogg Foundation, and last fall the Department of Agriculture awarded a Community Foods Project Grant that will provide $300,000 over 3 years. "The wealth gap in this country is serious. People in positions of power need to use their standing to leverage funds flow." More people need to act, but, sadly, Turner states, "People want to believe that someone will be a hero, but it is not them."[2]

Turner has learned a few key lessons. Foremost is that he finds it difficult to work with many traditional organizations—"the usual suspects." He feels that they delay getting to the real work of changing lives and alleviating disparity by engaging in dilatory discussions on things, such as a "consensus" plan. Turner feels that authentic consensus can only be built once partners are thoroughly engaged in the work and understand in a comprehensive way the issues through the lens of those affected.

His enthusiasm for the work is palpable. "This is my life! I gave up many things," meaning the traditional perks that accrue from a regular job, including health insurance and retirement benefits. He works from 6:15 in the morning to 10:00 in the evening at least 5 days a week. But Turner is quick to say that everyone does not have to give up their regular 9-5 job. He believes that every person can and should use the power that they have in their regular positions to open resource opportunities for people like him who are willing to work in community, or establish protective environments and positive attitudes to stem the loss of these young men from the social and economic mainstream and into the criminal justice system.

His own primary motivation was to address the literacy rate among the population. Today, Turner states, "I do this work to grow organizers, to grow transformative leaders. Transformative education is what I do; I just happen to be doing it in a garden."[3]

For more information, visit http://www.facebook.com/pages/Our-School-at-Blair-Grocery/180311562018355 and http://www.nytimes.com/2011/01/16/education/16blair.html?_r=1.

---

1. Author Interview with Nat Turner, September 2011.
2. Ibid.
3. Ibid.

## Notes

1. www.childrensdefense.org/child-research-data-publications/data/cradle-prison-pipeline-summary-report.pdf for Culture of Punishment. February 19, 2009, p. 1.
2. Author interview with Donna Brazile, May 2008.
3. Author interview with Joe Brooks, December 2009.
4. Ibid.
5. Lewin, Tamar. "Black Students Face More Discipline, Data Suggests." *New York Times*. http://www.nytimes.com.
6. Adams, Caralee J., Erik W. Robelen, and Nirvi Shah. "Civil Rights Data Show Retention Disparities." *Education Week*. http://www.edweek.org.
7. "Race Against Time: Educating Black Boys." National Education Association. http://www.nea.org.
8. Ibid.
9. "Minorities in Special Education: A Briefing Before The United States Commission on Civil Rights Held in Washington, DC, December 3, 2007." U.S. Commission on Civil Rights. http://www.usccr.gov/pubs.
10. Steele, Claude M., and J. Aronson. "Stereotype Threat and the Intellectual Test Performance of African Americans." *Journal of Personal and Social Psychology*. 1995;69:797–811.
11. Schott Foundation for Public Education. "New Report, 'Yes We Can' Shows America's Public Schools Fail Over Half the Nation's Black Male Students." http://schottfoundation.org
12. Harper, Shaun. "Black Male Student Success in Higher Education." National Black Male College Achievement Study. https://www.gse.upenn.edu/equity/sites/gse.upenn.edu.equity/files/publications/bmss.pdf
13. Strayhorn, Terrell. "The Role of Supportive Relationships in Facilitating African American Males' Success in College." *NASPA Journal* 2008;45:26–48.
14. Bonner, Fred A. *Academically Gifted African American Male College Students*. Santa Barbara, CA: Praeger, 2010.
15. Ehrenreich, Barbara. "Is It Now a Crime to Be Poor?" *New York Times*. http://www.nytimes.com/2009/08/09/opinion/09ehrenreich.html.
16. Ibid.
17. Ibid.
18. Harper, Cynthia C., and Sara S. McLanahan. "Father Absence and Youth Incarceration." *Journal of Research on Adolescence* 2004;14:369–397.

19. Gordy, Cynthia. "After Foster Care: What Happens Next?" The Root. http://www.theroot.com.

20. Bruskas, Delilah. "Children in Foster Care: A Vulnerable Population at Risk." *Journal of Child and Adolescent Psychiatric Nursing* 2008;21:70–77.

21. Juszkiewicz, Jolanta. "Youth Crime/Adult Time: Is Justice Served?" Building Blocks for Youth. http://www.cclp.org/documents.

22. Ehrenreich, Barbara. "Is It Now a Crime to Be Poor?" *New York Times.* http://www.nytimes.com/2009/08/09/opinion/09ehrenreich .html.

23. Coalition for Juvenile Justice. "Trying and Sentencing Youth in Adult Criminal Court." Coalition for Juvenile Justice. http://www.juv justice.org.

24. National Alliance on Mental Illness. "Department of Justice Study: Mental Illness of Prison Inmates Worse Than Past Estimates." http:// www.nami.org.

25. Zogby International. "Attitudes Toward and Support for Services to Successfully Reintegrate People with Felony Convictions Back into Society." Submitted to Community Voices, 2009.

26. Garland, Brett E., Cassia Spohn, and Eric J. Wodahl. "Racial Disproportionality in the American Prison Population: Using the Blumstein Method to Address the Critical Race and Justice Issue of the 21st Century." Center on Juvenile and Criminal Justice. http://www .cjcj.org.

27. Shrestha, Laura B. "The Changing Demographic Profile of the United States." Congressional Research Service. http://www.fas.org.

28. Ichikawa, Jenna and Peter Selby. 2009. "Children of Prisoners Empowered for Success (COPES) Mentor Program." Casey Family Programs. http://www.casey.org/.

29. Author interview with Doug Lomax, October 2009.

30. Binswanger, Ingrid A., Marc F. Stern, Richard A. Deyo, Patrick J. Heagerty, Allen Cheadle, Joann G. Elmore, and Thomas D. Koepsell. "Release from Prison—A High Risk of Death for Former Inmates." *New England Journal of Medicine* 2007;356:157–165.

31. Pager, Devah. "Sequencing Disadvantage: Barriers to Employment Facing Young Black and White Men with Criminal Records." *The ANNALS of the American Academy of Political and Social Science* 2009;623:195–213.

32. United States Department of Labor. "The African American Labor Force in the Recovery." http://www.dol.gov/_sec/media/reports/ blacklaborforce/.

33. Pager, Devah. "Sequencing Disadvantage: Barriers to Employment Facing Young Black and White Men with Criminal Records." *The ANNALS of the American Academy of Political and Social Science* 2009;623:195–213.
34. Author interview with Donna Brazile, May 2008.
35. Heredia, Christopher. "Dellums Panel Urges Help for Men of Color." *San Francisco Chronicle*. http://www.sfgate.com.

# CHAPTER 9

## A Public Policy Framework

*"Incarceration is becoming the new American apartheid."*
*—Marian Wright Edelman, President, Children's Defense Fund*

*The sun was shining as Martin walked over to the Saturday afternoon vegetable stand that Dorothea's organization was hosting. As soon as he turned the corner he knew he was in the right spot. Despite the throngs of women and children sorting through the bins of the fresh vegetables in season, Dorothea's broad smile stood out to him immediately. He walked up to her and introduced himself, and she remembered him instantly. She took him by the elbow and introduced him to some of the young people standing proudly by the bins of food they had grown themselves.*

*The group had taken over a small corner and filled it with table after table of gleaming produce. It was the height of summer, and the season had a lot to offer. Glimmering green beans sat next to red and green bell peppers, robust tomatoes, and sweet corn. In another row, teenagers patiently helped young families identify eggplant and okra, and were able to tell the three varieties of squash apart from the larger, greener cucumbers. Next to each bin sat stacks of recipe cards and sheaves of fliers advertising the next free cooking class at which families could bring their children to learn how to make quick and easy meals for the whole family.*

*As Martin wandered the aisles trying to decide what to purchase, a familiar face caught his eye. Walking past him was the young man he'd met a few weeks ago in the emergency room, and, before he could stop himself, he reached out to tap him on the arm and say hello. After a moment, Jamal's face slipped into recognition, and he reached out his hand to shake Martin's. They shared greetings and updates on how they were feeling.*

Acknowledging the impact of racism on the ill health of men of color is not an attempt to excuse poor health behavior, or even place the blame on individual discriminators. Understanding the context in which poor health decisions and behaviors are made helps guide effective intervention strategies. Racism is a system that impacts every area of policy making related to health equality and the practical and value-based assumptions that go into the making of those decisions. When we can be honest about where we are and how we got there, then we can be more effective at steering our communities in a healthier direction.

The status of African American boys and men represents the worst of what our public policy has to offer. To make the kind of real impact the current crisis calls on us to make, leaders are needed to understand and acknowledge the legacy of institutional inequity and power imbalance and take action to redress the harm that has been and is being done. We are all aware of our long history of racial inequality, but we are not as clear about how that history continues to inform our health policies today. Many of today's policies are rooted in an ideology that disadvantages men of color from the day they are born.

It is our own policy decisions that have prevented millions from voting, enrolling in and benefitting from Social Security, receiving aid, particularly dependent children, and fully benefiting from health care assistance from programs like Medicaid. Although the language we use to draft our policies no longer expressly states the intent to restrict access based on race and gender, the effect is the same, particularly when race intersects with the criminal justice system.

## Systems and Struggles

African Americans, particularly those struggling to find a way out of poverty, remain largely divorced from the economic opportunities that would afford them the kind of resources that equal improved health outcomes. Disproportionately, African American men and boys are not the people covered by our top tier private health insurers. They are less likely to live on safe, tree-lined streets with easy access to outdoor recreation. The grocery stores, pharmacies, and health clinics that serve them are ill-supplied, and neither preventive care nor informed care continuums are prevalent. These systems are related. The Dellums Commission identified additional roots of the crisis in economic shifts, such as American "deindustrialization, de-unionization, and the subsequent decline in jobs and wages for working class families, alongside ineffective drug laws; educational inequities; lack of social and legal services; and discriminatory housing policies."[1]

**REALITY CHECK   Food for Thought**

Poor nutrition, a factor in many diseases and conditions of mind and body, may be the only nutrition available for poor black families. For example:

In Baltimore, Maryland, 43% of predominantly black neighborhoods were in the top third of neighborhoods with the least healthy food options. Only 4% of "predominantly white neighborhoods were among the top third of neighborhoods with the least healthy food, and only 13% percent of the wealthiest neighborhoods were in that same group."[1]

In New Haven, Connecticut, researchers found that healthy foods were significantly less available in low-income areas than in wealthier neighborhoods; in addition, the produce that was available tended to be of poorer quality.[2]

## Beyond Bread and Water

In federal prisons, diets are usually carefully planned and standardized. Some facilities post the weekly menu, listing the caloric, fat, cholesterol, and sodium content of each food item. Federal prisons are meant to have a salad bar and offer a "heart healthy" version of the main meal. For example, baked or fried potatoes or French fries.[3]

- State prisons are another matter. Citing budget shortfalls, various state prisons are cutting back on the food they feed inmates. For example, Texas, Ohio, and Arizona no longer provide lunch on weekends, and there are reports of prisons accepting donations of food whose best-if-eaten-by dates had expired.[4,5]

- Prison and jail food services have been privatized to cut food costs as well. Sheriffs may be allowed to pocket extra funds left over after feeding prisoners. In Alabama, Sheriff Greg Bartlett was jailed by federal authorities for pocketing more than $200,000 allocated for meals for prisoners in the county jail. Prisoners had received fruit only three or four times during the 2-year period considered by the court, and prisoners ate hot dogs at every meal, because the sheriff got a deal on a tractor-trailer load of them. A federal judge found Bartlett had failed to provide the prisoners with "a nutritionally adequate diet."[6]

*(continued)*

**REALITY CHECK** **Food for Thought** (*continued*)

- As in the outside world, loss of control of what and when one eats can result in conflict and be used to add punishment and deprivation. Failure to provide adequate meals can lead to health-related problems or even violence by hungry and frustrated prisoners; food was a major issue in a major riot at Kentucky's Northpoint Training Center in 2009.[7]

1. Franco, Manuel, Ana V. Diez Roux, Thomas A. Glass, Benjamín Caballero, Frederick L. Brancati. "Neighborhood Characteristics and Availability of Healthy Foods in Baltimore." *American Journal of Preventive Medicine* 2008;35:561–567. http://www.ajpmonline.org/article/S0749-3797(08)00729-0/fulltext.

2. Bill Hathaway and Carly Keidel. "Healthy Foods Scarce in Poor Neighborhoods, Yale Researchers Find." Yale News. http://news.yale.edu.

3. Encyclopedia of Prisons and Correctional Facilities. "Food." http://www.referenceworld.com.

4. Fernandez, Manny. "In Bid to Cut Costs at Some Texas Prisons, Lunch Will Not Be Served on Weekends." *New York Times.* http://www.nytimes.com.

5. "Massachusetts Prisoners Receive Expired Food Rejected by Schools." Prison Legal News. https://www.prisonlegalnews.org.

6. Reutter, David M. Gary Hunter, and Brandon Sample. "Appalling Prison and Jail Food Leaves Prisoners Hungry for Justice." Prison Legal News. https://www.prisonlegal news.org.

7. Spears, Valarie Honeycutt. "Food Caused Northpoint Riot, Guard Says." Kentucky.com. http://www.kentucky.com/2009/11/07/1008801/food-caused-north point-riot-guard.html.

Society's safety net has been eroding for decades; yet, for African American men, that safety net was already whisper thin to nonexistent. After briefly narrowing, in the wake of civil rights advances, the life expectancy gap between African Americans and whites has grown dramatically over the past 40 years. The gap has widened primarily because of a rise in death from chronic diseases like heart disease, cancer, stroke, and respiratory disease. But health is also poorly affected by soaring divorce and high school dropout rates, by declining college enrollment and by rising incarceration rates. There is no way a community can flourish when the systems that hold it together are cracking at every joint and all of the individuals, either within or connected to that community, are compromised as its structures continue to weaken.

Black men and boys alone do not face the crisis; all of us are affected, including those who may falsely feel most insulated. As a society, we value safety, self-determination, education, equal treatment, equal access, equal opportunity, and the right to live a healthy life. Our reality fails to live up to our values. Nearly 46.2 million people are currently living in poverty; that is more than 15% of the total U.S. population and includes approximately 24.2 million children, which is the highest level of children living in poverty since 1993.[2]

As alarming as those numbers are, African Americans are living in poverty at nearly double the national rate. With 25% of African Americans living at or below the poverty line, compared with roughly 8% of whites, inequality has risen and the health gap has grown more uneven across the country. Although African Americans are certainly not alone in the struggle against poverty and the health issues it carries with it, African American boys and men carry far more than their share of the load.

## A Legacy of Inequality

As I show in Chapters 1, 2, 3, 4, 5, and 8, society has been quick to blame the poor for their problems. Rather than tackling inequality head-on in search of a real solution, our policies have focused on marginalization, exclusion, confinement, and punishment. It is difficult to explore the realities of racial health inequalities without being honest about the legacy of racism that is ingrained in our policies. Those of us working on dismantling this inequality understand that shedding light on this legacy, as well as both its lasting effects and current incarnations, is fundamental to breaking the cycle of health inequality.

Bias against young men of color, intentional or unintentional, has long guided public policy decisions with regard to housing, education, public assistance, policing, and employment. As growing fears about crime and personal safety took root over the past few decades, our policy responses have only aggravated the disappearance of men from African American communities. Despite their best intentions, many policy-makers find their hands tied by a system designed to permanently disadvantage people of color.

"The pattern," said Ehrenreich, "is to curtail financing for services that might help the poor while ramping up law enforcement: starve school and public transportation budgets, then make truancy illegal. Shut down public housing, and then make it a crime to be homeless. Be sure to harass street vendors when there are few other opportunities for employment. The experience of the poor, and especially poor minorities, comes to resemble that of a rat in a cage scrambling to avoid erratically administered electric shocks."[3]

Instead of working toward constructive solutions, misguided public policy decisions often force officials from our schools and our criminal justice systems to behave in ways counterproductive to increasing the health and wellness of men and boys of color and the communities in which they live. A small step back from the close-up imagery of young men of color as dangerous criminals with no stake in their own health and well-being would show quite clearly the public policy framework that leaves these young men few choices.

We have learned through Community Voices that, if we put fear-mongering aside and ask the community members themselves for answers to the problems that plague their lives and their communities, they have a far clearer vision of the policies that entangle them than one might think. Two examples come to light pretty quickly once we engage the conversation, and both are tied directly to the influence young men of color can have on their own lives, as well as that of their families, their communities, and society as a whole. The examples are illuminating, as they examine both the most intimately personal and externally political aspects of our lives: housing and voting.

## Public Housing: A Home or Just Another Type of Prison?

The same number of people reside in publicly subsidized housing, including housing projects and "Section 8" subsidized residences, as currently reside in America's prisons. Public housing used to serve as a means to an end—the end being the opportunity to move out of poverty and into independent living and eventual home ownership. The U.S. government began offering subsidized housing in 1937, during the height of the great depression. Over the next few decades, until the 1980s, millions of families who had fallen on hard times were able to secure safe housing with the kind of government assistance needed to get them up and on their feet so that they could move on.

The image of the black "welfare queen" raising generations of children in public housing, which gained popularity in the 1980s and 1990s, is distinctly related to public housing policies that penalized black men and actively separated them from their families. This began in the 1950s and 1960s when early attempts at welfare reform led to policies that imposed residency requirements on welfare applicants, including the "man in the house" rules that proved most devastating for poor black families. If it was proven that there was a man living in the home—particularly the husband and father in the family—then welfare benefits were immediately cut off. Although those laws were later found unconstitutional, the deep-seated problems they spawned had already been cemented. Countless husbands and fathers left their families so they could qualify for

**REALITY CHECK   Who's Getting Emergency Assistance?**

Temporary Assistance to Needy Families (TANF), formerly known as Aid to Families with Dependent Children (AFDC), has long been demonized as a government handout to lazy black women who do not want to work. In reality, blacks and whites receive nearly equal amounts of TANF assistance. The true numbers for who is receiving emergency assistance tell a more realistic story about poverty in America:

- Black 33.3%

- White 31.2%

- Hispanic 28.8%

- Asian 2.1%

- Native American 1.3%

- Other 3.4%[1]

1. Administration for Children & Families. "Characteristics and Financial Circumstances—FY 2009: Table 8." U.S. Department of Health and Human Services. http://www.acf.hhs.gov/programs/ofa/character/fy2009/tab08.htm.

assistance, and, long after the laws were rescinded, they remained alive in the public consciousness and impacted behavior.

The poorest men with the least employment opportunities were those forced to leave their families in a desperate attempt to secure their survival. With nowhere to go, they were often homeless, jobless, and open to arrest for anything from public loitering to simply "resisting arrest" if they could not immediately prove who they were, where they lived, and why they had a right to be standing on whichever street corner they were found. The "man in the house" rules for public housing were changed just as incarceration rates among African American men and boys were reaching epidemic levels.

Instead of having the effect of enabling families to reunite or stay together, the rules against men in the home were simply adjusted to have a similar affect. As the numbers of African American men and boys entangled by the criminal justice system shot up, rules against public housing residents with criminal backgrounds replaced the original "man in the house" rules. Suddenly, families whose husbands, fathers, and children were being released from incarceration found that those being released would not be allowed to return home. A tangle of new rules meant that, in the best of cases, a mother may have to choose between a father and son, or two brothers, and decide who would come home and who would be homeless. Even when one formerly incarcerated person is allowed re-entry to the family home, two may not be, depending on the terms of their release, because they were not allowed to associate with others with a criminal record. A housing decision is generally mediated by the parole or probation officer, and results vary, depending on each situation.

No other country on earth deprives people the right to basic housing after they pay their debt to society. These rules, ostensibly put into place to protect families and communities, actually stand in the way of our ability to redeem and rehabilitate people. Ironically, the protection these rules promise is a myth at best. In practice, violent felons—including the violently mentally ill—often have a much easier time circumventing public housing rules than those with drug convictions, since felony related drug convictions are often specifically flagged for notice and removal.

## How to Destroy a Family

When a father is released from prison and is barred not only from coming home to his family, but also from even visiting his children, families are destroyed. Compounding the impact on the family and community, the formerly incarcerated individuals are placed at far greater risk of returning to prison if unable to return home, since homelessness and residence in shelters are widely associated with increased rates of recidivism.

The reason I must refer to these rules in terms such as "most" and "often" is because the lack of fairness is the only thing these rules have in common. There is no single set of rules or guidelines that govern public housing policy across the country—often even across a single state. Each public housing authority is allowed to establish its own tenant policies. Tenants need not even have an arrest record or conviction to be banned from the home. Mere suspicion of criminal activity can be enough to remove a tenant—even a child—from the home. Once removed, appeals for return can take years.

Recent attempts to get a clear handle on how wide the variance is in policy and application have been met with resistance. In 2005, the Government Accountability Office requested race-based data on the people denied public housing placement or return due to drug-related criminal activity. Of more than 3,000 public housing authorities contacted, only

17 complied with the request and supplied data. That is less than one-half of 1%.[4]

Peggy Vaughn-Payne has seen the traumatic effects these policies can have on individuals and families up close in her work running the North-West Initiative in Lansing, Michigan. With a mission to create and sustain healthy families and communities in Northwest Lansing, Vaughn-Payne works directly with poor and low-income families, as well as with the formerly incarcerated. "In our area, there are very few places that people re-entering the community can go if they can't go back to their own personal residences," she said, "which is a lot of the time."[5]

Vaughn-Payne says that, oftentimes, people are denied release, even though they have completed their sentences, simply because they are unable to provide a home address to which they will be returning. "We're told in Lansing," she continued, "that the way it was written in the Lansing Housing Commission is there is a time frame that starts from the time that they were convicted, and it goes a number of years before they can return or re-apply to get into a subsidized housing unit."[6]

The barriers erected to living in public housing are only one side of the coin. The punitive policies established that break up families in public housing projects affect those already living in some of the worst possible conditions. As placement in publicly subsidized housing has become increasingly difficult, the available units remaining have become more like prison than ever before. Residents are subjected to random police sweeps, drug testing, and often-unlawful search-and-seizure with the only probable cause being their residence in public housing.

The psychic damage inflicted on families who have been told their families are, in effect, illegal and not worth maintaining is huge. Families whose options are housing projects or homelessness are already desperate. When we create situations, through our policy decisions, in which children are forced to hide their father's clothes so that social workers will not see them and to pretend that their father does not care for them, then we cripple entire generations of children who are already tackling the realities of poverty.

Sadly, when we create public policy, we often do so with blinders on. Just as poor public policy decisions helped create this crisis, equally poor policy decisions continue to make it worse. We already know that poverty is experienced differently by African American and Latino children than by white children. Poor children of color are far more likely to live in poor neighborhoods, filled with violence, and with little access to resources or role models that offer a chance at a better life.

Public housing advocates have long fought for reorganization of our approach to public housing. Unfortunately, the approach to that

**REALITY CHECK   A Natural Disaster for Housing**

Sometimes, humans and nature conspire. Fourteen months after Hurricane Katrina, 4,000 families had yet to return to New Orleans because of the remaining closure of public housing units. Rather than repairing the units, the federal office of Housing and Urban Development (HUD) and the Housing Authority of New Orleans simply boarded up the units and left them to rot.

In 2007, HUD demolished more than 4,500 units of public housing with no plan to replace them, prompting a huge public outcry. The public lost.

After the hurricane, tens of thousands of homes—mostly low-income rental properties—were destroyed. Currently, rent in the city is 35% higher than before the storm, far outside of the reach of the city's work force.[1]

The devastation of hurricane winds on lower income communities was not unique to Katrina. Hurricane Andrew (1992) destroyed 11,213 manufactured/mobile homes and 3,016 homes. In Homestead, a farmworker community, of the 1,761 mobile homes 1,167 were destroyed. Although standards for such homes were later revised/upgraded by HUD, the poor, the public, the most economically fragile lost.[2]

Question: Is planning for the safety and well being of the poor always an ex-post facto event? How do we determine risk and mitigate this before a disaster?

---

1. Seidenberg, Jennifer. "Cultural Competency in Disaster Recovery: Lessons Learned from the Hurricane Katrina Experience for Better Serving Marginalized Communities." Berkeley Law. http://www.law.berkeley.edu.

2. Pacenti, John. "Trailers 'Blasted'after the Storm." August 17, 1993. Ocala Star Banner, August 17, 1993, page 2B. http://news.google.com/newspapers?nid=hXZnTlglr50C&dat=19930817&printsec=frontpage&hl=en]

restructuring has too often been aimed at political gain, rather than improving the lives of those who are most in need. In Atlanta, for instance, there are no major public housing communities left. Instead, voucher programs send people into different communities all over town as the housing projects are bulldozed. Housing mobility programs designed to address the problem of concentrated poverty show promise and need to be brought to scale so more families can afford to move into safer neighborhoods. The relocation process is not without its bumps and bruises.

For the very poor, those same poor neighborhoods have often included extended family, friends, babysitters, and the entirety of their community support structure. When families are simply separated from their communities without taking into account the impact of that sudden loss of support, new problems arise.

Addressing the problem of housing, which, as we continue to wind our way through economic uncertainty, continues to take on even greater significance, can feel like wandering through a minefield when we are not looking at the problem through a systems-wide lens. Our policy approaches can keep us stuck in that same space of dynamic equilibrium whereby we attempt to fix one piece, only to see our "fix" create a new break.

## Deadbeat Dads—or Just Dead Broke?

Another example of the devastating effects of attempting to fix one symptom, while ignoring its system-wide impact, lies in an array of policies that serve to pile unmanageable debt on the shoulders of the poor. In the 1990s, the idea of the "deadbeat dad" gained prominence in popular culture. Television talk shows sprouted on every channel whose focus day after day was to exploit the image of poor families and sharpen the collective aim at society's age-old Boogie Man: the poor, young, black men.

Rather than parents struggling to find a way to support their families, our celebrity-starved culture began integrating new phrases like "baby daddy" and "baby mama" into our common language. Promoting fame at any cost, young parents were lured onto television with little more than the promise that, for 30 minutes, millions of people would pay attention to them. They could matter . . . until they were spit back out into their off-camera lives with little solved. As often happens, the lights and cameras stirred up a controversy that begged to be addressed, and an enraged public clamored for solutions.

As an attempt to address what was promoted as an epidemic of poor, young, black men fathering and then abandoning their children, child support laws were strengthened in states across the country. Leading the fight were women's rights groups who sought to enact laws that would bring support and fairness to the mothers left alone to raise their children without resources. Without addressing the systemic problems that led to such widely televised symptoms, once again, the solution served only to create a whole new host of problems.

Although the mostly-white, feminist organizations were certainly well-intentioned in their wishes to legislate support for poor mothers, because their frame of reference was predominately white and predominately middle and upper class, these organizations did not take into account all of those tennis balls already being juggled by these families in crisis. Leveraging child support orders on poor men who often barely even earned as much money as they now owed in child support became yet another approach whose effect was to criminalize the poor.

According to a 2003 study prepared for the California Department of Child Support Services, $14.4 billion was owed to parents in child support. Seventy-six percent of that $14.4 billion was attributed to parents unable to pay the debt. In California, these so-called "deadbeat" parents had a median annual income that was only 67% of what they actually owed, while still accruing monthly child support debt of up to $300 per month.[7]

Owing $300 per month, while earning an average of $500 per month and carrying up to $10,000 in debt, is a crushing sum. Because of the uproar in the supposed spike of "deadbeat" parenting, the courts were given little room to assign child support orders on a case-by-case basis. The study found that 71% of those orders were set by default. For those parents unable to pay, at minimum, they lose contact with their children; at maximum, they face jail time, during which their debt continues to mount and their ability to pay continues to decline.

It is becoming increasingly common for people to serve jail time as a result of their debt. Unreasonable levels of child support and harsh sentences for non-payment of child support (whether paternity is proven or not) are imposed. The average daddy may leave prison with $20,000 in past due child support payments. If he cannot find a job and cannot pay the child support, he is sent back to prison. The prisons have, in effect, become debtor prisons. Although debtor prisons have been explicitly banned by state constitutions, more than one-third of all states now allow borrowers who do not pay their bills to be jailed (they were supposedly outlawed in the 1900s; federal imprisonment for unpaid debt has been illegal in the United States since 1833). In many respects, as a result of nonpayment of fines arbitrarily imposed by judges and the rest of the system that knows full well that the man will never be able to pay the fees, fines, and child support, the man is remanded to prison. There are two major implications: daddy goes back into the jaws of the always hungry criminal justice "investment" system (as *someone* must benefit from the taxpayer's contributions); and, daddy may find it hard to hold up his head and be a man if he has to float under the radar at all times, hide from his children because he cannot take charge as a man, and hide from the law. In some ways, it may be easier just to go back to prison and stop running simply because he is a poor black man! Collection agencies are enjoying an uptick in activity as well. A report by the American Civil Liberties Union found that "people were imprisoned even when the cost of doing so exceeded the amount of debt they owed." And, because of "sloppy,

**REALITY CHECK   Child Support**

The Federal Agency for Child Support Enforcement reports that 70% of all back child support is owed by men earning less than $10,000 a year.

In addition, 29% of those fathers who are delinquent on their child support payments are institutionalized. Most of those who are institutionalized are actually in prison for failure to pay child support.[1,2]

1. "Child Support 'Talking Points.'" The National Center for Men. http://www.national centerformen.org.
2. Kouri, Jim. "Child Support Collections from Federal Income Tax Refunds." NWVnews. http://www.newswithviews.com.

incomplete or even false documentation," many borrowers facing jail time do not even know they are being sued by creditors.[8]

Programming without empathy, which is what I call this kind of system-blind approach to the symptoms of poverty and ill health, not only does little to improve the lives of the poor, but it in fact makes things worse. Where once you had a family with problems and few resources to address those problems, now you have that same family, with those same problems, and now you have added enforced estrangement between parents and children and probable incarceration. Until we have taken a walk through another's neighborhood in their shoes, we cannot possibly understand the effects of these kinds of genocidal policies. In an attempt to repair families and make them safer, we have actually ensured that the cracks continue to spread deeper and wider.

It is true, there are certainly young men who have no intention of caring for the families they create. However, despite popular belief, those men are in the minority. Most of those we would call "deadbeat" are, in fact, just dead broke, and once they have been targeted, their situation not only gets worse, but the avenues they have to pull themselves out of poverty and be a supportive force for their families diminish quickly.

Once a parent is incarcerated for his or her inability to pay court-mandated child support—whether or not the other parent wishes it—that parent can be sent to prison. Once sent to prison, their mountain of debt continues to grow not only from child support, but also from incarceration itself. In many states, prisoners are responsible for paying for their own health care. Emergency visits, doctor's care, prison uniforms, even room and board are tacked onto a growing mountain of debt that will follow that person out of prison and often leads him or her right back in after he or she has been released.

Prologue, chapters 1, 5, and 8 show that formerly incarcerated black men are less likely to get a job than formerly incarcerated white men. In fact, if we remember, formerly incarcerated white men are more likely to get a particular job than black men with no criminal history. With no way to earn the vast sums of money needed to get out of debt, the prison doors begin to revolve again and again for these men, endangering their health, lives, and children and families.

As discussed, once incarcerated, these fathers are prevented from re-entering the work force because of policies that encourage criminal background checks. These fathers are prevented from living either alone or with their families in public housing and government subsidized low-income housing units. They lose access to welfare assistance and are no longer eligible for emergency food stamps. They have their Medicaid benefits suspended on entering prison and, once released, must begin an often long and arduous road to get those benefits reinstated despite the need for a continuum of care to manage chronic disease and critical medication required to keep illness in check. These policies do not just affect the incarcerated parent; they affect the entire family.

## No Voice, No Vote

Worse for fathers re-entering the work-force after incarceration than the stripping of basic health benefits is that they now have no right to say anything about it. It is no coincidence that the surge in incarceration rates for African American men and boys coincides with our national war on the poor and legislation, such as the Voting Rights Act of 1965. As soon as the right to vote was firmly in place, states codified vastly increased means for arrest and conviction, and a huge amount of charges were elevated from misdemeanor to felony.

According to The Sentencing Project, 48 states and the District of Columbia currently prohibit inmates from voting while incarcerated for a felony conviction, 36 states prohibit former-felons from voting while on parole, and 3 states deny voting rights to *all* ex-offenders once their sentences have been served—many are barred for life. No other democratic nation disenfranchises people for life after completion of a sentence. In fact, many impose no restrictions at all on people with felony convictions. Once people have served their time, they are returned to the citizenry with an opportunity to rebuild their lives, which is denied here, at home, to millions of African American men.

**REALITY CHECK    Number of Black Elected Officials in the United States**

1875–1876: More than 1,500 during the Reconstruction, representing 4.5 million slaves[1]

1970: 1,469 . . . almost back to the levels reached during the Reconstruction[2]

2007: 9,100[3]

2011: More than 10,500[4]

Alabama, Louisiana, and Mississippi top the list of states that have elected the most African Americans to office.[5]

These are also the states in which the most violent voter suppression has taken place.[6]

These are also states with high rates of African American incarceration.[7]

Is it really a coincidence that, as blacks gain political power, policies continue to be strengthened to keep African Americans from the vote?

How do we explain the increase of legislation that has resulted in hyper-incarceration of African American boys and men in the face of increased representation by African Americans at the city, county, state, and the federal level? Does same race representation make a difference? If so, how? If not, why?

---

1. Office of History and Preservation, Office of the Clerk. "Black Americans in Congress: The Fifteenth Amendment in Flesh and Blood." http://baic.house.gov/historical-essays/essay.html?intID=3.

2. "National Roster of Black Elected Officials." The Joint Center for Political and Economic Studies. http://www.jointcenter.org.

3. Ibid.

4. Ibid.

5. "South Leads in Black Officeholders." Southern Changes. http://beck.library.emory.edu.

6. "Voter Suppression in America." ACLU. http://www.aclu.org.

7. "Mass Incarceration: Breaking Down the Data by State." Prison Law Blog. http://prisonlaw.wordpress.com.

As the result of felony conviction, more than 5.3 million Americans have lost their right to vote and, in effect, their voice in policy making decisions. Thirteen percent, 1.4 million, of those who have been disenfranchised are African American men. This number represents 7 times the national average.[9] At this rate, according to the Sentencing Project, 30% of the next generation of black men can expect to be disenfranchised at some point in their lives.

It is impossible to miss the fact that the past 40 years have seen both an explosion in the disproportionate incarceration and disenfranchisement of black men alongside their push for greater equality in power and representation. African Americans represent a significant and growing voting bloc. The representation of African Americans in elected office has similarly risen.

The formerly incarcerated are disenfranchised not just from the ballot box, but also from the entire political process, and they are not alone. They are joined by their entire community. When poor African Americans are disenfranchised, their entire community loses political power and access to resources. Even the simple act of writing a letter to your congressional representative is affected. If you write to your congressperson, that representative will scan your identity to see if you are a voter: if you are denied a vote, you are denied a voice. In addition, each of those letters is scanned for the zip code. Even if you have not been disenfranchised yourself, if your zip code has a low percentage of voters you are far more likely to have your opinions ignored.

## Policies and Politics

Financial and political resources are lost in urban communities with high felony conviction rates when inmates are incarcerated in prisons built in rural areas. Congressional representation, as well as federal and state funding, is budgeted based on population levels. When large portions of a community's population are removed and then placed into the less densely populated rural areas in which prisons are built at an alarming rate, the population is artificially ballooned in that rural area, as are the resources, funding, and representation. The U.S. Census Bureau counts the location of their prison, rather than their home, as an inmate's place of residence.

This is how a small town of 3,000 residents, when coupled with a prison population of 25,000, suddenly gains access to huge windfalls of public monies, whereas the urban communities from whence the inmates come—and to which they will return on release—are allowed to fall into decay. Rather than investing resources "where these inmates reside and improving the health care, education, job training, and reentry programs in underserved areas which would directly benefit children and families"[10] who are left to struggle in these communities, those resources are delivered to sparsely populated areas, allowing them to transition from ghost-town to boom-town almost overnight on the public dime.

When entire communities have their voice removed from the political process, it is left to leadership to intervene. Through our own policy decisions, African American men and boys are left homeless, incarcerated, uneducated, and disenfranchised. Families are broken apart and kept apart. These are the building blocks for an unhealthy population. If our own leaders can not look at this situation and respond, then what hope do these children have not only for a healthy life, but for any sort

 **TAKE A GOOD LOOK  Policy Maker**

Are you a policy maker or influencer? If not, can you image what it is like to be one? Look in the mirror and ask yourself:

- Is there any way for you to use your position, job, network . . . maybe your church or relationships, to bring together individuals that will work to redress stereotypes and foster social healing and change?

- If you cannot make a way out of what you may perceive as no way, what help do you need? How will YOU go about getting the help you need so forward movement can occur?

- Do you fear anything? If so, what? How do you address your fears?

- If you think things are just fine as they are, how will you go about maintaining the "civil society" you perceive as just fine for our children and our children's children?

- What, if any, is the risk to individuals and communities if one group is purposefully denied the right to vote?

- Who benefits when some segments of the population are restricted from free participation in the democratic process?

- What, if any, is the danger to society if all U.S. citizens, regardless of their engagement with the criminal justice system, are permitted to vote?

- Write one thing you are willing to do to support fair policies regarding incarceration and re-entry into society: _____

_____

of life at all? It is unfair to place the burden for reversing generations of discrimination solely on the shoulders of those who have just not been able to break out on their own.

If you feel it makes sense to revoke a person's right to vote once they have been convicted of a felony, it might help to take a look at our international neighbors and friends, as well as the international agreements to which we are a part. Most democratic nations have limited or abolished voting restrictions imposed on ex-offenders (Article 25 of the International Covenant of Civil and Political Rights) and argue that restrictions on the right to vote be based on grounds that are "objective and reasonable." Notably, Maine and Vermont are the only states that permit those with felony convictions to vote. Most demographic nations also argue that such policies violate the International Convention on the Elimination of All Forms of Racial Discrimination (CERD), ratified by the United States in 1994. The scope and increasing racial impact of such disenfranchisement violates CERD's command that states eliminate legislation that restricts the right to vote in a racially disparate manner.

We cannot continue to claim support for family values when our policies are devastating to millions of families. We must hold our leadership accountable, from the federal level down to the local level and in our communities. Although there are many groups working on separate pieces of this puzzle, we will continue to find ourselves drowning in that lake of dynamic equilibrium until we begin to work together on a systems-wide approach.

At Community Voices, we convene members of the Georgia Black Caucus on the Morehouse campus to address this issue. We develop relationships with policymakers, with the local and national media, and with community members. "It's easier to do nothing," someone once said in a meeting, ready to throw up his or her hands in exasperation at the sheer scope of the problem.

---

## LEADERS AND HEROES

### Debra Fraser-Howze, Founder, National Black Leadership Commission on AIDS (NBLCA) and Senior Vice President, Government & External Affairs, OraSure Technologies, Inc.

According to the U.S. Department of Justice, an estimated 17–25% of people living with HIV in America pass through the correctional system. Debra Fraser-Howze decided to do something about the widespread extent of the disease, but her route to that mission began with pregnant teenaged girls.

She was working at the Urban League when "One day, one of my colleagues called and told me about a 19-year-old young man who had a pregnant girlfriend and a 1-year-old by another woman. What was the outlook for the mothers and children? I did not know anything about HIV+. I called a doctor, and he just told me that everybody needed to be tested. Everyone was tested, and all were positive. I was shocked. I called an emergency meeting of clergy, media, and people from business and other community organizations. It came home to me and to us that these were not gay white men, these were people from the black community. The clergy said they were burying people. The funeral parlors were reporting funerals for people with the disease. Even beauticians and barbers knew, as there were changes in the hair."[1]

Out of that one incident, Fraser-Howze founded the National Black Leadership Commission on AIDS (NBLCA) in 1987, and, today, the NBLCA is "the oldest and largest non-profit organization dedicated to eliminating the AIDS epidemic in our nation's African-American communities. Through a network of affiliate organizations in 11 cities, its mission is to educate, organize, and mobilize black leadership to meet the challenge of fighting HIV/AIDS. NBLCA conducts public policy, advocacy, and research on HIV/AIDS issues and ensures the effective participation of its leadership in all policy and resource allocation decisions at the national level."[2]

"NBLCA has served thousands of organizations and institutions through community development, technical assistance and formulation of public policy; helped to raise billions in federal funding for HIV/AIDS and public health-related direct service organizations serving communities of African descent; and created the first programs for Black clergy to strategically address problems caused by HIV and AIDS."[3] During her years as President/CEO, Fraser-Howze advised two presidents, while serving on the Presidential Advisory Council on HIV/AIDS from 1995 to 2001.

Today, NBLCA works to "establish and implement a comprehensive national AIDS strategy that adequately addresses the needs of the African-American community, for the passage of HR 1964, the National Black Clergy for the Elimination of HIV/AIDS Act, to fully fund and provide adequate resources for HIV/AIDS programs, including HIV prevention and services in communities of color, and implement comprehensive HIV/AIDS prevention programs in prisons and other correctional settings."[4]

Fraser-Howze believes that NBLCA was respected immediately because she came out of the Urban League, a trusted community organization. She adds, "And I always talked about the issue from a business perspective, and this endowed some moral authority so people had no choice but to respond."

*(continued)*

## LEADERS AND HEROES

### Debra Fraser-Howze, Founder, National Black Leadership Commission on AIDS (NBLCA) and Senior Vice President, Government & External Affairs, OraSure Technologies, Inc. (*continued*)

Then, in 2004, tragedy struck: her 25-year-old college student son was killed by the police. "At that point, my life changed. I resigned as soon as I got back to work after my son's death with no plans, except to raise money for the Commission."[5]

She decided to move into the corporate world and is currently the Vice President of Government and External Affairs for OraSure Technologies. Fraser-Howze is the only African American and the only woman on the executive team. She made the move because she realized that the corporate world could have profound impact in the fight against HIV/AIDS and that a strong partnership between both the community and corporate worlds was needed. She wanted to be that link. She says she chose OraSure Technologies because of its commitment to the communities most affected by AIDS and because they manufacture rapid oral fluid testing, which she says is the single most important tool in HIV prevention. This method of testing is fast, easy, requires no blood samples, and the kits are not considered toxic after use. "With OraSure, I found that I could work with an organization that had a test to diagnose HIV quickly so that they could then get themselves into care quickly; they did not have to die."[6]

After her son was killed, Fraser-Howze says, "I sat and prioritized. Fighting for my community was at my core. One of the ways I was going to find my compass was to find work that still allowed me to serve my community. Being at OraSure has allowed me to continue my commitment to community on a larger and even more effective scale. We can diagnose people when they are most vulnerable and give them tangible options. I have got to find some peace in this space. Serving my community does that."[7]

To learn more about the National Black Leadership Commission on AIDS, please visit http://www.nblca.org/.

---

1. Author interview with Debra Fraser-Howze, March 2012.
2. NBLCA Web site. http://www.nblca.org.
3. Ibid.
4. Ibid.
5. Author interview with Debra Fraser-Howze, March 2012.
6. Ibid.
7. Ibid.

Personally, I believe that statement could not be further from the truth. It may seem easier to throw up our hands, bury our heads in the sand, and hope the problem solves itself. But history shows us that the longer we do nothing, the worse the problem gets—and the further it spreads.

## Notes

1. The Dellums Report. "Joint Center for Political and Economic Studies Health Policy Institute." http://www.jointcenter.org.
2. Tavernise, Sabrinia. "Soaring Poverty Casts Spotlight on 'Lost Decade.'" *New York Times.* http://www.nytimes.com.
3. Ehrenreich, Barbara. "Is It Now a Crime to Be Poor?" *New York Times.* http://www.nytimes.com/2009/08/09/opinion/09ehrenreich.html.
4. Randolph-Back, Kay. "Public Housing Policies that Exclude Ex-Offenders: Divided." Community Voices. http://www.community voices.org.
5. Author interview with Peggy Vaughn-Payne, October 2009.
6. Ibid.
7. "Examining Child Support Arrears in California: The Collectibility Study." The Urban Institute. California Department of Child Services. http://www.cafcusa.org/docs/DCSS_2003_collectability_study.pdf
8. Diamond, Marie. "The Return of Debtor's Prisons: Thousands of Americans Jailed for Not Paying Their Bills." Think Progress. http://thinkprogress.org.
9. Fellner, Jamie. "Losing the Vote: The Impact of Felony Disenfranchisement Laws in the United States." The Sentencing Project. http://www.sentencingproject.org.
10. Williams, Natasha H. "Where are the men? The impact of incarceration and reentry on African-American men and their children and families." Community Voices. National Center for Primary Care. http://www.communityvoices.org/Uploads/wherearethemen2_00108_00144.pdf

# CHAPTER 10

# The Media and African American Boys and Men

## *Another Take*

*"It really boils down to this: that all life is interrelated. We are all caught in an inescapable network of mutuality, tied into a single garment of destiny. Whatever affects one directly, affects all indirectly. I can never be what I ought to be until you are what you ought to be. This is the interrelated structure of reality."*

—*Dr. Martin Luther King, Jr.*

*Jamal and Martin decided to meet at Safe Haven, a church-managed day center that allows them to have a snack without charge, to receive mail when their housing is unstable, and to try to refer them to jobs and other social service needs. Safe Haven is a place to rest, to take a shower, to stay warm on a cold day, although they must leave by 5 p.m. They were sitting and watching the news and heard a white politician say, "We have to take our country back!" Martin and Jamal exchanged disgusted glances, and Jamal asked, "Who is this 'we' they are talking about? What exactly are we taking back? We are taking 'what' to where? We are taking it from whom?"*

*The other men in the center watching the news commented that it did not matter much, since life in this country has continuously excluded the black man. He has no health insurance unless he gets desperately ill with a disability—or is incarcerated. If he is healthy and poor, he is often hired for part-time, low-wage jobs that do not provide health insurance or provide insurance with a very high co-pay. Robert, another man sitting around said that he heard that "Obamacare" will finally provide insurance for poor men, but he doubts that the politicians will let that happen. Harold, in a rare fit of anger commented, "The only real 'insurance' that a poor black man has in America is the guarantee of going to jail or prison if someone just decides to send him away, regardless of the nature of the offense . . . if there actually was an offense." His friends tell him that they get health care, but even in prison they are beginning to charge a fee. They too wondered why the reporter, who happened to be black, did not ask the politician any tough follow-up questions. A young man who had just been released mused out loud, "They don't care about us. Man, they don't even see us. We are invisible!"*

Some version of this clueless-media scenario gets played out over and over again, day in and day out. Whether new or traditional—television, radio, newspapers, magazines, books, movies, blogs, Web sites, podcasts, you name it—the media are the conduit through which misinformation, biased information, and partial information gets communicated. The media are where only some stories get covered and only some people are shown. Media are a major source of our stereotypes. They set the stage on which society acts and, thus, are, in good part, why this book needs to be written.

The lack of fair and complete coverage exists, in part, because African Americans (and other people of color and other minorities) are not properly represented among the media-makers. But, in addition to the likely deep-seated and often unacknowledged biases of the people creating and delivering media, media itself has a built in flaw in that it must attract and please advertisers. Some would argue—and I would agree—that alternative or public media are doing a better job than mainstream mass media. But this form does not have as big an audience and advertising is inexorably part of their bottom line too. Some pin their hopes on the new digital and social media. It is true that these forms have a huge role to play and, so far, have been mostly open and democratic. But such open media is not only at risk of becoming less open, but it can also be a conduit for racism and lies as much as for truth and fairness. As Daniel Patrick Moynihan once quipped, "Everyone is entitled to his own opinion, but not his own facts." Today, we brush facts away if they do not suit our message.

## Media Matters

We are all formed by media and culture, and beginning at an early age. According to the Web site Tolerance.org, "Stereotypes are based on images in mass media, or reputations passed on by parents, peers and other members of society. . . . Social scientists believe children begin to acquire prejudices and stereotypes as toddlers. Many studies have shown that as *early as age 3* [emphasis added], children pick up terms of racial prejudice without really understanding their significance. Soon, they begin to form attachments to their own group and develop negative attitudes about other racial or ethnic groups, or the 'out-group.' Early in life, most children acquire a full set of biases that can be observed in verbal slurs, ethnic jokes and acts of discrimination."[1]

The media, then, may well have it within their power to shape the entire narrative around the well being of African American boys and men. There are endless snapshots, sound bites, and perspectives that feed the eyes and ears of the American public around the sensational that far too often are not positive. What, too, many learn, including many African Americans, is to fear, to be careful, to avoid danger, to stay away from men of color and, particularly, African American men. Countless boys and men tell of women clutching their purses, of people crossing to the other side of the street, of drivers clicking the lock button on their car doors when they walk by, of being followed by store detectives, all because they are black and male.

As bad as this is, the trouble does not end there. In contrast to the constant roar of negative images and stories, there is a deafening silence about the hope extinguished with every violent act. Rarely do we hear of the dreams deferred, damaged, and never-to-be because of profiling and inordinate direction into special education, jails and prisons, and alternative schools simply, it seems, because the dreamers are black. The media have not given us options around what to believe. They have not given us different ways to analyze individual actions and situational ethics. Perhaps the producers, writers, and reporters do not know the various storylines that could be told around every apparent tragedy, nightmare, failing . . . or success. For some reason or reasons, many in the media are not able to pursue the untold story of what it is like to be black and male of any age, in this nation, because of their own circumscribed background. Sometimes, the inability has its roots in money—sensationalistic stories increase an audience and that drives up advertising rates. This seems to be no secret. The Pew Foundation Center for the People and the Press noted that only 19% of Americans believed the primary concern of news media was keeping them informed. The major goal was to gather the largest audience.[2] Sensationalism sells. We all know it, and we watch it and believe it anyway.

Perhaps the tide is turning, though. The news coverage of the killing of 17-year-old Trayvon Martin in Florida in February of 2012 serves as a guidebook for breaking the silence that surrounds the profiling, stopping, searching, and disrespectful, and often rough treatment of young men whose only crime is to be dark skinned and looking "suspicious." Trayvon Martin's parents were savvy and hired a lawyer to pursue legal action and convince the media to report the case. Family members were also available to the various media to answer, over and over again, the same painful questions about their son. It probably did not hurt that many of the journalists who initially covered the story were black and that Facebook and Twitter served as further vehicles for the story to go viral. Although it took 10 days for the story to spread beyond the Florida media, the story was soon picked up by national news venues, including CBS News, The Huffington Post, and CNN,[3] and hundreds demonstrated in the "Million Hoodie March"—in a nod to what Trayvon was wearing when he was shot—shouting "Am I suspicious?"

And the higher a black man climbs . . . even high office does not make him immune from unseemly critique and disrespect and simple fairness. Now that there is an African American president, a typical news cycle fills the ears of the public with innuendo. One potential presidential candidate says, "that president . . . he thinks he's so smart, that he knows everything," and, to the ears of all of us who are black, we hear that old refrain . . . "he's an uppity black" . . . an "elitist" who thinks he is better than us (whites). Or, those negative old timey negative voices of the "bosses" say "we will defeat this legislation" and this will "break" this uppity president. Poor people, people of color recognize this term "break" as meaning breaking down the will and elimination of the spirit of an African American slave. We in communities of color have also heard "we will take this President's legislation/ideas" and "shove it back down his throat" . . . intimidation based on violence, scary indeed in that so much violence has been carried out against African American men just because they were African American and male. And the message to the African American men and boys listening is "be careful, be very careful, very, very afraid; do not risk interaction." They do understand that it is important to "stay in their place . . . " whatever that means. But one cannot stay in place and thrive. Does the media "call the question" when these remarks are made? What are the ethical standards to which the media adheres?

If the news is the barometer of what happened and what it means, then the news seems to have become less "news" and "truth" and more a thinly veiled veneer quite willing to keep the old ways of doing and ruling in place possibly because it is not challenged. And, it is those old ways that are killing the spirit, destroying the souls of far too many young males, who yearn to be men, but who know the inherent danger in standing up, in speaking out, in talking back. The mainstream media in the United States, despite the valiant efforts of some, may, by its silence, inadvertently protect cultural practices, ideology, and human marginalization actions from bygone eras. Those old days are gone and will never come again; or will they? Even when commentators or their guests use terms

## If Words Could Kill: The F-Word

Once upon a time, there was widespread use of the word "Negro" to describe the group of brown and black people of African origin. Over time, there were those who corrupted the pronunciation of this word Negro, and many began to say "Nigra," although we think they knew better. Peer pressure wields a heavy social bludgeon, we suppose. Then, those who were really mean-spirited corrupted further the name Negro to one that was pronounced just plain "nigger." Perhaps the phonics teacher got the pronunciation wrong, or maybe these were just very poor students. Yes, that must be it.

Not all lapses in how words are used, however, depend on differing pronunciations. Consider the word "felon," which refers to a level of criminal offense. The offense might historically have been a misdemeanor, but it was important to capture more as felons so they could be helped longer and so there could be assurances that their lives would more than likely be ruined. Now, they are not just someone convicted of a felony offense, they are a "felon" . . . no, a "FELON"! As in, "Didn't you know he was a 'FELON'?" the newscaster, the television judge, the others say. You, as a god-fearing citizen who believes in redemption, might have just thought the individual before you was just a child of god who had seen the errors of his ways and who has paid his debt to society through incarceration (although his debt to the sheriff and judge is harder to get rid of, because they keep on piling on the fees). So, he is not Harold, Robert, Jesus, Abraham, John . . . he is FELON! He might as well change his name to FELON. And do not forget that nobody wants you to go near that person lest they somehow find his or her way back into the world and not back into prison where he or she makes some people rich while his or her difficulty finding work increases overall community poverty.[1,2]

---

1. "Root Causes: Recidivism." PolicyforResults.org. http://www.policyforresults.org.
2. "From Prison to Home: The Effects of Incarceration on Children, Families, and Community." U.S. Department of Health and Human Services. http://aspe.hhs.gov/.

such as "the America people think," it is clear that the poor communities of color are vanquished, are made invisible.

In another sense, they are made all too visible and out of proportion to the truth. For example, during the Los Angeles riots in 1992, the way the events were presented led one to believe that the black community was solely responsible for the riots and other disturbances. Yet, "according to reports, of those arrested, only 36% were black and of those arrested, more than a third had full-time jobs and most had no political affiliation. Some 60% of the rioters and looters were made up of Hispanics and whites. Yet the media did not report this underlying fact."[4] So, it is, too, with the reportage of other "race" riots that may be more about underlying conditions than about race per se.

A powerful and comprehensive *New York Times* bestselling book about the media entitled *News For All the People: The Epic Story of Race and the American Media*, by Juan Gonzalez and Joseph Torres, puts race at the center of American news media and delineates the role that America's racial divisions have played in the creation of the country's media complex. The narrative takes us from an exploration of the "cotton curtain" and the practice of interdicting mail from abolitionists to the South (below the Mason-Dixon Line) to other forms of suppression of the discussion of racial equality throughout the nation. *News For All the People* provides details on how publishers and broadcasters actually provoked

---

 **REALITY CHECK   Diversity Still Lags in TV Management**

The 2010 census looked at the stations owned by ABC, CBS, Cox, FOX, Gannett, Hearst Argyle, Media General, Meredith, NBC, and Tribune. The census found that, even though people of color comprise about one-third of the U.S. population, only 12.6% of managers in these TV newsrooms were people of color. In addition, 82 of the stations had no people of color at all on their news management teams.

The census also found that "of the 1,157 executive producers, assignment managers, managing editors, assistant news directors, news directors, and general managers who work at these stations:

• 1017 (87.9%) were White

• 81 (7.8%) were African American

• 42 (3%) were Hispanic/Latino

• 16 (1.6%) were Asian

• 1 was Native American"[1]

---

1. Tene Croom. "NABJ Makes a Big Push for Diversity in Network Newsrooms." National Association of Black Journalists. http://rbr.com/

communities to violence. The writers, as well, give attention to the few times that the media actually promoted racial equality. We did not come to this place by chance. Herbert Hoover's Federal Radio Commission "eagerly" awarded a license to a notorious Ku Klux Klan organization in the nation's capitol. Hoover knew the power of the press to provoke, to incite individuals to war with one another. The conclusion is crystal clear. If media is responsible for leading us to this place of confusion and lack of understanding, what is it that prevents them from reversing the tide and leading us to a level playing field that is replete with understanding and concern for all Americans?

## Who Wrote That?

In America, the major mainstream media have predominantly white reporters and serve a mainly white audience. To correct this, in 1978, the American Society of Newspaper Editors set a goal to achieve minority employment at daily newspapers "equivalent to the percentage of minority persons within the national population" by the year 2000. Writing in 1999, Jeff Cohen found that "Racial minorities now constitute 11.6 percent of news staffs but 27.3 percent of the country's population. At the rate newspapers are going (ASNE last year extended its deadline by 25 years), they won't reach their goal until late in the next century."[5]

Cohen continued, "Slightly more diversity can be found in TV news staffs, and far less in magazines. But few top news executives in any medium—real decision makers—are people of color. This lack of diversity has consequences in terms of content."[6]

More recently, we see how times have changed—for the worse. The latest survey of journalists of color in newspaper and online newsrooms showed that people of color, especially African American staffers, declined for the third year in a row. And, 441 newspapers in 2010 had no minorities on their full-time staff.[7]

What is not covered can also be telling. For example, for years prior to the Oklahoma City bombing, the militia movement in the United States remained largely ignored. But think about it, and flip the colors around. As Cohen pointed out, "If hundreds of heavily armed units of African-Americans were training across the country and talking of the inevitability of violent clashes with the federal government, we'd have seen massive, hysterical coverage—and not just from white talk radio."[8] Could this lack of coverage be due to the fact that most reporters are white and most white people think white people are not "that dangerous"—or simply have the right to walk around heavily armed?

A report by the Joint Center for Political and Economic Studies, a black-led think tank, concludes that "whites and persons of color occupy distinctly different cultural spaces and that the implication of racially distinct media choices appears to be heightened interracial alienation."[9] One wonders, therefore, why the newscasters, the pundits, those that tell the story do not grasp the practices and trends that keep stereotypes and discrimination alive. Failure to make the connections that indicate that those old days are still with us means that insufficient numbers of well meaning commentators are giving chase to "those days" in numbers sufficient to eliminate the "respectability" of discriminatory words and deeds.

The Opportunity Agenda, also black established and led, issued a report that concluded there are distorted patterns of portrayal in the media.[10] These include under-representation of African Americans (and black males in particular) in a variety of roles, such as "talking head" news experts, computer users in TV commercials, and "relatable" characters with well-developed personal lives (e.g., fathers). The report also concludes that exploration of real problems may result in reinforcing the "problem frame," unless a delicate balance is reached in the discussion. It notes that distorted media representations can create attitudinal effects, ranging from general antagonism to higher tolerance for race-based

 **REALITY CHECK  The Opportunity Agenda Report**

The Opportunity Agenda conducted three research studies that examined perceptions of and by African American men and boys and their relationship to the media. The studies concluded:

- Producers themselves may have distorted perceptions or may make incorrect assumptions about what audiences want to see or who their audiences are.

- Media makers may be accurately reflecting the appetites and preferences of consumers who prefer these distortions.

- Media makers may be working toward political ends by trafficking in stereotypes.

- The media present little information about structural factors affecting life outcomes for black men and boys and that limited public awareness results in little understanding.

- There is a paucity of African American producers, journalists, invited guest experts, and other shapers of content.

socioeconomic disparities and reduced attention to the social determinants of health and well-being, all of which may result in increased punitive approaches.

So, would it help if more reporters were African American? Maybe. Maybe not.

In 1987, Kirk Johnson studied 30 days of news coverage of two mainly black neighborhoods in Boston. He found that mainstream media overwhelmingly focused on crime stories, especially violent crimes or drugs. About 85% of the stories reinforced negative stereotypes about blacks.[11] Conversely, when he looked at how the same two neighborhoods were covered by four black-owned news outlets during the same period, the coverage was more diverse. Although they covered crime, they also covered local business, school achievement, and community cleanup campaigns. As a result, 57% of the stories showed a community hungry for education and business success and eager to clean up poor living conditions made worse by bureaucratic neglect.

This suggests that a more equitable distribution of reporters would help improve the coverage of the news. Joseph Torres and Juan Gonzalez, the authors of the aforementioned book, *All the People: The Epic Story of Race and the American*, are not so sure. In an interview on NPR radio, Torres said, "unfortunately, at times journalists have been afraid to get involved because they are going against the corporate desires, let's say, of their owners to own more property and make more money."[12] In their book, they write about journalists who have, in fact, actively fought against discrimination in media. But, Gonzalez said, "You do [still] see it but unfortunately the pressures of today in newsrooms where everyone is downsizing in the commercial media and the advertiser-driven model of most of the news media in the company is falling apart, that there's a lot of fear in newsrooms today, fear of are you going to be the next person laid off. Are you going to displease your media supervisors, editors, and owners?" Gonzalez completes the thought: "And so I think that that level of fear is dissuading many people from the kind of entrepreneurial or courageous reporting that we've seen in the past."[13] National Association of Black Journalists President, Gregory Lee, agrees, "The relentless attack on newsroom diversity continues under the guise of a failing economy."[14]

Lack of diversity is an age-old problem found in most professions. Diversity alone may not be sufficient in that the health professions have made fits and starts to diversify the workforce. The impact of medicine's venture into diversifying the workforce has yet to be proven successful given the persistent health disparities, particularly when we find that African American men have greater health disparities than any other group

**✔ REALITY CHECK  The Incredible Whiteness of Media**

The media may over-represent blacks as criminals and druggies, but they are under-represented as experts and analysts.

In the late 1980s and early 1990s, according to FAIR:

- 92% of *Nightline*'s U.S. guests were white.

- 90% of the *PBS NewsHour*'s guests were white.

- 26 of 27 repeat commentators on National Public Radio during a 4-month study were white.

- According to Jeff Cohen, "Minority experts tended to be ghettoized into discussions of "black" or "brown" issues."[1]

_____

1. Cohen, Jeff. "Racism and Mainstream Media." *FAIR.* http://www.fair.org.

regardless of their income. Business and business schools seem to have less of a problem with diversity, as there appears to be a clear understanding of their goal: targeted SELLING to a multicultural audience that is easily measured by income generated. The profit motive appears to incentivize diversity. This "story" of workforce diversity is also not told by the storytellers. There is an opportunity to "address obstacles," rather than solidify African American men's place at the bottom of the ladder, with no health insurance or any other useful rungs on the ladder toward upward mobility and equality.

Also, the discussion of media and opportunities must be balanced by taking a realistic look at the pipeline. The pipeline discussion brings us back, yet again, to the story of the education of African American boys. A report by the Maynard Institute[15] surmises that, unless we do something about education, we may not have African American men to tell the story of the news, even if the doors open to them.

### An Untold Story: Affordable Care

In previous chapters, I tucked into the "Reality Checks" the astonishing figures that tell the true story of the health effects of our current justice system. My purpose is to begin to chip away at the inaccurate story told by the mainstream media. In this age of 24-hour-cycle news and endless punditry, we are de facto told or receive subliminal suggestions about what

**TAKE A GOOD LOOK   Media Maker, Media Consumer**

Are you a media maker? We are all media makers and consumers in this age of digital communication! And we are all influencers. Look in the mirror and ask yourself:

- Does someone have to die to mobilize a nation . . . for a time? If you think this is not the case, then what does it take and what can you do to help tell the story that does not require death (e.g., Emmet Till, Trayvon Martin, and perhaps countless others who are withering away in prison . . . a slow death)?

- How will you frame your letter or op-ed piece in a way that will persuade a jaded editor who believes he or she has seen and heard it all that you have a fresh perspective?

- If our world remains the same with marginalization, stereotyping, profiling, and discrimination, who will you identify as the major perpetrator, and why?

- What would you do to educate the reporters or commentators, the pundits?

- If you agree that the race and, perhaps, the ethnicity of the reporter, whether print, visual, or online, is important, what do you think you can do to encourage greater diversity?

- If you feel that the race and, perhaps, the ethnicity of the reporter, whether print, visual, or online, is NOT important, what do you think you can do to encourage reporting that is positive, that pays attention to the profit motive, and that improves the health and well-being of African American boys and men?

- What could you do to have news outlets in your community commit to producing a more balanced view of issues faced by each group in the community?

- Write one thing you are willing to do to use the media to tell an untold story:

_____

_____

to believe versus what to think about, reflect on, speak up about so that the truth, whatever its consequences, will improve our neighborhoods. Amid all the negativity, the issues, constraints, stresses, and strains experienced by black men, often regardless of their income, are rarely discussed.

When you look at the facts, it is clear that the level of health care given may be compromised simply because the consumer is African American. Has the media told the story of how Medicaid came into existence as a result of southern lawmakers refusing to make Medicare available for all Americans? Has the mainstream media spoken of the impact of the lack of coverage on disability and mortality in Black America? For example, in their discussions of the impact of the Affordable Care Act, has the media educated the public about who the new recipients of insurance will be and how these new recipients will benefit?

The changes "occurring as a result of healthcare reform will significantly affect the ways in which justice involved individuals can access public health insurance and services. Estimates indicate that at least 35 percent of new Medicaid eligibles under the Affordable Care Act will have a history of criminal justice system involvement."[16]

## An Untold Story: What We Spend on Prisons

If we want to know why we are where we are in this nation, follow the money. Many of our media elites, the pundits, focus on the debt in which our nation finds itself. They focus on what is owed to other countries. They wax eloquently and at length about what is spent in entitlement programs, supports for the poor, the safety net. But they are silent on the $75 billion plus spent every year on prisons in this nation.[17] No one knows what is spent on all jail care in the United States, as they are so numerous and there is no central reporting framework. The amount is likely in excess of $200 billion per year. Is this a debt we want our children to inherit if we do not change, just as they will inherit the overall national debt? And are the two debts not related, as individuals not in the workforce are not contributing to the tax-base? Conversely, these tax dollars could address obstacles.

## An Untold Story: The "End" of Slavery

How can one tell the story of those "missing" from their communities as a result of stereotyping and hyper-incarceration in a way that people can understand and relate to something that is familiar? Human trafficking refers to "Minors (under age 18) involved in commercial sex; adults age 18 or over involved in commercial sex via force, fraud, or coercion;

and a category too often overlooked by most, children and adults forced to perform labor and/or services in conditions of involuntary servitude, peonage, debt bondage or slavery, via force, fraud, or coercion. This includes agricultural work or housekeeping, both of which are widespread throughout the US . . . "[18] Therefore, I use in this chapter the term "human trafficking" to include the incarceration practices: Money is made in exchange for the use of the human body in the cell.

The comparison of human trafficking is undergirded by the stories and conclusions in Douglas Blackmon's book, *Another Form of Slavery* (that has also been made into a PBS documentary), that describes the transport of African American males to the North to work in the steel mills from the southern jails in which they had been incarcerated, as a way of having them pay for their expenses while in prison (and providing free labor to the steel mills), although the sheriff was paid. Nobody knows the names of most of these men. Nobody knew what happened to them. They were not paid. They had no access to health care. We know now that the graves are there, up North and scattered around the South. Many probably were just told that "he ran away" . . . from his family, his responsibilities. Not much has changed. Where are the storytellers? When will they tell us that modern prison takes them far, far away for years and years and that he (or she) may never come home, unless we change our system? Prisons are now opening nursing homes, because some have nowhere to go, as they have been away so long nobody is left to welcome them home. Many in this nation do not know anything significant about the prisons and the burden and unraveling they cause in families and communities. Who will tell the people?

## Telling the Story: Alternative Media

We do see the emergence of some alternate outlets that offer new ways of knowing and an examination of media practices. The GRIO (thegrio. com) and The Color of Change (colorofchange.org), among others, along with a handful of African American newspapers both online and print, are available, but these target the African American community primarily and do not regularly reach the general public, unless commentators are used on the major television/cable networks. Cultural segregation remains in place.

## Telling the Story: The Academic Press as Leader in Educating the Public

*The American Journal of Public Health (AJPH)* was the first premier academic journal to courageously embrace and publish special theme issues on the health of poor men of color; of the health of those in prison and re-entry into community; of oral health, mental health; and substance use disorders affecting communities that are poor; of poor men of color. This journal was the only major venue that opened the door to an exploration of issues not viewed as politically correct, or as of interest to the public. Several research studies have noted the opportunity to improve the health of the community,[19] including a little-thought-about topic, oral health,[20] by providing appropriate and comprehensive treatment to people while they are incarcerated. Since these original *AJPH* issues, several journals have been initiated both nationally and internationally affirming that there is interest and support at least among the academy. One suspects that, among the thousands of individuals with relatives incarcerated, there might be similar interest in articles in newspapers, on regular and cable television, and on the Internet. The Association of Healthcare Journalists (www.healthjournalism.org) has not published substantive stories or investigative reports that state the cost to society. The Association has not reported on what it means to individuals to live in a nation without access to health care and who cannot provide income to their families or meaningful support to communities in the form of taxes on earned income.

### Telling the Story: Solutions Journalism

Although the true nature and extent of the problems must be the basis for some of the stories that need told, there is another side of the coin. Where is the good news about people who are making a difference, no matter how small? An opinion column in the mainstream newspaper, the *New York Times*, seeks to shine a beacon of light on "solutions" to problems, not just the problems themselves. It is called "FIXES" and it is written by David Bornstein.[21] He explains the premise: "Fixes looks at solutions to social problems that can counterbalance stereotypes and reduce feelings of isolation." He acknowledges that "reporters will always be needed to play the crucial watchdog role—uncovering malfeasance, corruption, and betrayals of trust. But increasingly, there is a new problem that the press needs to be addressing as well—it's not so much about people doing terrible things that are hidden from view, it's about people doing remarkable things that are hidden from view." [22] This sentiment, this insight, is at the heart of Community Voices and this book. Scholars have described the tremendous explosion of nonprofits, nongovernmental organizations, social-purpose businesses, "benefit corporations," dot-orgs, dot-nets, and so forth, as a major global "power shift"[23] and, by Paul Hawkin, as the "largest movement the world has ever seen."[24] Taking it a step further, Bornstein admits that there is a danger in "writing about something I think is sensible, effective and efficient only to discover that it's wrong-headed, harmful and wasteful."[25] So, he invites feedback from readers, hoping to learn from their "criticisms, experiences and expertise" . . . "a reader's role can include action and social responsibility."[26] In my own world view, this is one way YOU can be part of the solution.

## Breaking Free

What, exactly, is the problem? Is it that we are still trapped in an era of political correctness? If we are, how does one break free? If we are already free, what is holding us back?

Clearly, it would not hurt to broaden the range of leaders working in service of healthy young men and boys of color. Media outlets—local and national—often have people of color who are reporters, editors, and producers who are sympathetic to the issue. There are a few hopeful signs, but these are mainly through the way that some choose to use their individual voice, the bully pulpit in which they may find themselves. Some networks do more than others to reach a new accommodation with the need for diversity and balance in broadcasting, although prime time positions are not equitably distributed. There are few "stars," however, whose opinions matter to a large audience. MOST are not people of color. And fewer are African American men. Through Community Voices, we have created an important partnership with CNN's Soledad O'Brien. Her *Black in America* series has made huge strides informing the nation about how far African Americans have come as a community and how far we still have to go. (See the Heroes and Leaders section within this chapter.)

The influence of the media does not just include national television. The power of the pen could be better used to motivate people on a large scale. One area in which we can showcase our leadership is to reach out to small, local and regional newspapers, online news sites and blogs, as well as talk radio stations. What would it take to encourage talk show hosts to commit one or two shows per month to take up an aspect of this issue and raise awareness?

We have seen the devastation that occurs when our own leaders are not actively driving media attention to the growing crisis. Unabated, negative media images shape the white majority's reaction to minorities, especially young men. Worse yet, these same negative images shape the view these young men have of themselves. News and entertainment industries perpetuate and profit hugely from the negative images that forestall empathetic responses to the systemic roots of current-day realities. Yet, the reality of the crisis continues to go unreported.

HISTORY OF CHANGE   **THE "WORD" CAN INSPIRE
AND FOSTER SOCIAL JUSTICE**

### Frederick Douglass, Orator, Writer, Statesman

*"Those who profess to favor freedom, yet deprecate agitation want crops
without plowing the ground, want the rain without thunder and lightning, and
the ocean, without the awful roar of its mighty waters!"*

*—Frederick Douglass*

The Power of the Pen . . . the media, such as it existed in the past, was powerful
enough to inspire action, to even foment civic unrest and rebellion that ultimately
led to substantial progress for Blacks in America. From out of the mists come leaders
of humble origin who just decide not to take it anymore. Frederick Douglass (born
Frederick Augustus Washington Bailey) led the way. Frederick Douglass escaped
from slavery and became a prominent leader of the abolitionist movement. Douglass
remains one of the most quoted speakers and writers as a result of his incisive and
pithy messages that offered metaphoric contrasts that illuminated the plight of slaves,
the shame of slavery, and the power of people to take up the cause for social justice
for ALL human beings and promote change. "I would unite with anybody to do right
and with nobody to do wrong" resonates today among those seeking freedom from
discrimination and protection from the bias induced by stereotyping.[1]

---

1. Family Search. "About Frederick Douglass." https://www.familysearch.org/. From a
speech "The Significance of Emancipation in the West Indies." Speech, Canandaigua, New
York, August 3, 1857. In *The Frederick Douglass Papers. Series One: Speeches, Debates,
and Interviews.* Volume 3:1855–63. Edited by John W. Blassingame. New Haven: Yale University Press, p. 204.

---

LEADERS AND HEROES

### Soledad O'Brien, Media Maker; CNN News Anchor

Soledad O'Brien is always after the real story, and she advises others in the media
who are after the truth to "develop the real estate that will support their deciding when
and where to tell the story about African American boys and men. In other words, they
have to continually make the topic something that they stay tuned in to and then know
when the time is right to put a story out there. I do not believe that one should just do
a story. They need to cover the waterfront, establish their own real estate around the
issues; then they know what to place and when to get it to the public."

Since O'Brien joined CNN in 2003, she has been reporting breaking news from around the globe. She has produced award-winning, record-breaking, and critically acclaimed documentaries on important stories facing the world today. She hosted the extremely successful multi-part series of documentaries, *Black in America*, which focused on successful community leaders improving the lives of African Americans, a youth empowerment program, and the state of black America 40 years after the assassination of Dr. Martin Luther King, Jr. The series became one of CNN's most watched programs. "Several viewers of the first episode were so inspired by the program that they launched BlackInAmerica.com, an online community and social network for black Americans who want to address the issues and challenges of Black America."[1] O'Brien "has also reported for the CNN documentary *Words That Changed a Nation*, featuring a look at Dr. King's private writings and notes, and investigated his assassination in *Eyewitness to Murder: The King Assassination*."

She recently covered the devastation in Haiti, which has provided her with an apt metaphor for the danger of feeling overwhelmed by huge, heart-breaking stories. She recalls, "I asked some of the missionaries there how they stood it; what kept them going? Their response was to quote the proverbial story of the starfish and the miles-long beach. Each person that they helped is saved, and they work one by one, as with throwing the starfish back into the water so that they can live. The way to tell the story amidst that overwhelming event was to tell it one by one, one person's story, one community story, so it make sense to the audience. Anyone, whether in media or elsewhere, has to figure out what it is that you want to and then can do and work in your little space. One of those starfish might be the big story, and your friends and supporters may resonate with the theme. I do my job and try to highlight interesting stories and make news when I can."[2]

We may think we know the story, but when reporting you need to be open to surprises. O'Brien reminds us that the problems that we face are a result of multisectoral issues: poverty, lack of hope, and feeling that getting ahead is not for them. Many face challenging issues at home that we know nothing about. She says, "I interviewed two students at Morehouse College, a place where many imagine that people go who have families with assets. But the responses that these two young men gave surprised me. One said, 'I am so glad not be hungry all the time, because now I am on the meal plan.' The other one said, 'The heat is on when it is cold outside.' I thought they would focus on the Spelman College girls, the city of Atlanta, sports teams, but NO; they talked about hunger and heat!"[3]

O'Brien says she does not do a story simply because she thinks it is a "good story." It has to be dramatic, colorful, interesting. For example, she says, "Nobody is interested in poverty as the story. You have to be smarter about telling the story. Framing the story is important. If a father goes to prison and his children follow him, how do

*(continued)*

## LEADERS AND HEROES

### Soledad O'Brien, Media Maker; CNN News Anchor (*continued*)

we get the media there, interested in that story? People do not want to talk about the 'prison population.' The stories must be about human beings and the implications of what is happening for the individual and beyond."

"There are some obstacles, certainly. Funding for a story is always an issue. Then there are people who see things differently. The bigger problem that we have is the lack of coverage and lack of stories at all. I have tried to open up opportunities for stories to be told. People need to have had success with the documentaries primarily because they were well done. Well-done documentaries beget more documentaries, and these allow stories to begin that all provoke conversation. Or some topics just may not be popular immediately. Another very real obstacle is competing interests. Other people have ideas about what the story should be and how it should be framed."[4]

In addition, she points out, "we have too few African Americans and Hispanics and virtually no Asians in their vast diversity, nor Native Americans. I try to inspire others to enter the field and stay in the field. I have to sometimes convince people to stay, because they do not feel valued. I tell them, 'You cannot make changes if you are disheartened. There is nothing that you can do about the way people treat you. You cannot make any difference at all if you leave.' Things go unchallenged on up to the next level if there is no diversity. However you define diversity, it is not authentic to move forward on a story if it is not 'informed' by diverse perspectives."[5]

According to O'Brien, "We also can see how people will put stories out, build a narrative based on things that are not true. In that case, it is the job of media to bring in the content and context. Media must ask questions that clarify. There must be nuance in the conversation. My job is to obsessively lead in to a story but always do so with respect for the person I am interviewing or profiling. After all, no one lives in a singular dimension."[6]

For more information about the documentary series *Black in America*, please visit http://inamerica.blogs.cnn.com/category/black-in-america/.

---

1. Author interview with Soledad O'Brien, March 2012.
2. Ibid.
3. Ibid.
4. Ibid.
5. Ibid.
6. Ibid.

## Notes

1. Teaching Tolerance. "Test Yourself for Hidden Bias: Teaching Tolerance." http://www.tolerance.org/hiddenbias.
2. "Public More Critical of the Press, but Goodwill Persists: Online Newspaper Readership Countering Print Losses. June 26, 2005. A Publication of the Pew Research Center for the People and the Press." Of the People's Press or The Pew Research Center for the People and the Press. http://www.peoplepress.org.
3. Stelter, Brian. "In Slain Teenager's Case, a Long Route to National Attention." *New York Times*. http://www.nytimes.com.
4. Balkaran, Stephen, "Mass Media and Racism." *The Yale Political Quarterly* 1999;21(1). http://www.yale.edu/ypq/articles/oct99/oct99b.html.
5. Cohen, Jeff. "Fairness & Accuracy in Reporting." *FAIR*. http://www.fair.org.
6. Ibid.
7. Turner, April. "America's Newsrooms Fail to Match U.S. Diversity." National Association for Black Journalists. http://www.nabj.org/.
8. Cohen, Jeff. "Fairness & Accuracy in Reporting." *FAIR*. http://www.fair.org.
9. Entman, Robert. "Dellums Report: Young Men of Color in the Media: Images and Impacts." Joint Center for Political and Economic Studies. http://www.jointcenter.org/.
10. This research was authorized by Topos Partnership (Executive Summary; Social Science Literature Review: Media Representations and Impact on the Lives of Black Men and Boys; and A Review of Public Opinion Research Related to Black Male Achievement) and Marc Kerschhagel (Media Market Research: Media Consumption Trends Among Black Men), with consultation from Janet Dewart Bell and Eleni Delimpaltadaki Janis of The Opportunity Agenda, who contributed to the design and analysis of the research and edited the report. Christopher Moore designed the report. Jill Bailin, Judi Lerman, and Loren Siegel also assisted in the editing of the report. "Opportunity for Black Men and Boys: Public Opinion, Media Depictions, and Media Consumption." The Opportunity Agenda. http://www.nationalhomeless.org/factsheets/veterans.pdf
11. Johnson, Kirk. "Black and White in Boston: A Researcher Documents Disturbing Biases in Mainstream Coverage of Blacks." *Columbia Journalism Review* 1987;26(May/June).
12. "Racist History of American News Media." http://www.npr.org/2011/11/25/142704489/racist-history-of-american-news-media.
13. Juan Gonzalez. http://www.npr.org/2011/11/25/142704489/racist-history-of-american-news-media "Racist History of American News

Media?" NPR. Tell Me More, hosted by Tony Cox. http://www.npr.org.

14. Posted by April Turner. "AP Lays Off Diversity Advocate Robert Naylor." National Association of Black Journalists. http://www.nabj.org/news/82840/ .

15. Richard Prince's Journal-isms. "Report Calls Underachievement a 'National Catastrophe.'" Maynard Institute, 2010. http://www.maynardije.org/richardprince/will-black-boys-have-skills-be-journalists.

16. Department of Justice. Federal Register. 2011;76(129):39438–39443. http://www.gpo.gov/fdsys/pkg/FR-2011-07-06/html/2011-16844.htm.

17. "Billions Behind Bars: Inside America's Prison Industry." *CNBC News.* http://www.cnbc.com/id/44762389/.

18. Archer, Dan. "Slavery Lives on in the United States." Truthout. http://www.truth-out.org/human-trafficking/1329157025.

19. "The Health Status of Soon-to-be-Released Inmates: A Report to Congress." National Commission on Correctional Health Care, 2002. http://www.ncchc.org/pubs/pubs_stbr.html.

20. Treadwell, Henrie and Allan Formicola. "Improving the Oral Health of Prisoners to Improve Overall Health and Well-Being." *American Journal of Public Health*, 2005;95:1677–1678.

21. Bornstein, David. Opinionator. Fixes. *New York Times.* http://opinionator.blogs.nytimes.com.

22. Bornstein, David. "Why 'Solutions Journalism' Matters, Too." Opinionator. Fixes. *New York Times.* http://opinionator.blogs.nytimes.com.

23. Mathews, Jessica T. "Power Shift." *Foreign Affairs.* http://www.foreignaffairs.com/articles/52644/jessica-t-mathews/power-shift.

24. Hawkin, Pawl. *Blessed Unrest: How the Largest Movement in the World Came Into Being and Why No One Saw It Coming.* New York: Viking Press, 2007.

25. Bornstein, David. "Why 'Solutions Journalism' Matters, Too." Opinionator. Fixes. *New York Times.* http://opinionator.blogs.nytimes.com.

26. Ibid.

# CHAPTER 11

# Looking for Real Community Values? Follow the Money

*"Far too often we become cowards when faced with individuals who have strong leadership abilities, individuals who often do not want social revolution as much as they want personal power."*

*—Shirley Chisolm, Former Congresswoman,
New York's 12th Congressional District*

*Jamal had not known about the vegetable stand, but was passing by after seeing the doctor about his back. After sitting in the clinic for a couple of hours, the doctor turned out to be a nice older man who had seen cases like Jamal's before. He took some blood and some x-rays of his spine and concluded that years of poor diet, posture, and stressful sleeping conditions had left him with premature spinal arthritis. Jamal was given advice to monitor his diet and continue his regimen of over–the-counter pain medication.*

*The doctor promised to have him come back to the office after the results of his blood work were returned. Although his back was not necessarily feeling better, Jamal felt that finally someone had taken his pain seriously. After years of being ignored by prison health services and rushed out of emergency rooms with no treatment, there was a doctor who offered him a diagnosis and committed to following up with him.*

*Walking down the street, enjoying the sunshine after the hours inside the clinic, Jamal could not believe his luck when he happened on what looked like an outdoor market. He was remembering the doctor's advice to add more fresh fruits and vegetables to his diet. Standing right by a pile of tomatoes was the most beautiful woman he had ever seen with a smile that took his breath away.*

*As he slowed his step, he felt a hand on his arm and saw the old man he had met at the emergency room. After sharing greetings, Martin followed Jamal's gaze and introduced him to Dorothea. Dorothea started helping Jamal pick out a few vegetables to take home. By the time they were done speaking, she had agreed to give him a personal cooking lesson.*

Who benefits from our system in which disorder is heaped on injustice, which piles on top of human misery, lost children, fractured families, and disproportionate resource allocation? The benefit can perhaps be assessed in a variety of ways, but the most direct and telling assessment would be by simply following the dollars. With the singular exceptions of Mahatma Ghandi and Martin Luther King, Jr., it is difficult to find those that seek power and prestige without the concomitant accrual of extraordinary resources.

Even simple decisions (i.e., where to site a prison or a school or a hospital) are generally linked to: Who will benefit the most? Does the African American community benefit when census count and ensuing community block grant development dollars are linked to where people are incarcerated versus where they lived—usually a resource-poor neighborhood that helped drive them into the way of the criminal justice system? This is not to suggest that environment alone is responsible for behavior that leads to incarceration, but the statistics are clear: if you are born and live in poverty, your risk of incarceration is greater. Is it because you are poor or is it because you are profiled?

There have been no studies that have seen the light of day that completely dissect the pathway of the billions of dollars that enter communities from state Departments of Corrections. We know that prisons are economic development incentives for rural communities just as cotton was when cotton was king and there was free labor to harvest the cotton. The source of the income is different, but the population central to the success of the economic scenario is the same: black and male. What do we have to do to break the pattern? My answer: follow the money, and then tell somebody, anybody who will listen, what tax dollars are doing that is ultimately destructive to the fabric of democracy. Crime rates are down, have been down. But investments continue, if not in the public sector, then in the private sector. If it is not about making communities safe, then what is all of this prison industry about? We end where we began: WHO BENEFITS? Take a further look . . . stay with me here.

The connection between our public policy decisions and the healthy life opportunities of young men and boys of color is real and direct. Because these policies do not operate in a vacuum, all of us, leaders and

HISTORY OF CHANGE **TITLE VI OF THE 1964 CIVIL RIGHTS ACT**

No person in the United States shall, on the ground of race, color, or national origin, be excluded from participation in, be denied the benefits of, or be subjected to discrimination under any program or activity receiving Federal financial assistance.

ordinary citizens alike, must take the time to try to understand the motivations behind the policy. Leaders and policy makers are often motivated by a genuine desire to make a positive difference, but they can also be swayed by popular imagery that demonizes black men.

Well-intentioned leaders can be misdirected or driven by political pressure to place misguided law and order goals ahead of a systemic analysis of the problem that could lead toward lasting healthy solutions. These ideological detours cause much needed resources (i.e., money) to be diverted to actions that wind up making things worse, so that, once again, our leadership fails to act in ways both inclusive and redemptive.

## Who Benefits? Who Pays?

Today, the disease, victimization, miseducation, and incarceration problems suffered by poor people of color are leveraged as revenue sources for localities seeking to boost their recession-starved coffers. Yet the monies raised to address these problems rarely find their way to the people they are meant to serve. If the people, families, and communities in need are not benefitting from the resources spent, then we can only ask ourselves: who *is* benefitting? An even more urgent focus for the question is for our leadership, in every field, to develop and articulate a strategic plan to ensure that the communities in need are actually given access to expanded opportunities provided by the resources secured on their backs.

The amount taxpayers spent on federal, state, and local corrections rose from about $9.6 billion in 1982 to $57 billion in 2001.[1] That is an astonishing 540% increase in less than 20 years. From 1980 to 2010, the federal prison population grew by 800%, whereas the federal prison budget grew by a whopping 1,700%.[2] The number of federal inmates continues to grow by about 3% per year. And it is not over yet. According to a Pew report, by 2008, states alone were spending $51.7 billion per year. The reported average inmate cost was $79 per day, nearly $29,000 per year, and including local, federal, and other funding brought the national correctional spending total to $68 billion.[3] In 2011, the taxpayer burden was more than $75 billion for corrections. Only 1 in 10 federal prisoners are incarcerated because of a violent crime—more than one-half are drug offenders, often serving mandatory long sentences, aiding the population explosion. "Increasing funding for more prison beds has been shown to be a self-fulfilling prophecy. . . . If you build it, they will come," notes the Justice Policy Institute.[4]

In 2006 National Public Radio news broadcasters brought the rampant spending into full relief when they discussed such spending in light of housing. "For more than a decade," they said, "the greatest increase in government-subsidized housing has come in the form of cells."[5] What legacy is the reckless spending that builds this mountain of debt for our children and our children's children with no clear public benefit given the continually declining crime rate? Or . . . could the answer lie in the profit motive in incarceration?[6]

Some police officers, who are or have been "in the trenches" are beginning to speak out and advocate for change and prioritizing funds toward education. For example, Neill Franklin, who was a narcotics officer and a commander of training during his 34-year career with the Maryland State Police and the Baltimore Police Department, wrote in the *New York Times*, "If we have any hope of healing the deep wounds of race in this country, we've first got to stop the bleeding caused by mass incarceration and the other ill effects of the failed 'war on drugs.' Perhaps if we spent less money in a futile attempt to eliminate drug use through suspicion, arrests, prosecution and punishment, we could invest resources in improving our schools to ensure that more of our young people get the preparation they need to succeed."[7]

Louisiana has the highest incarceration rate in the United States: 1 in 86 adults is "doing time"; in new Orleans, 1 in 14 black men is in prison. And, as the *Times-Picayune* thoroughly and heartbreakingly documents in its eight-part series published in 2012, "Louisiana Incarcerated," this means money. "Each inmate is worth $24.39 a day in state money"— enough for inmates to "subsist in bare-bones conditions with few programs to give them a better shot at becoming productive citizens." It also means that "sheriffs trade them like horses, unloading a few extras on a colleague who has openings. A prison system that leased its convicts as plantation labor in the 1800s has come full circle and is again a nexus for profit," according to one of the articles in the series. The article quotes Burk Foster, a former professor at the University of Louisiana-Lafayette and an expert on Louisiana prisons: "You have people who are so invested in maintaining the present system—not just the sheriffs, but judges, prosecutors, other people who have links to it. . . . They don't want to see the prison system get smaller or the number of people in custody reduced, even though the crime rate is down, because the good old boys are all linked together in the punishment network, which is good for them financially and politically."[8]

It is difficult to argue against economic development schemes that provide livable wages in rural America. But is this benefit coming at the expense of urban America? And, as one analyzes the initial investment in infrastructure, then in continuing support services (food, transportation, and other ancillary services), where are the funding streams flowing? To contractors? To businessmen? To transportation agencies? Again, these are all needed ancillary services, but is there a better way to feed the need of the community without the feast being borne disproportionately by one group of people that have, as we have discussed, no voice, no vote? If we could follow the muddy footprints that track where the money has gone, we might find the real beneficiaries and, with them, if they would, find a way out of this crucible of pain and destruction.

"We don't take the long view in our society," said Brooks. "If we leave these men behind we are all going to suffer in the future." Not addressing the problem, and the resource drain connected to it, only costs us all even more long term. "We're talking about impairing our economic competitiveness," Brooks continued, "losing the skills and talents of future generations to not only be competitive in local markets, but in the global economy. We're also tying our hands by not supporting them, because they will become a tax burden through the high costs of incarceration, welfare, etc. It's not in our long-term economic interest to have anybody caught between the cracks."[9]

Meanwhile, public housing is being destroyed across the country, even as homelessness rates soar. It is difficult to correctly estimate the exact number of homeless people, because the estimates vary widely and depend on the methodology used. One approximation, by the National Law Center on Homelessness and Poverty, estimates that between 2.3 and 3.5 million people experience homelessness each year. In Georgia, there were nearly 20,000 homeless people in 2007, the majority of whom were children. That includes nearly 3,300 homeless veterans. Approximately 56% of all homeless veterans are African Americans or Hispanic, even though they represent 12.8% or 15.4% of the U.S. population, respectively.[10]

One-fifth of the homeless population is veterans. The majority are from urban areas and suffer from mental illness, substance use disorder, or have co-occurring behavioral issues. Notably, about 1.5 million other veterans are at risk of being homeless because of poverty, lack of support networks, and dismal or overcrowded living conditions.[11] The lack of access to mental health services, as well as to other services (e.g., oral health) unless the problem is service related, makes their maintenance of good health difficult, as they are, in many cases, without adequate health care services. These people are provided no insurance and poor access, despite their service to their country.

## Money Lost

Although we hear the constant refrain that there is not enough money, the truth is that the money is going through the systems at an alarming pace. We are not seeing, however, the change to reflect the investment we are making. So what is happening? Tens of millions of precious dollars slip through ever-widening cracks every year. Denial of education and employment, widespread refusal of federal benefits, such as welfare, food stamps, public housing eligibility, and the disproportionate loss of voting rights, in communities of color create gaping holes in the ability of communities to sustain themselves. States provide training for some but then will not hire these same individuals because of their felony conviction. The real question becomes one of investment before incarceration. We KNOW that young men (and increasingly women) are dropping out of school earlier and that they are on the road to prison; the data show that. Yet, we do not require that school accreditation be based on the numbers of boys being retained and graduating. Our standards have not evolved to reflect today's greatest challenges. Who sets the standards? What are they thinking? What should they be thinking? What should/ must they do?

Since the onset of the recent recession and the resultant decimation of state and federal budgets, the enormous financial toll represented by our growing prison industry has finally gotten more attention. There has been a great deal of motion, outrage, and even some activity, but the outcry is still not big enough, nor has it received the level of funding necessary to grow to scale and succeed. A notable article in the *New Yorker* by Adam Gopnik[12] reminds us (or perhaps TELLS some of us) that there are more black men in the grip of the criminal justice system—prison, probation, and parole—than there were in slavery in 1850 in this nation. In addition, in the past 2 decades, the money that states spend on prisons has risen at 6 times the rate of spending on higher education.

When speaking to an audience of Community Voices leaders held at the Morehouse School of Medicine in early 2009, Civil Rights Veteran and U.S. Congressman John Lewis said, "As a society, we must find a way to get in the way. We must do better to help people rebuild their life with dignity and respect." Despite popular belief, government agencies are not our only hope for large-scale intervention. Private funders can play a critical role in dealing with the re-entry of formerly incarcerated

**TAKE A GOOD LOOK**  **Citizen Taxpayer**

Are you a taxpayer? Do you donate to private charities or work for one? How would you prefer to see your tax money or donations spent? Look in the mirror and ask yourself:

- Would you rather we spend our collective money on great schools, public parks and libraries, an engaging public environment, healthy community activities, gathering places, and opportunities for connection?

- Or would you prefer to spend our collective money on incarcerating millions of your fellow citizens who suffer from a crushing lack of these very things that so many millions more take for granted every day?

- How could you step out of your comfort zone so your volunteerism becomes more than episodic community service if you think your volunteerism can mean more in terms of sustained impact?

- What will your volunteerism mean to "the least of these" in our nation? Is this enough?

- Would you like for your children to "inherit" the tax bill for a prison system that does not reduce crime since crime rates are down?

- Write one thing you are willing to do to increase the amount of money available and that it is spent effectively: _____

_____

people into society by investing long-term in programs that get people integrated back into community, jobs, and with their children, when possible. Funders can also use their convening power to bring others into the construction of programs that include hiring. If nobody hires, the training is not useful. There remains a damaging lack of hard data to track the impact of the cradle-to-prison pipeline on communities of color. Public and private investment in research studies and pilot programs, focused on long-term results, will make a critical difference. It may take 10 years to get it right, but that is a short period considering it has taken decades for us to reach this nadir in the American Dream. Only then will we know if we are spending our money wisely and, if not, point the way to a better use. We face what is akin to a cancer on the American body politic. Finding the "cure" for ravaging illnesses takes years. We must expect to be patient and to stay the course.

Funders often label prisoner re-entry projects as "high risk," but the fact is we cannot make the changes needed by relying on anecdotal evidence alone. Instead, in meeting after meeting, many of the largest funding organizations refuse, year after year, to work on improving conditions for the growing prison population. The irony is that, in the same breath, they express their interest in helping vulnerable children. As we have seen again and again, helping the prison population *is* helping vulnerable children. Without comprehensive, system-wide change, those vulnerable children will soon be a part of the prison population. Until we strengthen the healthy life opportunities of the incarcerated and formerly incarcerated, the children they leave behind remain in danger of falling through the cracks. It only makes sense that addressing the health crisis of men and boys of color, especially around incarceration, should be the number one priority for everyone who wants to save children. But would funders rather continue throwing sprinkles of water on a raging fire? Admittedly, this work is not for the faint-hearted or for those who are risk averse. But, someone must carry the message, underwrite the work, and risk success!

Private funders are not the only people who shy away from supporting prison populations. Neighborhoods and communities routinely resist the location of halfway houses and safe spaces for recently released prisoners in their communities. The fact is that these people, having served their debt to society, have to go somewhere. They deserve a chance to rebuild their lives.

Our success is more about morality than money. Money is important, but the political will is key. Once we get the morality on the table, then we can get the money to finally break the crushing cycle of poverty and punishment that ensnares so many men of color from the earliest age and often never lets go.

## Where Should the Money Go?

Too often, there is more at stake than a lack of desire to invest in positive opportunities for men and boys of color. Time and again, there is a marked disinvestment in communities of color that are effectively locked out of the economy by policies and practices that actively discriminate against them. When they then find themselves desperate, with few options and vulnerable to the draw to an underground economy that will accept them, then they are once again locked out—from society at large.

Once these men return to their communities after serving their sentences, those same policies and practices promise them the same lack of support they received from childhood—exactly zero. When I was speaking with the office of Oakland Mayor Ron Dellums, his staff was quick to point out disparities in funding to provide post-release support

**REALITY CHECK   Investing in Education**

The National Urban League's 2007 Equality Index showed a real disparity between the educational investment made in our children—a disparity clearly based on race. The index divided education into five major categories—quality, attainment, scores, enrollment, and student status and risk factors. Each was given a particular weight. In all categories, black and white were not equal, and the overall index for blacks was 0.79, as compared with 1.00 for whites. Focusing on funding, the authors of the index report write: "Funding was measured per student in high and low poverty districts based on the total amount of state and local revenues each district received for the school year. Even after applying a 40% adjustment for low-income students, which takes into account the fact that these students need more support to reach the same level as higher-income students, there still remains a funding gap."[1] This is our money, our investment in our future. This travesty ensures that a healthy life and an opportunity-filled future are denied to a vast number of black children based solely on their race. We tell our children they must simply try harder, but, when they are running a race on uneven ground, trying harder means they can barely keep up—at best.

1. Thompson, Rondel and Sophia Parker. "The National Urban League Equality Index." http://academic.udayton.edu/health/syllabi/disparities/05RacialInequality/State%20of%20Black%20Equity.pdf.

to parolees. After fighting for years for just $2 million—barely enough to provide even the most basic services—the state of California finally decided to distribute funds. However, rather than funding the city of Oakland, which is home to more than 3,000 parolees, the relatively affluent city of East Palo Alto received $3.4 million in funding. East Palo Alto is home to just 160 parolees.[13] Oakland has yet to receive any funding at all, yet it is clearly in more need, as the Reality Check on page 178 shows.

Rather than getting stuck arguing about whether one community or another is worthy of support, our leadership can force progress by highlighting that every dollar spent increasing the healthy life opportunities of men and boys of color is an investment in our larger social and economic well-being over both the short and long term. We can choose to send our people to college or to prison. When we make the myriad policy decisions that set the path, we should ask ourselves which we prefer: a growing population of sick, helpless, desperate men with no

**REALITY CHECK   Who Needs the Money?**

In Oakland, households earning less than $20,000 per year spend more than one-half of their income on transportation.[1] A teacher of poorer students in Oakland Unified School District makes $14,000 less than a teacher of wealthier students in Piedmont Unified School District.[2]

According to the Alameda County Health Department, compared with a white child born in the Oakland Hills, an African American born in West Oakland is:

- 1.5 times more likely to be born premature or low birth rate

- 7 times more likely to be born into poverty

- Twice as likely to live in a home that is rented

- 4 times more likely to have parents with only a high school education or less

- 2.5 times more likely to be behind in vaccinations as a toddler

- 4 times less likely to read at grade level in the 4th grade

- Likely to live in a neighborhood with twice the concentration of liquor stores and more fast food outlets

- 5.6 times more likely to drop out of school

- 5 times more likely to be hospitalized for diabetes as an adult

- Twice as likely to be hospitalized for and die of heart disease

- 3 times more likely to die of stroke

- Twice as likely to die of cancer

- Expected to die almost 15 years earlier[3]

---

1. Lipman, Barbara. "A Heavy Load: The Combined Housing and Transportation Burdens of Working Families." Center for Neighborhood Technology. http://www.cnt.org/.

2. Matt Beyers, Janet Brown, Sangsook Cho, Alex Desautels, Karie Gaska, Kathryn Horsley, Tony Iton, Tammy Lee, Liz Maker, Jane Martin, Neena Murgai, Katherine Schaff, Sandra Witt, and Sarah Martin Anderson. "Life and Death from Unnatural Causes: Health and Social Inequity in Alameda County." Alameda County Health Department. http://www.acphd.org.http://www.acphd.org/data-reports/reports-by-topic/social-and-health-equity/life-and-death-from-unnatural-causes.aspx]

3. Ibid.

accessible experience outside of criminal activity or young men educated and empowered to build businesses, develop new products and services, and lead a new generation to do the same?

The choice is ours, and we make it every day for ourselves and for our children's children. It is time to come together and make these decisions about how our money is spent more consciously. It is not only the future of men and boys of color at stake—it is all of our future.

To begin gaining wider buy-in, we have to be honest about what is at stake. In funding meetings, town halls, community centers, and school board meetings, let us ask ourselves, our leadership, and our communities this question: What is something that everyone is concerned about? When we ask this question at Community Voices, the answers most often received are: crime; education; the right to believe what you want; to be treated in the same way by public and private agencies including doctors, health care providers, the education system, and the criminal justice system. The mantra: There HAS to be a better way!

 **REALITY CHECK  The Prison Population Is Aging**

Did we imagine that policymakers were designing geriatric systems of care when they hyperincarcerated? Did we imagine that we would keep them so long that there would be no place for them to go, no one to welcome them home? After all, they were gone for a long time, it cost a lot of money to place a call to them, and then the system wanted a poor, struggling family to pay for certain expenses, to put money into their account so they could pay for their health care, for toiletries? The data on those aging in prison are sobering. The general population of the United Sates is getting older, and it should be no surprise that the prison population is not staying forever young either. This is having an enormous impact on the health and health care of prisoners. For example, according to the Human Rights Watch:

- The number of U.S. state and federal prisoners age 65 or over grew at 94 times the rate of the total prison population between 2007 and 2010.

- The number of prisoners age 65 or older increased by 63%. There are now 26,200 prisoners age 65 or older.

- There are now 124,400 prisoners age 55 or older.

- Fourteen percent of federal prisoners are age 51 or older.[1]

(continued)

**REALITY CHECK** **The Prison Population is Aging (continued)**

## Impact on Health Expenditures

- Chronic diseases, including dementia; high blood pressure; diabetes; incontinence, frailness, and mobility; and hearing and vision impairments are skyrocketing.

- It costs 3–9 times in medical expenditures for older prisoners compared with other prisoners.

- In Florida, 16% of prisoners are 50 years of age or older, yet they account for more than 40% of all episodes of medical care and nearly 48% of hospital stays.

- In Georgia, prisoners 65 years of age or older cost an average of $8,565 for medical care compared with $961 for prisoners younger than 65.

- In Michigan, a prison inmate's average annual health care cost is an estimated $5,801; those go up as age goes up, from $11,000 for those between 55 and 59 years of age to $40,000 for those 80 years of age and older.[2]

---

1. "Old Behind Bars: The Aging Prison Population in the United States." Human Rights Watch. http://www.hrw.org/reports/2012/01/27/old-behind-bars-0.
2. Ibid.

## Big Returns: Wise Investing

Whether it is encouraging small businesses, making microloans, feeding children nutritious food, or mentoring programs, wise investments—no matter how modest—can pay off big time. Along these lines, there are a number of agencies and organizations that need to be pressed into doing a better job supporting not only the formerly incarcerated, but poor communities in general. The Small Business Administration, for example, can set aside more pro-active opportunities to provide start-up small business capital to people with viable business ideas. This not only supports one individual with an idea, but the larger community that benefits from local businesses, job opportunities, more money circulating in the local economy, and healthy people with an investment in looking out for each other and the neighborhood.

"It's not enough to just counsel kids," said Tony Iton. "You've got to give them something that means opportunity." [14] Iton himself piloted a micro-loan program to develop businesses and independence as part of the larger investment in tackling public health disparities in struggling Oakland communities. With small investments, the program is already showing signs of promise in improving health by improving social and economic realities. By helping people earn an income and accumulate real assets, which can expand micro-enterprise opportunities, while also supporting job creation and local economic growth, Iton believes that the program can make an impact at the systems level, far beyond the single individuals to whom the loans are made.

Investments that are critically imperative to making the kinds of systemic changes to which Iton is committed include expanding early childhood opportunities by investing in good schools; making sure children get adequate nutrition; and helping families learn to provide nurturing, support, and a sense of ambition to their children—including teaching parents those principals if they were unable to get them from their own families. Investments made early in life, including at the pre-natal level, make an enormous difference.

Think of these systems changes as a target on which we launch intervening missiles as one of the many tools in our arsenal. By doing so, we can imagine how much easier it is to aim our missiles from the launch pad—the earliest stage in a life—than while the missile is in mid-course. By the time the missile is about to land, it is often too late to course correct. Many men have already lost the opportunity for a long, full, and healthy life. However, we can still reach into our toolboxes and find ways to help them salvage what opportunities may remain for them to live healthy, fulfilling lives. Of what materials is our toolbox made? Public policy.

Although state and national public policy investments are crucial, we also have the power at the community level to make meaningful investments in the healthy lives and opportunities of young men and boys. "We are our brothers' keepers," said Pastor Donna Hubbard, "and it can be very easy for us if we have a nuclear family, if we're making a good salary and living a decent life, not to notice that half a block down the street there's a woman struggling to raise three kids. One of her children happens to be a son. When we get our own son and put him in the car to take him to the Atlanta Falcons game, why not go down the street and get that boy who doesn't have a father and take him to the game too? What's the worst thing that can happen? That he might learn to be accountable? The thing is, if you don't hold yourself accountable, then later you may see him standing down in the street, and you may be afraid of him. But this is the same boy who grew up right down and street, you didn't take the time to invest in him."[15]

We all have to step outside of our comfort zone if we have any hope of stemming this crisis. The health realities of poor men of color are an economic nightmare, but investing in the necessary turnaround is the right thing to do. Once we understand the ramifications of this situation, then we have a responsibility to act and to act comprehensively without excuse or apology. We have to demand that our leaders take on the tough issues and demand results. We each have the power to hold our leadership accountable for systemic change, and we can each start with ourselves.

Leadership discussions are a dime a dozen, but toward what end are we talking aloud without the context of a real example of what we face and without insisting on results? We cannot allow this to continue. Even where I am, in the "mecca" of Atlanta, our leaders do not respond, even when doing so would be a win/win situation for everyone. Recently, Fulton County District Attorney Paul Howard was allowed the opportunity to have a large facility for next to nothing, which could be used to provide services to the community. A school that had closed down was being offered to the county for just $1.00.

Mr. Howard had a plan to work on purchasing the building and putting it to work, until his office had its priorities turned around by political pressure. Rather than purchasing it far below market value, renovating it, and using it to provide low-cost services, housing, or office space for advocacy, the building was sold for a bit of money. The money received for selling the building does not compare to what Fulton County and its residents could have gained from executing a shared vision.

Part of that shared vision lies in providing the kinds of services that often get overlooked. Peggy Vaughn-Payne does just that at Lansing, Michigan's Northwest Initiative. "It's hard sometimes for me to separate an ex-offender from a low-income person or an immigrant," she says. "We've inherited quite a few immigrant populations from around the world, and I look at our form that folks have to fill out to get food stamps or Medicaid—it's a difficult form for a college educated person to fill out, let alone someone who is poorly educated or doesn't speak English very well. It's crazy to think that people can do this by themselves. Then, once they get them filled out, it seems the workers mentality is to deny, deny, deny. I've seen workers search to find anything to make people ineligible after they've jumped through every hoop they've been presented."

"We have a very non-service-friendly system," Vaughn-Payne continued. "I understand that nobody wants to see abuse of the system, but the way the economy is here in Michigan, it seems that there should be an easier way to help people get back on track."[16]

This is when we must ask ourselves the biggest question of all: With the kind of inaction we continue to see, is it possible we don't really care about the money we spend or results we receive?

President Robert Franklin used his leadership position to ensure that Morehouse College joined the Morehouse School of Medicine in a "Promise Neighborhood" pilot to lead by example. Because both campuses sit directly in an African American community and bring together young African American men from every background, we are uniquely seated to

---

## LEADERS AND HEROES

### Sally Dorsey, Community Volunteer Fundraiser

Many people in our society fear other people and appear to want to be away from them. They do not seem to care about those "other people" . . . THEM. Sally Dorsey could have taken that route, but she did not. "I grew up in the old South and my family was not open to different cultures and races," she recalls. "My family was not angry at black or Asian or other groups of people; they just thought of them as different. So I did not grow up thinking the way I think now. As I travelled and met new people of many cultures and races, I realized all that I had been missing. Since then I have wanted to learn about everybody's issues and experiences."[1]

Dorsey has chaired major fundraisings for organizations such as Project Open Hand, the Shepherd Clinic, the Swan Ball, the Alliance Theater, the WXIA, 11 Alive, WATL TV Community Awards Gala, and the Soledad O'Brien Freedom's Voice Awards for Community Voices of the Morehouse School of Medicine. Millions of dollars have been raised under her leadership. In 2007 she was named as one of Atlanta's 50 most beautiful people.

The common denominator in all that activity is health. "Health—what makes people healthy—is what concerns me," says Dorsey. "If we can help people make healthy choices for themselves, and raise awareness about what makes them unhealthy . . . lifestyle, diet . . . then we can change things. If a person is desperately poor then let's get them some help, such as we provide at Project Open Hand."[2]

"Project Open Hand's mission is to help people prevent or better manage chronic disease through Comprehensive Nutrition Care™, which combines home-delivered meals and nutrition education as a means to reinforce the connection between informed food choices and improved quality of life."[3] Project Open Hand delivered nearly two million meals in 2011 and since its inception in 1998 has served 20 million meals. Dorsey chaired the Development Committee for a Capital Campaign

(continued)

LEADERS AND HEROES

## Sally Dorsey, Community Volunteer Fundraiser (*continued*)

that raised $4.5 million for the construction of a start of the art facility to allow Project Open Hand to continue its important work of delivering healthy, nutritious meals to those that need them—sometimes, just for awhile, until they are able to get back on their feet.

Dorsey continues, "And what a HUGE problem it is to have so many people in prison. I never thought about this before I began to meet even more people with experiences different than mine. But that does not excuse me. I am a privileged person. I have everything I need, and more. But I was not put on this earth just to be a rich white girl. If people are desperate, poor, depressed, it is because they have no power. I want to help give them power. Otherwise we will have to pay for them and suffer through their anger and sickness. It is better if they can have control of their own destiny."[4]

"I spend much of my energy with Project Open Hand. I did not know anything about people who were poor, shut in, with chronic conditions such as diabetes, blindness, severe hypertension, people on renal dialysis who are disabled . . . who needed not just something to eat, but a nutritious meal and some information that could help them make healthy choices in things that they ate that were not delivered by Project Open Hand. We have phenomenal success stories. I would never have known this if an individual had not cornered me at a reception and 'educated' me. Once I KNEW, I had to act."[5]

"I am also interested in the arts and like to raise money for the arts in Atlanta and throughout Georgia. But for the most part I prioritize my volunteering, my work on major fundraising and capital campaigns. I want to make sure that what I am doing is important, that it makes a difference. Otherwise I need to move on. I love what I do. I am so fortunate to be able to dedicate much of my life to helping change the outcomes for those who have less than I do. I am thankful for my gifts everyday.[6]

For more information about Open Hand, visit: http://www.projectopenhand.org/index.asp

---

1. Author interview with Sally Dorsey, March 2012.
2. Ibid.
3. Project Open Hand web site. http://www.projectopenhand.org
4. Author interview with Sally Dorsey, March 2012.
5. Ibid.
6. Ibid.

make the kinds of contributions that bring about systemic change; however, we are far from the only people who have the opportunity to leverage our unique gifts. The next section provides some enlightening case studies of organizations and individuals who have found amazing success at developing interventions that work. We also look at some of the missed opportunities and discover what lessons we may learn from them.

## Notes

1. Butterfield, Scott. "With Longer Sentences, Cost of Fighting Crime Is Higher." *New York Times*. http://www.nytimes.com.
2. "The Expanding Federal Prison Population." The Sentencing Project. http://www.asca.net.
3. "1 in 31 U.S. Adults are Behind Bars, on Parole or Probation." Pew Charitable Trust. http://www.pewcenteronthestates.org/.
4. Ridgeway, James and Jean Casella. "Obama Budget: Grow Prisons and Keep Gitmo." *Mother Jones*, February 22, 2012.
5. "Ex-Offenders: Who Needs Housing First?" *NPR*. http://www.npr.org.
6. Blow, Charles M. "Plantations, Prisons and Profits." *New York Times*. http://www.nytimes.com.
7. Franklin, Neill. "Spend Money on Schools Instead." *New York Times*. http://www.nytimes.com.
8. Chang, Cindy. "Louisiana is the World's Prison Capital." *The Times-Picayune*. http://www.nola.com.
9. Author interview with Joe Brooks, December 2009.
10. "FAQ about Homeless Veterans." The National Coalition for Homeless Veterans. http://www.nchv.org/background.cfm.
11. Ibid.
12. Gopnik, Adam. "The Caging of America: Why Do We Lock Up So Many People?" *The New Yorker*, January 30, 2011.
13. "City of East Palo Alto: Parole Re-entry Program." City of East Palo Alto. http://www.ci.east-palo-alto.ca.us/.
14. Author interview with Tony Iton, November 2009.
15. Author interview with Donna Hubbard, December 2009.
16. Author interview with Peggy Vaughn-Payne, October 2009.

# PART THREE

# Building Healthier Opportunities

# CHAPTER 12

# Leadership Models That Work

*"If you've got this many unhealthy people in a community, there's no way that the community itself can be healthy."*

—*Congressman Danny Davis*

*Dorothea and Jamal quickly became close. After his roommate, Benjamin, found long-term work on a construction site and began filing for shared custody of his children, Jamal moved into his own apartment. Benjamin tried to get Jamal on the job with him, but his incarceration record was too much of a barrier for the employer who worried about his bonding status.*

*Jamal worried about finding more permanent work to cover his rent, and the added stress only served to aggravate his back. Fortunately, Dorothea was able to find him work through the community-based organization at which she worked. It was just some cleanup work at the offices, but it was steady and the people were friendly. Having Dorothea in his life was a wonderful change for Jamal, who had never been in a real relationship before. He made her laugh and showed his appreciation for her in a hundred ways a day. She helped him learn to make easy, healthy meals and take better care of himself.*

*Through Dorothea, he also learned more about the state of the community in which he lived. Jamal learned that, contrary to what he saw on television and in the movies, poor health and nutrition were even more prevalent problems for men in the community than violence and safety. Dorothea had such passion for her work that it was infectious.*

*Fed by her inspiration, Jamal began taking better care of himself than he ever had. Even more, he began getting more involved with community work during his off hours. In addition to participating and organizing a nutrition group training where Dorothea worked, Jamal began to volunteer at the community health clinic at which he first felt heard. He was getting his life back, slowly but surely, and it was beginning to feel wonderful.*

I regularly travel across the country, helping inform people of the real toll each of us is paying for our current state of power failure. In my work, I speak to leaders in communities of all sizes and shapes and in every arena of power, including all areas of government, philanthropic organizations, faith communities, and medical and health care leadership. Whenever I travel, I always take Martin and Jamal with me. Their stories help sustain me and keep me going in my work designing intervention strategies, building health clinics, and raising and allocating funds to help a population many wish to sweep under the rug.

I do this every day, and I do not do it alone. Once made to understand the issues, many people agree that something is wrong and that something must be done. Moving forward into taking action, however, is the more difficult step. Yet the more we help each other understand the true despair that people feel, how they feel trapped, juggling far too many balls with no rest on the horizon, the closer we get to eradicating the power failure that keeps us stuck. The power lies within each of us to move our leadership out of power failure and into a time of genuine hope in which we can hold our leadership accountable to the promise of hope and justice that put us all in leadership positions in the first place.

Health inequity is just the tip of the iceberg. There must be a marriage of public policy with practice, deeply anchored in the values of social justice. We have already reviewed a bit of what is standing in our way of bringing hope and healing to black men and boys. We know we have to hold the mirror up to ourselves and challenge ourselves to see what is holding us back individually. Some leaders, even entire communities, are stymied by stigma.

Embarrassed about the sorry state of our situation, too many of us do not want to speak up, because we do not want to create waves. Even worse, there are many of us who feel we need to draw a deep line between ourselves and those *other* black men out there having a hard time. It is easier to look at poor men and boys of color—particularly those who have been incarcerated—as the "other," rather than understanding these are all of our issues, all of our concerns.

There are some leaders who are getting it right. They understand that, by wedding the practical with the academic, community leadership with government accountability, we can achieve the kinds of lasting, solid change so sorely needed. This chapter looks at some of those positive examples of true leadership to see what people are doing right.

By exploring examples of what has been working in areas, such as government, the faith community, the medical and health care industries, and philanthropy, as well as community-based interventions, we can lift up the approaches that are working and we then know what to emulate and how to spread the positive work from community to community.

## Going Viral—in a Good Way

There is a popular catch phrase in the business community that explains how you can create something small and watch it gain popularity and spread around the world. The phrase is: Going Viral. In health care settings, we spend a great deal of time fighting and preventing viral infections. However, I would like to see positive solutions and effective interventions catch on and spread like wild fire. We can only do so by finding what is working and spreading the word. This chapter and the Appendix are filled with examples that could "go viral."

Who are the people who have moved the human spirit and, in so doing, have advanced social justice? There are many, like my Aunt Modjeska (in Chapter 6), who have carried history forward in ways that sow the seeds of empowerment that last for generations. However, although each of us has a role to play in the solution, we are more effective when we work together, rather than alone. By focusing not on one or two individual success stories, but on system-wide successes, we can ensure that those individual success stories grow in size and number until they go viral and become a thriving movement.

If we were to ask the leaders who are making a positive imprint on their communities and actively addressing the ongoing health crisis of black men and boys what stands in their way from making their work more effective, the number one response would be funding. Ask, and you will hear that money is not going to the right communities or is not allocated to the best projects and, most importantly, there just is not enough money directed to the kind of interventions that can make a difference. When we think about where that money can or should come from, we most often think of government, business, or philanthropy.

Many people and organizations profess a desire to see a more active involvement of the business community in funding projects that promise to make communities not only healthier, but more productive overall—a win/win for both business and communities. The more I look around, the more I see it is just not happening. I have asked several people why there is not a bigger investment in health and wellness on the part of business when they can only gain both in active consumers and productive workers. "I don't know what business is anymore," said Tony Iton, former director of the Alameda County Department of Public Health, who has also spent time thinking about this question. "Aren't we all business?"[1]

"The Fortune 500 is in Belgium," he continued. "Small business is poor too. The biggest industry in Alameda County is the government. The second biggest industry is agriculture. There is next to no manufacturing. The biggest sector overall is the service industry in both the formal and informal arena. The next biggest is government, then retail."[2] Iton's answers highlight a few important facts: The American business community has changed in many important ways. Very few of the companies whose names and products most people can identify are based in any of the communities in which we live. Small businesses, those more likely to have a stake in the communities in which they are based, are also struggling, in many cases for their own survival.

Most importantly, the biggest employer left in many American cities and towns is actually the government, or government agencies. The government, using our tax dollars, has an obligation to care for the people it exists to serve. Yet, the truth is that, where there is government, there are politics, and, oftentimes, the political ladder can be an awfully steep one to climb. "The poor, incarcerated, and African American communities are viewed as not being politically influential," said Marc Mauer, executive director of the Sentencing Project. "It's been politically popular to demonize these communities. People feel that they do not make major campaign contributions and overall are viewed as not being responsive."[3]

Still, locally and federally, steps are being taken in the right direction. "There has been growing recognition in people needing to be treated," said Mauer. "The Reentry Movement and the Second Chance Act are becoming a little more popular. I am encouraged by the new developments taking place, but, at the same time, the scale of the problem is so enormous and there has not been a significant shift."[4]

## Project Choice

Project Choice, a city funded initiative seeking to offer hope, support, and accountability to juvenile and young adult offenders re-entering the Oakland community, is one of those opportunities to see movement toward that significant shift. The city of Oakland is home to nearly 3,000 parolees every year. Unfortunately, many of those who come home on parole soon return to prison.

Recognizing the need to support the successful reintegration of ex-offenders from the criminal justice system back into the community, the city launched Project Choice in 2001 to provide those re-entering their communities with tools to help them become successful, contributing members of the community.

The fact that the city of Oakland has recognized that successful re-entry is critical to the city's public safety agenda, as well as to any real commitment to building strong, healthy communities, is promising. From the Alameda Department of Public Health to the office of Oakland Mayor, Ron Dellums, this Bay Area city and county are offering real leadership in addressing the health crisis of black men and boys, and of the thousands of families facing problems stemming from incarceration every day. As the Mayor attests, "Investing in these individuals not only helps them to succeed, but also positively influences the young people who witness their achievement, rather than their repeated incarceration."[5]

Those who participate in Project Choice are young people between 16 and 30 years of age who are returning to Oakland from San Quentin State Prison and California Youth Authority facilities in Stockton. Through a broad partnership between the Department of Corrections, Parole Division, state prisons, the mayor's office, the city council, the police department, the Department of Human Services, Workforce Investment Board, and county health care services agency, county social services, and other broadly identified community stakeholders, the project crosses the boundaries from inside the prison gates to outside on the city streets.

What the project offers its young parolees is an intensive coaching and case management relationship that begins 6–12 months prior to their release, while they are still serving time in prison. The service then continues to support their successful community re-entry after their release and throughout their time on parole. In addition to coaching and case management, Project Choice works with a variety of community agencies to ensure its participants access to a full spectrum of services that pivot on their holistic health and wellness, including substance abuse treatment, mental health services, intensive employment and training support, health care, and housing.

Project Choice has been so successful that it has continued to be supported by violence prevention legislation, Measure Y, which was passed by California voters in 2004. In early 2009, the program was featured as a part of CNN's *Black in America* series. During the segment that focused on black men, CNN's Soledad O'Brien and Stan Wilson visited San Quentin prison and explored the case of ex-offender Chris Shurn. Since his release, Shurn has returned to San Quentin, but not as an inmate. Instead, he works with Project Choice to help other young men identify routes to a successful re-entry.

Still, the journey has not been easy. "Every day of my life," Shurn told CNN, "with or without work, I feel vulnerable." His vulnerability and his ordinary aspirations are exactly the kind of story we need to keep sharing to humanize a community that far too many have dehumanized for far too long. "I want to have a family," said Shurn. "I want to own a house. I want to have everything that an average American would want; a good-paying job, a career."[6]

In the state of California, there is a 70% rate of recidivism within the first 24 months after returning from prison. Most of those who return to prison have not committed a new crime, but because their parole has been revoked for often minor violations. Those violations can stem from their inability to access the fundamentals we all need to keep healthy and safe: housing, work, and health care. Programs like Project Choice are an important way that government—in partnership with health care providers and community-based organizations—can make a difference in the lives of those returning from prison, as well as their families and communities.

Unfortunately, Oakland is in many ways a unique case. When I look around the country to see where and how initiatives like Project Choice are being emulated, I quickly realize that there is not much. Oakland has the benefit of having an engaged mayor, an engaged public health department, and a progressive population. This is the kind of political trio that provides the ideal conditions for the kind of system-wide interventions needed to make lasting change. However, no matter where we live and no matter what the political climate, it is within our power to go to policy makers and demand action.

The key here lies not just in being unhappy with the current state of affairs, but in being willing and having the courage to make the connections necessary to encourage change among ourselves and among the leaders we elect and appoint. Locally, better leadership from political groups like the National Conference of Mayors could make a significant difference in urban metro areas, much like the City of Oakland. By taking models that work and building campaigns around them that can grow from city to city, we can move closer toward our end goal of policy and systemic change.

### Federal Legislation

Young black men and boys face a wide berth of health and wellness problems. There are several examples of a promising shift in federal legislative priorities in this regard, including the Second Chance Act and the Men and Families Health Care Act.

### Second Chance Act

Signed into law in the 2008, the Second Chance Act is a federal bill designed to help improve outcomes for people re-entering their communities after incarceration. The Second Chance Act represents an important first step in terms of federal legislation to address the ongoing health crisis so deeply tied to incarceration and inequality. The Act "authorizes federal grants to government agencies and nonprofit organizations to provide employment assistance, substance abuse treatment, housing, family programming, mentoring, victims support, and other services that can help reduce recidivism."[7]

Illinois Congressman Danny K. Davis sponsored the Second Chance Act and has long been a champion of improving the chances of those returning from prison to have a positive shot at life. In its first year, the Act was minimally financed. Without a firm investment in its success, it is easy for naysayers to accuse the legislation of being unsuccessful. For its second year, funding more than quadrupled from $25 million to $114 million for fiscal year 2010. The increased funding is a hopeful sign, but the fact is that the funding allocations are still far below what is needed to bring any of the successful programs to the scale needed for systemic success.

Representative Davis is aware that the bill sparks mixed feelings even among many supporters. "There are millions of people who themselves are not sure about how they feel about criminality, about crime and punishment, who should be punished," he said when addressing a 2009 Community Voices health summit. "People want programs, but they tell you take them to the other side of town, don't put them in my back yard. We call it the NIMBY attitude, not in my back yard. Don't put a halfway house here, take it up the lakeshore, take it to California, take it to New York or somewhere."[8]

### Men and Families Health Care Act

To underscore the lack of prioritization the health of men and boys of color receives, we only need to search for federally funded sites of the Office of Men's Health to find out what they are doing about the crisis. The only trouble is that none exist. The U.S. Department of Health and Human Services created the Office of Women's Health under its auspices in 1991. Since then, branches of that office have been created in 41 states from coast to coast, including both Alaska and Hawaii. The fact that there is no comparable office focused on the unique health needs of men is telling. Given the disturbing morbidity and mortality rates among all men of color and African American boys and men, specifically, makes rational people wonder why there is no Office of Men's Health.

In 2009, Pennsylvania Congressman Tim Murphy set out to change that by introducing the Men and Families Health Care Act of 2009 to the House of Representatives. In introducing his bill, he highlighted the following facts, among others, as a reason the bill was so urgently needed: "men are leading in 9 out of the top 10 causes of death; 1 in 2 men versus 1 in 3 women in their lifetime will be diagnosed with cancer; the life expectancy gap between men and women has increased from one year in 1920 to 5.2 years in 2005; and studies show that women are 100 percent more likely than men to visit a doctor, have regular physician check-ups, and obtain preventive screening tests for serious diseases."[9]

These facts are relevant to all men, yet we know that the statistics are even more troubling for men of color. With regard to the incarcerated and formerly incarcerated, using an Office of Men's Health to establish a re-entry network that addresses the health needs of men and boys whose lives are interwoven with the criminal justice system can go a long way. Such a network can address such medical and social needs from establishing a clinic at which those re-entering the community can be immediately received and screened for services to establishing comprehensive, culturally competent case management services that address housing, employment, job training, drug abuse treatment and mental health treatment in addition to the widespread chronic illness concerns that afflict young men who have had minimal access to health care in the first place.

## The NorthWest Initiative

As discussed, one of the barriers standing between power failure and true leadership on this issue is fear. Stories like that of Sturn and Project Choice are an important step toward humanizing the young men and boys of color who have made a mistake, yet still deserve a second chance at a healthy life. Simply because people have been put into a savage situation does not mean they are savages. Media intervention on a wider scale is needed to help spread the stories of hope and opportunity. In turn, more and more political leaders will find the courage needed to stand up and take action.

"The people that are on the inside of government are afraid to speak up about injustices of incarceration, because they are very successful and they want to separate themselves from the stigma of incarceration," agrees Alex Busansky, former Executive Director of the Commission on Safety and Abuse in America's Prisons. "One of the biggest fears is that, if they show too much concern about these issues, then their personal relationships will be exposed. We do so much to isolate and distance ourselves from stigmas. When it comes to issues around the criminal justice system, who you are means a lot."[10]

Peggy Vaughn-Payne, the executive director of Michigan's NorthWest Initiative, also agrees, but she also offers a different perspective. "There are so many things we can do without government," she said, "to find resources to do or fix whatever it is. Government may be a piece, but we don't need them to come in and fix the whole thing."[11] Vaughn-Payne works at the crossroads between government support and community organization. A true example of leadership, she has worked tirelessly to address the many road blocks faced by men returning from prison into the East Lansing community her organization serves.

One such barrier in Michigan has been that individuals are required to have a valid state identification to access health services. Prison IDs are not accepted as a legitimate form of identification. "If someone has been locked up for 20 years," Vaughn-Payne said, "what ID do you think they'll have?"

Rather than allow this unfair barrier to stand, one that crippled her attempts to make an impact even without government assistance, she went to Capitol Hill and took on the problem directly. "We were able to work with our Michigan Department of Corrections and our Secretary of State, getting them to agree that, if we can help those returning home to get a birth certificate, then the Secretary of State will accept their Michigan Department of Corrections ID as a second identification so that they can get some state ID."[12]

This is a problem that stretches far outside of the state of Michigan. The City of Oakland has also worked to eliminate the identification barrier by creating City IDs, which enable people to access services. For those re-entering, a lack of identification can be a major barrier not just in accessing health care services. "There are so many of those simple barriers that exist," said Vaughn-Payne. "People don't really look at how incarceration impacts families—there's a lot of emotional guilt." Everything from finding employment and housing, to petitioning for visitation rights with children, to the successful transfer of prison health records can be dependent on a formerly incarcerated individual's ability to obtain legally recognized identification. [13]

## Getting Creative

In addition to the expanding use of public service announcements, an accessible route for celebrities and other public figures to lend their voice to eliminating the crisis, it is heartening to see government and community organizations exploring innovative ways of getting health and wellness messages out to the public. The Health "Mobilegram" is

LEADERS AND HEROES

## Lee Baca, Los Angeles County Sheriff

Sheriff Baca has been a teacher on many levels, but he is now a sheriff in the most populous county in America in the state with the largest jail population in the country. Because of overall volume and overcrowding, the system is under order to bring the prison population down from 170,000 to 130,000. That is a lot of people re-entering society. Will they be ready? Will they be able to stay out?

Sheriff Baca has a plan: the Education-Based Incarceration (EBI) initiative. Instead of the punitive theory of incarceration that is prevalent in the United States, EBI focuses on "reducing and mitigating crime by investing in its offenders through education and rehabilitation. To accomplish its mission, EBI uses a comprehensive educational curriculum designed to reduce recidivism by increasing the educational, civic, social, economic, and life skills and engagement of its participants."[1]

Launched in 2010, EBI might sound like an expensive idealistic throwback to the 1960s and 1970s, but Baca believes that, thanks to his education background and Ph.D. in public administration, he knows that "the human mind can change." And, he is working within the budgetary constraints imposed by the fact that the program is paid for from the Inmate Welfare Fund (money from vending machines, pay phones, and other services paid by businesses that operate them).

Interested inmates are evaluated and are assigned to a course of instruction tailored to best address their needs. The classrooms are the cells themselves, and modern technology—DVDs, closed-circuit TVs, computers, MP3 players, and so on—are the teachers. Inmates get self-study workbooks in a variety of disciplines, including mathematics, history, English, social studies, and writing. Educational TV programming features segments on history, science, world geography, career education, social sciences, and important literary works. The inmates respond, because they really want to spell, read, and hold conversation, Baca states. "We reward our inmates in the education system when they excel. They are placed into a merit-based dormitory where they have a great deal of autonomy over what they do every day."[2]

"We have a parolee program, emerging leaders academy, that prototypes teaching adults who have been incarcerated. So the men come in and see themselves as people who can make a difference. When they complete the 3-month training program, they receive a signed certificate that they have gone through the training and have the ability to succeed." Baca says preliminary results indicate that those receiving the certificate are having an easier time getting a job and that recidivism is lower. He and his team believe they can get recidivism down to 20% versus the 70% that exists now. "Our system is more intellectual, whereas many others are still more labor oriented, teaching people things like cooking, cleaning, and other types of manual skills. Education, not skills, is the key."[3]

He isn't getting much pushback since many people seem to believe in a redemptive type of corrections. He believes that "we have to have a better person coming out of incarceration or we cannot justify the cost. We have to build self-esteem in the person. We want them to be a good father, husband, and mate. We have to remember that people in jail have been living in the negative part of life for a long time. They are experts at negativity. We help them to see and live the positive." [4]

"All individuals have a mind, and the development of the mind is all important. We have to save the mind. The human mind is a miracle. We cannot stop everyone from going to jail, but we can use the jail time as a 'pause' . . . a time that frees them up to think, to go to school, to reflect. They do not have to hustle for jobs, food, or housing when in jail. They can find themselves if we create the space of education versus solely the ethos of security."[5]

Sheriff Baca's unique viewpoint is that "many of the acts that get people locked up are a result of their decision-making that is, itself, a result of a lack of education. The idea that being locked up keeps people safe is a fair enough idea but it is not enough. When people are locked up, there is no personal decision-making. This constant decision-making by others removes all responsibility from the individual and removes their own moral authority over who and what they can do and be." Many of these individuals, Sheriff Baca feels, still have the mind and decision-making references and capacities of a child in an adult body. "They are still children," he says, "But when we do our programs, they change."[6]

Baca says the California State Prison System is looking at what it is doing and is considering implementing this in the facilities. There is a prison in Louisiana doing a great job, and others in Maryland. "There are over 3,000 counties in the US and each has a sheriff with responsibility for a jail. Those sheriffs have to make a decision that they can get a better result, use their time and that of their staff better and more effectively. These sheriffs have it within their power to try something new, and education is a better use of our time and resources."[7]

Creating an education-based system, he says, "is the right thing to do, but it takes more dialogue. I push my literature into the hands of other sheriffs, because, to bring about change state-wide and across the nation, a culture change is required." Specifically, Sheriff Baca states, "Corrections officers must change their role from one of security to one of security and education. This change can occur, and there is no need to spend more money as there is no more money. We have to set more roads in place for the people that we see to go down, to find their rightful place. We are the ones who have to be the bridge so that they can cross over from the cycle of

(continued)

## Lee Baca, Los Angeles County Sheriff (*continued*)

negative to positive achievement and contribution to community." The prisons may look to the federal government for cues. With jails, the sheriffs must lead. "This work comes from your heart. If you do not care about redemption and helping people regain what they lost, we will not win."[8]

For more information about Education-Based Incarceration, please visit http://www.lasdhq.org/divisions/correctional/ebi/index.html.

---

1. "Education-Based Incarceration." Los Angeles County Sheriff's Department. http://www.lasdhq.org.
2. Author interview with Sheriff Baca, March 2012.
3. Ibid.
4. Ibid.
5. Ibid.
6. Ibid.
7. Ibid.
8. Ibid.

---

another one of those innovative interventions. The "Mobilegram" campaign, designed to work in conjunction with a larger, multi-media social marketing approach, compliments sister initiatives, such as the "Health Is Power" and "Don't Check Out, Check In" campaigns. Since studies have shown that women generally make the health decisions in their families, the "Mobilegram" program utilizes cell phone technology to allow a woman to send messages to the men in her life. When he answers her phone call, he will instead be routed to appropriate health resources through an automatic triaging system.

Interventions like these highlight the opportunities that exist for creative thinking to make a dent in our growing crisis. If we push our leadership to expand this thinking to corners of health and wellness we often do not think about, then we can only expand on the benefits we reap. Dental health, for example, remains an issue we just do not talk about. Although we know that dental health is a critical aspect of good health, many men and boys of color have limited to no access to dental health services. Even among the health clinics that exist to serve them, dental health access is the exception, rather than the rule.

We can also begin exploring other ways, much like what Alameda County's Camp Wilmont Sweeney is doing, to increase the employability of young men and boys. The "camp" is actually a residential treatment program that houses 90 young men and boys, providing them with career training, including training to become an emergency medical technician (EMT). Young men and boys who are ordered by the Juvenile Court to be committed to Camp Sweeney complete the 6- to 9-month rehabilitation and educational program. After they complete the in-camp program, the youth graduate into a 6-month supervised furlough. The success of the program lies in its focus on rehabilitation, rather than simple punishment, which enables the young men to graduate into expanded, rather than contracted, opportunity. Other examples are a fast-track GED program to help young men obtain an equivalency degree and no-cost bonding programs to give employer incentives to hire qualified ex-offenders.

To those who would protest the cost, I would say the cost of not taking action is so much greater than the cost of eroding opportunity that it would seem to automatically erase the "we can't afford it" arguments levied at those who propose innovative programs and initiatives.

As we have seen, health inequalities among African Americans, Hispanics, and whites cost the health care system dearly—nearly $24 billion in 2009. What is worse, the Urban Institute estimated that over the next decade the cost of health inequality will come to $337 billion.[14]

---

## ✔ REALITY CHECK   What a Waste!

Excess health care costs for African Americans under Medicare and Medicaid total $12 billion per year.[1]

In addition, 30% of direct medical costs for blacks, Hispanics, and Asian Americans were incurred because of health inequities—more than $230 billion over a 4-year period.[2]

When additional indirect costs are added, including lost wages and absenteeism due to ill health, family leave, and premature death, the total for the period between 2003 and 2006 reaches more than $1 trillion.

---

1. Waidman, Timothy. "Estimating the Cost of Racial and Ethnic Health Disparities." The Urban Institute. http://www.urban.org/.

2. LaVeist, Thomas A., Darrell J. Gaskin, and Patrick Richard. "The Economic Burden of Health Inequalities in the United States." Joint Center for Political and Economic Studies. http://www.jointcenter.org/.

No matter how you slice it, the government—and the taxpayers—are already spending far more than they can afford. Rather than argue about what we can afford to spend, the question should be what are we getting for the money we spend and how can we spend that money better? Certainly not by continuing business as usual.

## Private Money

Until we ensure that our leadership fully understands the consequences of the laws and policies they enact, we have little hope to secure adequate public funding of the innovative systemic solutions that will bring an end to this growing health crisis. However, as Vaughn-Payne said, we also have other avenues to explore outside of governmental resources. Private foundations offer one of our best hopes at funding the kind of research and initiatives that can help light the way toward a permanent solution. Two that I am most familiar with are the W.K. Kellogg Foundation and the former H. Jack Geiger Congressional Health Policy Fellows program.

The W.K. Kellogg Foundation, for whom I used to direct major community-based programmatic priorities and at which I was proud to help fund some of the most innovative work in the public health field, continues to lead the national effort. Among the examples that offer hope are those that prioritize increasing the diversity of those policymakers who decide what funds are leveraged and to what end. In 2005, the W.K. Kellogg Foundation joined the Aetna Foundation and the Annie C. Casey Foundation to fund the Center for Advancing Health's groundbreaking H. Jack Geiger Fellowship program.

The H. Jack Geiger Congressional Health Policy Fellows program provided congressional caucus groups, health committees, and offices on health disparities and health policy with highly trained minority health policy advisors to participate in the national public policy decisions that affect the health of minority populations. The Program's stated purpose was to "bring widespread attention to healthcare access and health disparities issues of minorities and underserved populations in the U.S.," and to "expand the nation's capacity for research, leadership and policy development to more effectively address the broad range of factors affecting minority health."[15]

The truth is programs like these have an impact far beyond the actual fellows they produce. The opportunity to support young men of color in their journey up the career ladder in the health field does not just affect our health priorities now, but far into the future. Operating from an interdisciplinary model that brings together health research, public health interventions, social policy, and budget and legislative policy development brings the work closer to the development of systemic advancement than any of these fields can achieve working alone.

Brandeis scientist Dolores Acevedo-Garcia has also leveraged private funding from the W.K. Kellogg Foundation to strengthen the Diversity Data project. This initiative seeks to chart racial and ethnic equity in cities across the country. "My goal is to make it a more comprehensive and useful data-driven tool for people working toward improving the lives of vulnerable children," Acevedo-Garcia said. "I'm looking to incorporate information on policies that may help those children and promote equity."[16]

In the same interview, Acevedo-Garcia also described how the lack of diversity she encountered in college helped her understand the importance of having a wide range of perspectives at the decision-making table. "I have a clear memory of the people working in the dorms and kitchens at Princeton," she said. "Many of them were African-American. And yet it was very rare to find an African-American graduate student attending classes there."

"After that," she continued, "I was always aware of how opportunities differ for so many reasons, including geographic, racial, and socioeconomic reasons." The inequity that Acevedo-Garcia observed is everywhere to see for those who would take the time to notice it. Racial, and gender for men of color, inequality is not even hiding in plain sight. Rather, the glaring omission of men of color from academia, research, and health policy fields is impossible to miss. The difference that makes effective leadership is being willing to take the bold step between observing the problem and taking action to solve it.

## Closing the Gap between Rhetoric and Action

Robert Ross, Director of the California Endowment, points out, "When you watch Tavis Smiley bring together Cornel West and Henry Louis Gates and other intellectuals who have tremendous insights on the issue, you can get a lot of very fine rhetoric that engages the choir that has them rousing on their feet—that's a good thing. But it's insufficient as a way to move towards a well-resourced, defined strategy, and we've got to find a way to close that gap. What we need to move forward is to engage others in a way that's concrete, meaningful, and pragmatic, and understand that it's going to be a long haul."[17]

Ross, whose Board of Trustees has committed his foundation to a minimum decade-long investment in making a dent in the health and wellness crisis of men of color, does not participate in that rhetoric by simply speaking about the need to take specific steps. He outlines what is needed and then sets out to get it done. According to Ross, researchers, funders, and policy makers must come together to "agree to a basic set of metrics, and measure that to illuminate the past, then join hands and move ahead."[18]

If everyone in the community can come to see themselves, as well as the organizations, communities, and families that they lead, as a part of something bigger, then we can work collectively toward changing policies and making significant strides toward healthier individuals who are a part of healthier communities. "The importance of being connected to something bigger than yourself," said Ross, "is that it interrupts the feelings of isolation and outsized risk that can stand in the way of leadership." "There's never a substitute for hard work," he said, "and mentors along the way who've said, 'yeah, you're not crazy, that is the right method, let's work to get there.'" Working in conjunction with others across disciplines to obtain compatible goals brings us all into the fold of a larger social movement that takes into account what each of us can do to make us *all* healthier.

### Collaborating with Faith-Based Organizations

A recent collaborative effort between Morehouse School of Medicine-Community Voices and the Georgia State Board of Pardons & Paroles was developed with this same strategy in mind. What we have done differently is acknowledge that the faith community is a crucial community stakeholder and included them in the process. By leveraging the resources of the faith-based organizations for parolees returning to the Atlanta-Fulton county population, we have the opportunity to reach far more people and integrate them in even deeper ways than can be achieved by governmental agencies alone.

Evidence is beginning to support the fact that involving family, peers, and employers in the re-integration of ex-offenders, together with faith-based and non-profit organizations, can make a big difference in the lives of those re-entering society. Faith-based organizations generally have long-standing ties to the communities they serve. Their unique understanding of the local culture and the community's needs makes them an important ally in bringing whole-life wellness to individuals and families that can spread throughout the community and beyond.

To accomplish its goals, the Board of Pardons & Paroles utilizes the Parole Officers to identify the needs of the parolee and matches their needs to faith-based organizations within Fulton County. Engaging faith-based groups alongside civic organizations and forming strategic alliances, as well as providing additional supervision to help guide the process, enables the collaborative to provide shelter, job training/employment, food, transportation, counseling, and other services to the parolee population. Using a systems approach to reducing Fulton County's exorbitantly high recidivism rates provides formerly incarcerated people with a broad base of available resources to aid in re-acclimating to their communities.

Engaging faith groups has the added benefit of pushing past the "us" versus "them" mentality that saddles young men of color with the kind of "otherness" that allows leaders to continue to ignore their plight. Until the entire community gains the sense that the crisis is not about someone else, but about all of us, we cannot engage people into the leadership needed to achieve a solution.

## Working with the Medical Establishment

We cannot underestimate the importance of the medical establishment's involvement in working toward a solution. When it comes to health care access, the first thing that comes to mind for many is access to health insurance. Although most people get their insurance from employment, many African Americans are low wage earners or are in part-time positions, neither of which offers health insurance coverage. Men and boys who are sick, and getting worse, do not have time to argue the political merits of expanding health care coverage. What they need is help.

## We Are the Power System

"Being an American has become a spectator sport," wrote *New York Times* columnist Bob Herbert, in an op-ed piece. "Americans have tended to watch," he continued, "with a remarkable (I think frightening) degree of passivity as crises of all sorts have gripped the country and sent millions of lives into tailspins. Where people once might have deluged their elected representatives with complaints . . . the tendency now is to assume that there is little or nothing ordinary individuals can do about the conditions that plague them." Herbert believes, "This passivity and sense of helplessness most likely stems from the refusal of so many Americans over the past few decades to acknowledge any sense of personal responsibility for the policies and choices that have led the country into such a dismal state of affairs." I, too, have watched as our leadership has slowly resigned itself to push only as far as the power structure will allow. What we must all realize is that *we* are the power system, and not just because we have the power to elect our political leaders. Whether the leadership is political or corporate, faith- or community-based, people can only lead so long as others are willing to follow.[19]

So much more is possible than the limited options to which so many of us have resigned ourselves. Rather than allow ourselves—and our friends, neighbors, colleagues, family members—to fall into the knee jerk attitude of questioning why we should care, let us encourage each other to ask "why not" instead. Yes, we are all busy, and the battle requires a long uphill climb. But, as Herbert said, "It can start with just a few small steps. Mrs. Parks helped transform a nation by refusing to budge from her seat. Maybe you want to speak up publicly about an important issue, or host a house party, or perhaps arrange a meeting of soon-to-be dismissed employees, or parents at a troubled school. It's a risk, sure. But the need is great, and that's how you change the world."[20]

People in powerful positions should come together to determine what the barriers are to investing in change and then, together, eradicate those barriers. If medical agencies want to offer services to communities but find that they do not have insurance, then let us find a solution that will get them the insurance they need to obtain the services to help them get and stay well. Isolated approaches often fall apart simply because of their single-minded approach. Unfortunately, failure of an attempted program has become an easy excuse to give up on trying to make a difference. "The helplessness," said Herbert, "is beginning to border on paralysis."[21] Everything is related.

Doug Lomax embodied this approach in his work with the Boston Municipal Court. "One of the things I did," he said, "in my groups here in the court, is require that all my men have a primary care physician. It's mandatory. If you're 45 and over, you have to have your prostate exam. I promote good health, good eating, exercise, and we lead by example, and the men seem to want to do it once they passed the barrier of that fear and maybe this can help me or maybe I should know."[22]

Lomax's integration of medical education into a community setting is precisely the kind of multi-tiered approach that makes an impact. The fact that his work was housed and funded by the City of Boston's criminal court division makes it doubly important. The Institute of Medicine has talked about the quality and availability of health care and education for years, but never have they said a word about prisons. When we expand the opportunities that men of color, especially those embroiled in the criminal justice system, have to access culturally competent health information, then we expand their ability to access and benefit from the services that will keep them well.

Programs like those I have highlighted are too often short-lived and underfunded. It is within the power of our current leadership to ensure that promising models like these do not fall by the wayside for lack of financial and political investment. The success and survival of these programs do not depend only on political and organizational leaders. They also rely on the engagement of "ordinary" people committed to making a difference.

When we commit ourselves to pushing past the helplessness and paralysis that Herbert described as taking over the American conscience, we come closer to eliminating the disproportionately poor health and limited life opportunities of young men and boys of color in communities across the country. Many people, including both established and potential leaders in every area of life, find it difficult to see beyond a limited scope of influence to draw the connections between themselves and the larger communities in crisis. Missing the forest for the trees, we can easily get caught up in specific policies and forget about the full environment. As leaders, it is important to recognize that the time has come for us to engage in a full 360-degree analysis of what it is that makes people sick or keeps them well and then figure out where our work fits into that equation.

Each of us matters. Every moment we are not spending working toward a solution we are complicit in cementing the problem even deeper. Chapter 13 begins to explore some specific steps toward success that we can begin to take right now, from wherever we are. But before you even turn the page, take a moment to look around your own community. Where are the successful models of leadership—both large and small—in your area that are making a difference in the health and wellness of young men and boys of color? How can you help?

## Notes

1. Author interview with Tony Iton, November 2009.
2. Ibid.
3. Author interview with Marc Mauer, October 2009.

4. Ibid.
5. Author interview with Ron Dellums, October 2009.
6. Wilson, Stan. "Behind the Scenes: Life after San Quentin." *CNN Living*. http://articles.cnn.com/
7. "Second Chance Act." Justice Center. http://reentrypolicy.org/government_affairs/second_chance_act.
8. Author interview with Danny K. Davis, October 2009.
9. H.R. 2115. Men and Families Health Care Act. http://www.govtrack.us/congress/bills/111/hr2115#.
10. Author interview with Alex Busansky, October 2009.
11. Author interview with Peggy Vaughn-Payne, October 2009.
12. Ibid.
13. Ibid.
14. Bower, Garrett, Matthew Buettgens, Lan Doan, Irene Headen, and John Holahan. "The Cost of Failure to Enact Health Care Reform: 2010-2020." The Urban Institute Study. http://www.urban.org.
15. "H. Jack Geiger Congressional Health Policy Fellows." Center for Advancing Health. http://www.cfah.org/activities/geiger.cfm.
16. Author interview with Dolores Acevedo-Garcia, October 2009.
17. Author interview with Robert Ross, October 2009.
18. Ibid.
19. Herbert, Bob. "Changing the World." *New York Times*. http://www.nytimes.com.
20. Ibid.
21. Ibid.
22. Author interview with Doug Lomax, October 2009.

# CHAPTER 13

---

# Opportunities for Success

## *What You Can Do and How*

*"When leaders have fulfilled their functions, it's time for them to retire."*
—*Nathan Hare, Ph.D., Psychologist and Co-founder,*
*The Black Think Tank*

*For a week or two, Martin was frequenting the vegetable stand, and his eating had improved considerably. Then he began to fall back on old habits. He took a job that required him to work far from home on Saturdays, and soon he was back to subsisting on the processed food available at the 24-hour market near his home.*

*It was only a few days into his old eating habits that Martin began feeling poorly. The same symptoms he had before were creeping back up. At first, Martin brushed off the nausea, exhaustion, and tingling sensation he felt at odd times. He had been so used to feeling poorly that he thought, if he just got home a little earlier, got more rest, he could sleep it off.*

*Dorothea and Jamal also had not seen their friend, Martin, in a while. They knew he was not feeling well and decided one Sunday afternoon, after spending the morning at Pastor Hobson's church, to pay him a visit. As soon as Martin opened the door, they could tell just by looking at him that he was not doing well. The clinic was closed, but Jamal convinced Martin to let him take him to the emergency room.*

*It was nearly the following morning when Martin was finally seen by a doctor and learned he was even sicker than he thought. Martin was suffering from end-stage renal failure, the doctor told him, without looking up from his clipboard. Because he had no medical insurance and had precious little time or hope for a kidney transplant, even if he could afford it, his only option was dialysis.*

209

*The physicians recommended Martin be admitted to the hospital to begin treatment immediately. Shocked and afraid, Martin agreed to admit himself, but because he knew he might be in the hospital for a while, he asked them to postpone his admission until the morning. He wanted to go home, get his affairs in order, and pack some belongings for his stay.*

In conversations about how we can improve the health and lives of men and boys of color we often struggle to think as big as the crisis requires. Rather than looking at the problem from a systemic angle, we focus on individual changes that people can make, leaving the argument in the "blame the victim" territory that has helped the situation grow out of control. We begin to feel helpless, as if any response larger than what an individual can do for himself is beyond our control.

It is certainly advisable for each of us to encourage others not to drink or smoke, to eat nutritionally sound foods, and to get adequate exercise. By resting there, however, we miss the opportunity to make an even more significant impact by gathering together with our families, friends, and neighbors to make community-wide changes that affect the larger environment in which we live. Simply working with local city councils and regional boards to increase park space, expand sidewalks, and install adequate lighting can create a safer place that is more conducive to exercise.

Working with local farmers and nutritional organizations to ensure neighborhood access to fresh foods can positively impact the nourishment, health, and vitality of the entire community. By getting involved with local school boards, we can make a difference in the kinds of education available to the children in our communities. Taking collective action gives everyone a chance to make a difference, both for themselves and for the entire community.

Making sure that men and boys of color have equal access to a healthy life requires that we tackle many problems at once. To accomplish this, one of the first things we can do is look around ourselves and take stock of who is doing the work, what they bring to the table, and what tools and skills are missing. Once we know what we are working with, we can know what to look for when we go back into the community to develop new leaders. Only by having a firm understanding of the people and capacities at our disposal are we able to build a successful team.

Effective teamwork often requires us to move beyond our comfort zone and reach into the community for leadership and direction. Community-driven leadership development is an iterative process. We cannot simply go into a community once, gather people together, ask them for their input, and then leave—never to be seen again. The most successful models for leadership discussed in the previous chapter began by going to community members and asking them directly what they thought were the worst problems and what ideas they had for effectively solving them.

Confronting power failure requires us to implement our work in more creative ways: Develop a varied incentive base to get people in the door and keep them coming back. Know what potential leaders may need and find ways to help them meet those needs directly, whether that means offering public transportation vouchers or offering free lunch. Show the community you understand its problems holistically, rather than from a single-issue perspective, and its members will begin to not only take your involvement seriously, but also think themselves toward more holistic solutions.

We must begin to build deep and lasting relationships. Rather than just making telephone calls, we can take the time to visit every local community organization in person and see what kind of work they are doing and who is doing it, as well as listen to the stories people in the community have to tell. In their stories may lay a path toward change that would otherwise escape us. Then identify champions who understand the importance of the work—both inside and outside of organizational settings—and who are invested in creating change.

The relationships built this way will then lead to more relationships as each budding leader introduces new potential leaders into the process. We can then begin building the kinds of communications tools that take some of the heavy lifting out of growing the community. Social media networks are already gravitating in that direction. Tools like Facebook, MySpace, Twitter, and others offer the ability to build an online community of like-minded people who not only believe in your cause, but bring their own cultural, social, intellectual, and monetary capital to the table. We then have the opportunity to use that media to develop specific action plans and deliver messages in a much more targeted way.

Community-based organizations are not the only organizations that can utilize media—be it social, paid, or earned media—to build community and deliver targeted messages. Many corporations have developed public relations campaigns to champion specific social issues that help reinforce their own positive images in the community. By tying their own brands to issues the communities they serve care about, companies are able to build consumer loyalty and keep their names in public conversation.

Those of us committed to healthy communities can begin to work better with these companies to help them understand the importance of their consumers' health to their own bottom line. A healthy customer is a repeat customer. Messages like these can help us gain corporate support, and resources, to further our shared goals.

In addition to leveraging their media reach for health promoting messages, both the corporate and small business communities offer an opportunity to develop a wide range of partnerships. In addition to rethinking our funding practices with an eye toward long-term investment, we can also imagine anew what that funding means. Developing loan programs, from standard small business loans to micro-loans, to give young men with felonies a way to start their own businesses has an enormous impact on their ability to live healthier more fulfilling lives.

Because formerly incarcerated men of color face such an uphill battle to employment, starting their own businesses gives them the kind of security and community investment they need to become leaders in their own right. We must find a way to put people to work and help families break the cycle of poor health and limited opportunity. Working toward an Internal Revenue Service policy that provides a significant deduction for businesses that hire formerly incarcerated persons is a promising option, as is working with rotary clubs and small business administrations to develop the kinds of job programs that guarantee employability. Finding business mentors or even including incubator arrangements as a part of the loan process to help them learn to manage their businesses helps guarantee loan repayment and the kind of business success that has a ripple effect on the entire community.

Increasing both governmental and private sector funding for community and mental health centers so they can adequately meet the needs of men and boys in crisis can go far, both in addressing health issues and offering opportunities for employment. We must begin prioritizing the recruitment and retention of African American men into the mental health workforce. We can begin by taking a hard look at admissions policies and practices, reducing financial barriers to mental health professions training, and offering mechanisms to encourage support for diversity efforts. Through actions like these, we can help increase the numbers of men and boys of color who access those services by eliminating the stigma, integrating services into the wider circle of care, and offering culturally competent caregivers who intimately understand their struggles.

There are benefits to operating in the new environment in which hope and change are considered worthy causes. One is that there are people at the federal level talking seriously about directing much needed funding to historically black colleges and universities (HBCUs) to implement in-depth research on this issue of men's health. It is critical that we increase the available documentation of health inequities. This will not only help

> As a child all I wanted to do was go to college and further my education.
>
> —*Wayne Stern, ex-offender*

generate the funding we need to address those inequities, but lead to greater buy-in from a wide variety of stakeholders to tackle the myriad problems that keep the crisis going.

The Institute of Medicine could be directed by Congress to do a study on the health of poor men of color. Federal legislation was introduced to fund this type of study, but it has yet to pass. Without proper documentation, communicating the urgency of the crisis at hand is an uphill battle, particularly when men and boys of color are already an un-prioritized community. The Institute of Medicine's landmark 2003 study, *Unequal Treatment: Confronting Racial and Ethnic Disparities in Health Care*, documented the disproportionately poor health of African American men and boys.[1] It is time to begin undertaking an *Unequal Treatment II*, which will track the crisis over time and tease out what has really happened to poor men of color.

Policy makers must begin to implement social impact studies as a part of every level of health and social policy passed. Policies have so often worked against poor communities, especially poor communities of color. We know this, but we must generate more scientific evidence to support the volumes of anecdotal evidence community groups have to offer. We know it is real. It is time to show it with the numbers so we can get added buy-in to take action.

Thinking more broadly about how government-funded research is handled would allow Historically Black Colleges and Universities (HBCUs) and other community stakeholders to take a systems approach to their research. Currently, the National Institutes of Health and other governmental funding agencies, whose priorities tend to set the national research agenda, focus their funding on specific health barriers, such as heart disease, drug abuse, or prostate cancer. However, what we need is to support more innovative approaches research, such as a cross-cutting study that looks at how a wide swath of health issues affects African American men and boys in a way that directly contributes to the health crisis at hand. If we set our grant-making priorities so the institutions who have the most at stake in solving the crisis—such as HBCUs, Hispanic Serving Institutions, Native American Tribal Colleges, and others—have the support needed to do the work, then we will soon see a much broader perspective represented, along with more creative approaches to solution.

Changes like this do not happen just because the community wants them to. Community groups know it does not necessarily take money to get started taking action; however, we also know, no matter the size of our institutions, that we will never get the funding needed without a well-designed plan. What does it mean when a large percentage of a community's population is taken away with no hopes of redemption because of the collateral damage of a felony conviction? Working together, we can begin to ask the necessary questions that will guide our plan and move us toward systemic solutions.

Charting the impact of policy also requires that we look at how we develop our laws and policies in the first place. If a law passed will cause significant damage to the larger society, how can we identify that potential damage and work to adjust the law toward the positive outcome we seek? We must look at our investment in crime prevention programs and see what is working and why so we can spread that model. At the same time, we need to look deeply at what kind of damage our punitive approach to public safety visits on our communities and hold our leaders accountable for the damage they inflict in the heat of a political and ideological moment.

For instance, Mercer Law School recently released a report detailing how the state of Georgia's existing laws and policies erect devastating barriers for those re-entering their communities after incarceration. These policies make it next to impossible for people to get back on their feet and rebuild their lives, which, in turn, increases the rate of recidivism and has been found to produce excessive social and economic strains on Georgia taxpayers. By picking up on studies, such as the one recently completed by Mercer, we can document destructive law and policy so we can take the actions needed to change it.

Creating the necessary networks between community organizations, public health departments, and the criminal justice system offers a unique opportunity to approach the issue from many sides. By working with district attorneys' offices to help them understand the real impact that certain sentencing decisions have on neighborhoods, families and community groups can have a hand in helping criminal justice professionals understand the collateral consequences their decisions have.

Rehabilitation should begin the moment a person enters prison. Rather than breaking people's spirit, they should work on how they can become a positive contributor to society and have the most fulfilling life possible—even while incarcerated. Similarly, working with congressional committees and public health departments to help them understand that incarcerated people must still be considered a part of their home communities, we can break the cycle of the funding drains that remove necessary assistance and health care access from the communities that need them most.

Communities must demand increased investment in programs that provide comprehensive family reunification services. At the same time, we must press our leaders to critically investigate the impact of policies, such as the 1997 Safe Families Act that makes children available for adoption outside of the family if parental caregivers are imprisoned for more than 6 weeks. Working to restore voting rights to formerly incarcerated people so they can be full citizens with the kind of political clout that forces leadership to listen offers another route. Lobbying our state legislatures to ensure people re-entering their communities after incarceration have access to emergency food stamps until they can get on their feet offers yet another. If coming home from prison does not constitute an emergency case, then what is? Every major city should begin building a collaborative to address this crisis and make doing so a basic part of doing business.

In addition to working with mainstream health care and political leadership, the reinvestment of African American leadership is a critical key to making a difference. As we continue to work our way through how we balance race, class, and community progress, it is imperative that our leadership not check a large swath of the community at the door as we move ahead with our own advancement. We are developing a dangerously segregated class of African Americans who are involved in the community in some ways, yet separated from it in many others. The ascendency of President Obama, as promising and powerful as it has been, shows us how this segregation can work.

Although Obama's administration is widely diverse when it comes to race and gender, the vast majority of those people come from Ivy League backgrounds far removed from the problems poor men and boys of color face every day. Although they have certainly had to deal with racism in their rise to power, their understanding of race and racism has been filtered through a far different experience than those who are currently suffering.

African American leadership organizations face the same dilemma. Older generations would have found it unthinkable that groups like the NAACP could ever lose their relevance in the African American community. Yet, the membership base of these groups is both aging and shrinking. Younger people do not feel a connection to these groups, because their priorities do not seem in line with those of the communities in which they live.

If organizations like the NAACP are no longer robust in their programming or as embraced by the broader community as they have been in the past, then their leadership must begin to take stock of the situations in their communities—not just those at the top, but those at the bottom and those hanging on to stay somewhere in the middle. As long as mainstream African American leadership continues to keep their work close to their comfort zone, we lose potential new leaders with the tools and skills that could help make a difference.

We have got to reach out to our leadership with both criticism and compassion. Understanding the barriers that block them from taking on the problem and working toward solution is not a difficult task. The more successful African Americans become, the more frustrating and isolating their experiences can begin to feel.

African Americans who have worked hard to reach a pinnacle of success, whatever their field, are quickly confronted with the uniqueness of their existence at the top. One of the painful symptoms of that isolation can be found in the striking imbalance between finding support and appreciation for the hard work many of our leaders had to undertake to succeed and the pressing knowledge that they would not need to be alone if others had been afforded some of the same opportunities.

Leadership involvement in overhauling our broken public education system offers one of the most important opportunities for success. A nationwide campaign is needed to prioritize public education. We need to engage in real talk about teacher training and find new ways to reward teachers. School systems may consider evaluating teachers based on the numbers of young men they keep in their classrooms, rather than on the basis of test scores.

Part of our property taxes could be diverted to a state level school fund, which can then be distributed to schools equally to eradicate the necessity of children in poor communities suffering through a poor education. These are just a few of the opportunities we have to improve academic performance, achieve equity, and give all of our children the opportunity for a healthy and fulfilling life.

Today, we find ourselves living through an embarrassment of riches. Racial diversity is growing at all levels of leadership. If we do not begin to use this opportunity to demand these new leaders take real action to save poor men and boys of color, then we face the imminent destruction of a huge portion of our community. This is a death blow not only to communities of color, but to our larger society that needs the opportunity to benefit from the minds and talents of those we have been so quick to throw away.

The downward trend of wealth accumulation in black communities does more than speak volumes about the current health crisis. It offers an opportunity to see how the happenings in communities of color will

**TAKE A GOOD LOOK   Foundation Program Officer**

Are you a foundation program officer? If not, can you imagine what it is like to be one? Look in the mirror and ask yourself:

- What strategic approach can you take to introduce work with the incarcerated as a part of your portfolio? The mother, the father, the children?

- What collaborators can you identify as integral to your ability to make a sustainable difference in the lives of those who have been touched by the criminal justice system?

- Can the media be your partner? If so, in what ways might you engage potential writers and reporters?

- Can you find a way that enables others to "follow the money" in their storytelling about the criminal justice system if this is a way to enable understanding about cost and benefit?

begin to play out in our larger national society. After decades of growth, the concentration of wealth in African American communities has been taking a sharp decline in recent years. Levels of educational attainment have increased significantly; however, as African Americans have moved into the middle class, their wealth base has been concentrated in home ownership. It is telling that the biggest surge in black homeownership has taken place in the first decade of the new millennium, particularly because the recent recession has taken such a significant toll on home ownership. In yet one more way, African Americans have been disproportionately devastated by the downturn.

As after any major disaster, most communities take stock and begin making plans to rebuild. But a people cannot begin to rebuild if they do not live long enough to pour a new foundation or replace a lifetime of lost savings. The monetary, cultural, and intellectual wealth of the African American community is in danger of being lost forever. A people must live long enough to build wealth, understand the value of the wealth they have, and then have the opportunity to pass that wealth on to the next generation. We can no longer afford to stay silent. We can no longer afford to avoid action or to invest only the bare minimum into initiatives that stand little chance of making a difference. Our society is one in which the wealth and contributions of all of us are what make us unique. Each of us has the opportunity to be a leader, and every leader has the opportunity to make a difference. Together, we can put an end to the

LEADERS AND HEROES

## Jacqueline Martinez, Philanthropy, New York State Health Foundation

Jacqueline Martinez began to shape her work while earning her master's degree at Columbia University. She was very attracted to the work of Columbia professors Drs. Robert and Mindy Fullilove. Martinez contemplated studying medicine but realized she did not have to go to medical school to heal communities. Columbia afforded her the opportunity to work with Dr. Jack Geiger. Dr. Geiger was and is a leader in the movement to elevate the issue of health disparities, in particular, cardiovascular care issues in black men.

Martinez also had spent time prior to graduate school working with a well-known community organization, Alianza Dominicana. She attributes her effectiveness at Alianza to the fact that "I understood those issues, because I lived in the communities where we saw the issues."[1] There, she says, she gained invaluable experience in incorporating the ethos of community into addressing comprehensively community issues. This work, combined with her work with Dr. Geiger, is the foundation of her interest in and commitment to the social determinants of health.

After graduation she left Alianza for Columbia's Northern Manhattan Community Voices project, a part of an initiative funded by the Kellogg Foundation that focused on translating community-based information and findings into policy options for local and national decisionmakers. Martinez fine-tuned her community-based approach and became convinced it is social and family networks that have the greatest potential to protect people from drugs and prison.

As Senior Program Director at the New York State Health Foundation, Martinez now wants to gather the forces to inform policy even more. Martinez believes that philanthropy should invest wherever possible in programs that can inform national practice and policy. "One must work across sectors to find more global solutions. Local policy is important, but it must sometimes be fortified by policy deliberations and implementation at the national level," she says.[2]

Martinez finds that the constraints of decisionmakers and policy leaders in philanthropy often reflect contemporary values and do not necessarily embrace issues that may be of great concern in poor communities. She, nevertheless, says she sees incremental change, and this continues to give her hope. Although she believes "the collateral damage of incarceration is an issue that all of philanthropy should embrace," she can only begin to work on this issue at this time if it is directly related to incarcerated veterans.[3]

Martinez's work with veterans has allowed her to connect dots outside of mental health and post-traumatic stress disorder and to include housing and other issues that support an individual becoming reestablished in community. The veterans in trouble, says Martinez, "are not very different from the boys and men that did not enroll in the Armed Services and simply found themselves in trouble with the law earlier than those that go off to fight in a war and then return home with no greater skills that help them cope and even thrive. In fact, those that are dishonorably discharged come in higher numbers from communities that do not have adequate supports if you are poor, are from a racial group that has suffered historic discrimination, and if you are undereducated."[4]

The next frontier in philanthropy is investing in gathering data that will permit a more strategic programming based on what communities say and are experiencing versus what those on the outside "think" are the priorities. Martinez says she needs to remind herself that "it is important to keep my eye on the big picture, as the day-to-day experiences can be frustrating, can make one want to give up the work." Investment in the poor must take a realistic look at the data and a different perspective on sustainability, she believes. Sustaining work in poor communities takes longer, and there is often no resource stream to pick up work for populations that have been historically marginalized.[5]

Martinez concludes, "I want more data on who goes to jail or prison and why, so that we can plan to keep them safe and strengthen families. I have learned to be a strategic thinker. I have to remind myself to have the patience to learn from others and to most effectively translate to others what I am learning."[6]

For more information about the New York State Health Foundation, please visit http://www.nyshealthfoundation.org/.

_____

1. Author interview with Jacqueline Martinez, March 2012.
2. Ibid.
3. Ibid.
4. Ibid.
5. Ibid.
6. Ibid.

kind of power failure that has led to one of the most pressing crises in recent history. Together, we can take the power in our own hands, flip the switch, and offer rays of hope and possibility to millions living on the margins with little hope of reaching the center.

The heroes and leaders profiled in this book are of necessity in the limelight. The bottom line on most of the heroes in the world, however, is that they are often just regular people who keep their noses to the grindstone and fly under the radar, because, if people knew their entire agenda, they would be fired or marginalized. At Community Voices, I have to spend a lot of time just trying to keep some from walking away saying, "ENOUGH!" So here is my secret message: Do the work, but maintain a low profile and avoid the limelight. Perhaps your contribution starts with simply contacting one or more of the heroes profiled in this book and saying, "good job." Ask if they could use your help—you do not need to start a whole new project.

In closing, I wrote this book and this chapter not to overwhelm you, but to paint a picture in broad strokes to remind you of the kinds of things that could be done—and that must be done. You do not have to do them all—but maybe you could do one.

Write the one action you will take:

_____

_____

_____

*"Each time a man stands up for an ideal, or acts to improve the lot of others, or strikes out against injustice, he sends forth a tiny ripple of hope, and those ripples build a current which can sweep down the mightiest walls of oppression and resistance."*

—*Robert Kennedy*

## Note

1. Smedley, Brian D., Adrienne Y. Stith, and Alan R. Nelson, eds. *Unequal Treatment: Confronting Racial and Ethnic Disparities in Health Care*. Washington, DC: The Institute of Medicine, 2003.

# Epilogue

Jamal arrived at Martin's apartment first thing in the morning to pick him up and take him to the hospital. He had tried to go home with him the night before to help him pack, but Martin had begged off and asked to be left alone with his thoughts. Against his better judgment, Jamal agreed.

He knocked on the door for nearly 20 minutes before he went for help. Unfortunately, by the time he had found the superintendent and convinced him to let him in the apartment, it was too late. Jamal found his friend on the floor near the telephone. He was not breathing and looked as if it had been a while since he had.

The next few hours passed in a blur of ambulances and policemen, flashing lights, and emergency medical personnel. Dorothea rushed over to help, even though the best she could do was keep Jamal together. He was not prepared for how moved he would be by the loss of his friend. Martin's passing made all the things he learned from Dorothea about life, death, and the health crisis facing black men like himself more real than ever.

Jamal buried his friend and committed himself to becoming a part of the solution. The organization at which he worked gave him a promotion to community outreach worker, and he began working in the streets, documenting the stories of the men he found there, while directing them to service centers at which they could find help. One story touched him particularly deeply. It was told by an older man who appeared to have been living on the streets for some time. He met him one night outside the 24-hour market on the corner where he was begging for change. Jamal was not even on the job, but something about the man made him stop and listen to his story.

The story of how the man wound up in his present situation was heartbreaking, yet no more or less heartbreaking than the hundreds of stories Jamal had gathered during the several months he had been working in his new job. In the end, he realized that what had changed was himself. His commitment to helping others had brought him even more than he ever gave. He felt more a part of the community in which he had been born and raised than he ever had. The work he was doing gave his life a new-found purpose. Jamal realized an emotion that night that he had never quite felt before. He felt proud of himself: proud of the life he had built and the work he had done, proud of the smile he found on Dorothea's face every time he saw her, and proud to know that it was him who put it there.

For the first time he could remember, Jamal felt hope. He began to dream of the future, of the home, the life, the family he had always wanted. Even more, he began to believe in the possibility of those dreams. He knew it would not be easy, but, for the first time, it felt possible. With every person he helped through his work, it felt a little more possible that everything he had always wanted could come true—for him, for Dorothea, and for as many people as they could bring along with them into the light.

\* \* \*

# Appendix

There are many organizations working in communities across the nation. Clearly, there are not enough and more good ideas are always needed. We have just begun to scratch the surface on the issues we face, and community intervention alone will not likely be sufficient, as policies often cause the issues that communities face. In sum, this listing is not intended to be directive or exhaustive. The descriptions are necessarily brief and represent only the highlights—please visit the Web sites of any you are interested in learning more about. Much remains to be done by leaders, . . . those of you who are reading this book, who are capable of visualizing previously unimagined futures.

## 100 Black Men of Atlanta/Project Success

- Post-secondary preparation and tuition assistance program
- Mentors inner-city youth in at-risk environments
- Encourages academic success
- Helps develop educated, contributing community members
- Currently at capacity and is not accepting applications
- 100 Resource Learning Center, 241 Peachtree Street, NE, Suite 200 is open to public

**Contact:**
Ray Singer
100 Black Men of Atlanta
241 Peachtree Street, Suite 300
Atlanta, GA 30303
404-525-6220
rsinger@100blackmen-atlanta.org

info@100blackmen-atlanta.org
100blackmen-atlanta.org

\* \* \*

## 2025 Campaign for Black Men and Boys

- Seeks to create a society that inspires ambition and hope among African American men and boys
- Initiative for educational, emotional, social, spiritual, physical, political, and economic development and empowerment
- Connects community-based organizations, organizers, advocates, practitioners, and youth leaders with businesses, philanthropies, academics, and concerned individuals

**Contact:**
Landon Jermain Adams
CDA Inc./2025 Campaign for Black Men and Boys
1320 Petrel Alley
Columbus, OH 43219
614-313-1747
landon@cdatrust.com
2025bmb.org/thecampaign

\* \* \*

## Amachi

- Mentoring program to provide consistent presence of loving, caring people of faith
- Adult mentors meet weekly with a carefully-matched child
- Aims to significantly improve the life opportunities of the children
- Uses the Big Brother Big Sister (BBBS) mentoring model and congregational volunteers

**Contact:**
W. Wilson Goode, Sr.
AMACHI
2000 Market Street, Suite 550
Philadelphia, PA 19103
215-557-4497

wgoode@ppv.org
amachimentoring.org

\* \* \*

## Amer-I-Can of New York, Inc.

Consists of:

- Amer-I-Can Program: Life Management Skills curriculum
- Amer-I-Can Foundation for Social Change: non-profit organization that offers social support and services to underserved populations
- Founded by NFL Hall of Fame running back and motion picture actor, Jim Brown
- Recognizes that the attitude of the recipient is paramount for success

**Contact:**
Walter Beach III
Amer-I-Can of New York, Inc.
2010 Wienthrop Way
Macungie, PA 18062
917-838-4192
walterbeach3@aol.com
amer-i-can.org

\* \* \*

## America's Promise Alliance

- Collaborates with more than 300 national partner organizations and their local affiliates
- On-going Dropout Prevention works to ensure that all young people graduate from high school ready for college, work, and life
- Provides children key supports ("Five Promises"): safe places, caring adults, effective education, a healthy start, and opportunities to help others through service
- Commissioned Grad Nation to use evidence-based practices

**Contact:**
Charles Hiteshew
America's Promise Alliance
1110 Vermont Avenue, N.W., Suite 900
Washington, DC 20005
202-657-0613
charlesh@americaspromise.org
americaspromise.org

\* \* \*

## Aviation Explorers

- Tomorrow's Aeronautical Museum's elite group of young pilots who learn to fly at an adult flight school, Aero Squad
- Provides applied math and science in aeronautics, after-school and weekend tutorial services, computer lab and internet access, and women's studies
- Addresses nationwide problem of the lack of after-school activities, mentorship, and positive role models
- Provides skill sets (civic and personal duty readiness; ethics and career awareness; early teen living skills; mentoring) useful for any career and for lifelong benefit

**Contact:**
Robin Petgrave
Aviation Explorers
Tomorrow's Aeronautical Museum
961 West Alondra Blvd.
Compton, CA 90220
310-618-1155
robin@tamuseum.org
tamuseum.org/aviationexplorers

\* \* \*

## Baltimore Safe & Sound Campaign

- Improves conditions for health, safety, and well being of Baltimore's children and youth
- Made up of thousands of people from all walks of life

- Tracks progress against indicators of child well-being citywide, which are trending in the right direction for the first time in decades

**Contact:**
Fanon Hill
The Baltimore Safe & Sound Campaign
2 East Read Street
Baltimore, MD 21202
410-625-7976
fhill@safeandsound.org
safeandsound.org

\* \* \*

## Bethune-Cookman University's Black Male College Explorers Program

- Mentoring programs that steer more black men toward college
- Boys in 6th–12th grade meet weekly on campus to analyze the news, receive tutoring, and learn to play chess
- During the summer component, students focus on academics and learn more about colleges and universities

**Contact:**
Dr. Fredrick Milton
Bethune-Cookman University
Judson/McPhillips Office of College Advancement
640 Dr. Mary McLeod Bethune Boulevard
Daytona Beach, FL 32114
386-481-2000
bethune.cookman.edu
miltonf@cookman.edu

\* \* \*

## Black Men & Boys Coalition/Fresno West Coalition for Economic Development

- Mission and goal is to improve the socioeconomic and physical conditions of southwest Fresno residents

- Goals that guide its work: education and training; leadership/professional and personal development; neighborhood development; socio-economic development; health equity; justice and safety; community capacity, advocacy, and organizing; and the creation of leaders

**Contact:**
Jocelyn Chretien
Black Men & Boys Coalition
Fresno West Coalition for Economic Development
1350 E. Annadale
Fresno, CA 93706
559-485-1273
Jocelyn@fwced.org
fwced.org

* * *

## Black Men's Health Network

- Founded in 1987 to raise public awareness about the excessive morbidity and mortality rates in the African American community and especially among males
- Advocates and supports attention to the health needs of women and children
- Developed effective educational materials targeting low literacy populations, minority youth, and Christian organizations

**Contact:**
Jean Bonhomme
National Black Men's Health Network
250 Georgia Ave., Suite 321
Atlanta GA 30312
404-524-7237
info@nbmhn.net
www.nbmhn.net

* * *

## Boston Health CREW

- A program of the Boston Public Health Commission
- Trains and provides hands-on experience to young men of color who wish to become health educators in their communities

**Contact:**
Boston Health Crew
Boston Public Health Commission
1010 Massachusetts Avenue, 6th Floor
Boston, MA 02118
617-534-9647

\* \* \*

## The Brotherhood/Sister Sol

- Addresses the need for supportive programs for black and Latino youth
- Provides knowledge, resources, opportunities, love, and skills needed to understand and overcome the myriad negative pressures in their lives
- Provides opportunities to explore ideas, identity, and future among peers, with support and guidance from youths' immediate elders
- Addresses ten curriculum focus areas
- Enriching, educational after-school opportunities and summer programs

**Contact:**
Khary Lazarre-White, Executive Director & Co-Founder
The Brotherhood/Sister Sol
512 West 143 Street
New York, NY 10031
212-283-7044
klw@brothrehood-sistersol.org
brotherhood-sistersol.org

\* \* \*

## BUILD

- Aims to provide underserved students with educational and entre-preneurial opportunities that would otherwise not be available
- Helps youth gain an education, financial responsibility, and self-confidence
- Breaks the vicious cycle of high-school dropouts and socio-economic disadvantage via motivation and role models

**Contact:**
BUILD Headquarters
5 Palo Alto Square, 6th floor
3000 El Camino Real
Palo Alto, CA 94306
650-688-5840
build.org

\* \* \*

## Center for Community Change

- Founded in 1968 to honor Robert F. Kennedy
- One of the longest-standing champions for low-income people and communities of color
- Builds new politics based on community values to achieve social and economic justice
- Strengthens, connects, and mobilizes grassroots groups to enhance their leadership, voice, and power

**Contact:**
Mary Lassen
Center for Community Change
1536 U Street NW
Washington, DC 20009
202-339-9300
mlassen@communitychange.org
communitychange.org

\* \* \*

## CeaseFire

- Launched in 2000 by the Chicago Project for Violence Prevention
- One of the only proven techniques for making neighborhoods safer
- Takes an evidence-based, collaborative, public health approach to reducing violence epidemic of shootings and killings
- Uses highly trained street violence interrupters and outreach staff, public education campaigns, community mobilization, faith leader engagement, law enforcement coordination, and public education

**Contact:**
Candice M. Kane
CeaseFire Program
University of Illinois, Chicago
1603 W. Taylor St., MC 92
Chicago, IL 60612
312-996-8775
kanecm@uic.edu
ceasefirechicago.org

\* \* \*

## Communities in Schools

- The nation's largest dropout prevention organization
- Champions connecting "community resources with schools to help young people learn, stay in school and prepare for life"
- Brings "caring adults into the schools to address children's unmet needs," providing a link between educators and the community[1]
- Frees teachers to teach and students to focus on learning
- Works to ensure every child receives "five basics": a one-on-one relationship with a caring adult, a safe place to learn and grow, a healthy start and a healthy future, a marketable skill to use on graduation, and a chance to give back to peers and community

**Contact:**
Daniel Cardinali
Communities in Schools
2345 Crystal Drive, Suite 801

Arlington, VA 22202
703-518-2542
cardinalid@cisnet.org
cisnet.org

\* \* \*

## Community Oriented Correctional Health Services (COCHS)

- Non-profit organization that builds partnerships between jails and community health care providers
- Aims to establish "medical homes" for offenders in their communities so they stay healthy, can support themselves and their families, and stay out of jail
- Helps people with chronic and contagious diseases get the medical care they need

**Contact:**
Steven Rosenberg
Community Oriented Correctional Health Services
675 61st Street
Oakland, CA 94609
510-595-7360 x12
info@cochs.org
cochs.org

\* \* \*

## East End Neighborhood House

- Brings together the untapped resource of Senior Citizens with community youth
- Through the Neighborhood Foster Care Program, enables children to remain in their communities and achieve permanency in their lives
- Provides basic computer literacy classes for seniors, young people, and the general community
- Provides a Day Care and Head Start program and an extended before and after school
- A resource for families in crisis to access culturally sensitive, competent assessment, and other services

**Contact:**
Paul Hill, Jr.
East End Neighborhood House
2749 Woodhill Road
Cleveland, OH 44104
216-707-6000
nropi@aol.com
eenh.org

\* \* \*

## Family Justice

- Engages families with a loved one involved in the justice system or at risk of involvement
- Provides proven results in decreased drug use and recidivism and improved family health and well-being
- La Bodega de la Familia program partners with probation and parole officers—this Bodega Model® is used and refined nationwide
- Adapts the model to address truancy and gang involvement

**Contact:**
Justin Burke
Family Justice National Headquarters
625 Broadway, 8th Floor
New York, NY 10012
212-475-1500
jburke@familyjustice.org
familyjustice.org

\* \* \*

## Flip the Script Program/Goodwill Industries of Greater Detroit

- Assisted more than 1,000 young men since established in 2003
- Considered Detroit's premier minority male training program and one of the most respected in the nation
- Uses an intense gender- and culture-specific 18-week curriculum that focuses on math, reading enrichment, spiritual life, social skills, academic, and workforce development

- Addresses male responsibility, positive relationship development, conflict resolution, fatherhood, and financial literacy/wealth building
- Teaches young men to be economically self-sufficient, positive heads of households who take an active role in their community
- Includes job preparation, placement assistance, GED tutorial/preparation, In-School Youth Service workshops, and mentoring

**Contact:**
Keith L. Bennett, Program Director
Flip the Script Program
Goodwill Industries of Greater Detroit
7700 Second Avenue, Fifth Floor
Detroit, Michigan 48202
313-557-4848
goodwilldetroit.org/programs/flip-the-script.aspx

\* \* \*

## Gloucester Institute

- Committed to providing an environment for discussing ideas transforming them into practical solutions that produce results
- Provides a peaceful place to restore and refresh leaders and to train and nurture emerging leaders
- Dedicated to cultivating a society of "solutionists"; providing a safe environment for divergent views to resolve issues; equipping scholars with intellectual, moral, and financial support; and communicating this vision to the entire African American Diaspora
- Creates a unique Web presence as a portal to policy papers, conversation, news media, and career development

**Contact:**
Kay Coles James
The Gloucester Institute
100 North 5th Street
Richmond, VA 23219
804-644-6290
kjames@gloucesterinstitute.org
gloucesterinstitute.org

\* \* \*

## Healthy Black Family Project

- Provides activities that help individuals and families prevent diabetes and high blood pressure
- Provides assistance and support to individuals and families to help them make preventive lifestyle changes

**Contact:**
Kingsley Association (Headquarters)
6435 Frankstown Ave.
Pittsburgh, PA 15206
412-661-8751
cmh.pitt.edu/hbfp.asp

Hosanna House, Inc.
807 Wallace Avenue
Wilkinsburg, PA 15221
412-342-1344
cmh.pitt.edu/hbfp.asp

\* \* \*

## Homeboy Industries

- Supports youth and young adults to transition out of gangs in East Los Angeles, California
- A well respected, community-based, "gang-neutral" organization that uses job training, employment, and tattoo removal to help members create a new life
- Provides a "safe space" for individual therapy, family and marriage counseling, and treatment for trauma and substance abuse

**Contact:**
Father Gregory Boyle, Director
Homeboy Industries
130 W. Bruno St.
Los Angeles, CA 90012
323-526-1254
info@homeboy-industries.org
homeboy-industries.org

\* \* \*

## IMapAmerica

- Aims to guarantee every young person safe and accurate information so he or she can make better decisions
- Flips the conventional model of "we're doing this for youth" to "youth are doing this for themselves"
- Equips youth and adults with the ability to identify opportunities and services in their communities that are relevant to their needs and interests
- Allows young people to shape their own futures and the future of their communities, as well as the world beyond

**Contact:**
James Logan
IMapAmerica
2753 Broadway, #357
New York, NY 10025
646-794-4146
jlogan@imapamerica.org
imapamerica.org

\* \* \*

## LifeStarts Youth & Family Services

- Provides youth and their families with mentoring, life skills, coaching, support, and advocacy
- Serves more than 1,000 youth and their families per year
- Offers family-strengthening programs in school and after school
- Staff strongly connect with the youth they serve because of their similar backgrounds

**Contact:**
Curtis Watkins
LifeSTARTS Youth & Family Services
1115 Good Hope Road SE
Washington, DC 20020
202-610-9903
cwatkins@lifestarts.org
lifestarts.org

\* \* \*

## Men's Health Network

- National, non-profit organization that reaches out to men and their families where they live, work, play, and pray
- Founded in 1992 by health professionals and others; today, more than 800 physicians and key thought leaders on their Board of Advisors
- Helps men live longer, fuller, and happier lives; helps them implement positive lifestyles for themselves and their families; reduces the cycles of violence and addiction; energizes government involvement in men's health activities; and encourages women to expand on their traditional role as the family's health care leader
- Uses health prevention tools, screening programs, educational materials, advocacy, and patient navigation

**Contact:**
Ana Fadich
Men's Health Network
P.O. Box 75972
Washington, D.C. 20013
202-543-MHN-1 (6461)
info@menshealthnetwork.org
menshealthnetwork.org

\* \* \*

## National CARES Mentoring Movement

- Connects caring adults to the mentoring opportunities present in their community
- Building a mentor-recruitment program to fill the pipelines of the thousands of organizations serving black children desperately waiting for mentors

**Contact:**
Susan Taylor (Founder-CEO)
National CARES Mentoring Movement
408 W. 58th Street
New York, NY 10019
212-920-7750

Taylor@caresmentoring.org
cc: dparker@caresmentoring.org
caresmentoring.com

\* \* \*

## National Council on Crime and Delinquency

- The oldest nonprofit criminal justice research organization in the Untied States that prevents and reduces crime and delinquency
- Promotes effective, humane, fair, and economically sound ways to solve family, community, and justice problems
- Conducts research, promotes reform initiatives, and works with individuals, public and private organizations, and the media

**Contact:**
Christopher Baird
NCCD/CRC
426 S. Yellowstone Drive
Madison, WI 53719
608-831-8882
CBaird@mw.nccd-crc.org
nccd-crc.org

\* \* \*

## National Exhoodus Council (NEC)

- A coalition of leading U.S. anti-crime/anti-violence organizations
- Their leadership and management are individuals who are previously incarcerated
- Helps successful resettlement (re-entry) to the community from prison, creating jobs, and reducing gang violence
- Partners with the National Organization of Black Law Enforcement (NOBLE)

**Contact:**
Que English
National Exhoodus Council
633 Cheswick Road
Philadelphia, PA 19128

214-435-3694
que@thenec.net
thenec.net

\* \* \*

## National Rights of Passage Institute

- Provides training, programming, evaluation, international field trips, and information to develop a critical mass and community of leaders
- A developmental and transformational process that is culturally-specific and recognizes that entry into adult life involves the realization of social obligations and the assumption of responsibility for meeting them
- Fosters a sense of belonging in adolescents and adults who will become part of community life rather than lacking support, sanction, and purpose

**Contact:**
Zulma Zabala
2749 Woodhill Rd.
Cleveland, OH 44104
216-791-9378
zzabala@eenh.org

\* \* \*

## Network for Better Futures

- Serves high-risk men with histories of substance abuse, mental illness, chronic unemployment, and homelessness
- A collaboration of public services, including emergency rooms, mental health programs, treatment centers, jails, and prisons
- Offered to governments and health plans for a set price to manage the needs of this population

**Contact:**
Steven G. Thomas, President and CEO
Network for Better Futures
1017 Olson Memorial Highway

Minneapolis, MN 55405
612-455-6133
steve@networkforbetterfutures.com
networkforbetterfutures.com

\* \* \*

## New Heights Neighborhood Center

- Provides educational, career development, employment, social, and work support services to older youth who are out-of-school, out-of-work, and in transition
- Connects emerging young workers and untapped labor force with local businesses, strengthening the local economy and providing a route to self-sufficiency and advocacy

**Contact:**
Evelyn Fernandez-Ketcham
New Heights Neighborhood Center, Inc.
216 Fort Washington Avenue, 2nd Floor
New York, NY 10032
Dapheights@reachnewheights.org
reachnewheights.org

\* \* \*

## New Mexico Forum for Youth in Community

- Statewide network that acts as a catalyst and support to a positive youth development movement
- Seeks to achieve a transformative change in youth development through systemic changes simultaneously within and across different systems
- Provides youth practitioner training and field building
- Offers program and organizational development
- Works within public/private partnerships

**Contact:**
Everette Hill
New Mexico Forum for Youth in Community
924 Park Avenue SW

Albuquerque, NM 87102
505-821-3574
everette@nmforumforyouth.org
nmforumforyouth.org

\* \* \*

## No More Victims, Inc.

- A non-profit corporation founded in 1993 by Texas parole officer Marilyn K. Gambrell
- Reduces victimizing behavior in society by creating an atmosphere wherein each child, woman, and man can actualize his or her own worthiness
- Works to reduce crime and victimization by focusing on prevention, intervention, and rehabilitation and reducing the propensity for violent, abusive, and addictive behavior
- Offers programs to individual children and adults, school systems, adult and juvenile correctional and treatment programs, spiritual institutions, community-based programs, and civic organizations

**Contact:**
Marilyn Gambrell
No More Victims, Inc.
9688 Mesa Drive
Houston, TX 77078
832-922-0053
gmarilynk@yahoo.com

\* \* \*

## The Omega Boys Club/Street Soldiers

- Founded in 1987 to keep young people alive and out of prison by helping them move from the culture of violence to safer, more personally and socially productive alternatives
- Addresses the violence deeply ingrained in homes, on streets, in neighborhoods, in relationships with peers, in movies and music

**Contact:**
The Omega Boys Club/Street Soldiers
1060 Tennessee Street
San Francisco, CA 94107
415-826-8664
obc@street-soldiers.org
street-soldiers.org
omegaboysclub.org

\* \* \*

## One Vision One Life

- An initiative of the Allegheny County Department of Human Services Office of Community Services
- Works with targeted communities to reduce or eliminate crime and violence by reaching out and providing opportunities for a better way of life
- Identifies, trains, and develops teams of Community Coordinators to be active in and informed about their communities; systematically collects and utilizes "street-level intelligence to intervene in petty disputes, turf battles and gang/group incidents before they become shootings and homicides"; and reaches out to those at risk with services, jobs, and assistance to reduce their risk for violence[2]

**Contact:**
Richard S. Garland
One Vision One Life
564 Forbes Avenue, Suite 1302
Pittsburgh, PA 15219
412-434-1287
onevisiononelife.org

\* \* \*

## Project Brotherhood

- A clinic dedicated to improving the health and welfare of African American Men

- Provides primary, holistic health care and improves health awareness in black men
- Develops innovative strategies to recruit and retain black men into primary care
- Provides free haircuts and food, as well as transportation assistance for every clinic session[3]
- Provides resources and linkages to other Chicago area services

**Contact:**
Marcus Murray
Project Brotherhood
Woodlawn Health Center
6337 S. Woodlawn Ave.
Chicago, IL 60637
773-753-5543
projectbrotherhood@gmail.com
projectbrotherhood.net

\* \* \*

## Public Allies

- A national movement grounded in the conviction that everyone leads, and can make a difference
- Seeks to change the face and practice of leadership in communities by inspiring citizens of all backgrounds to believe in themselves, step up and act
- Advances new leadership across the United States to strengthen communities, nonprofits and civic participation

**Contact:**
David McKinney
Public Allies
735 North Water Street, Suite 550
Milwaukee, WI 53202
414-273-0533: X 2965
davidm@publicallies.org
publicallies.org

\* \* \*

## Roca, Inc.

- Uses a High-Risk Youth Intervention Model to help disengaged and disenfranchised high-risk men 16–24 years of age move out of violence and poverty and improve their health and well-being
- Helps young men learn skills to get and keep a job and curb violent behavior via substance abuse treatment, mental health counseling, and working in supervised crews cleaning, painting, and landscaping

**Contact:**
Molly Baldwin
Anisha Chablani
Roca, Inc.
101 Park Street
Chelsea, MA 02150
413-846-4301
Anicha@rocainc.com
BaldwinM@rocainc.com
rocainc.org

\* \* \*

## Student African American Brotherhood

- Mentoring and support groups to bring the message of empowerment and success to young men
- Offers conferences across the United States to bring together like-minded young men, professionals, community activists, and scholars

**Contact:**
Dr. Tyrone Bledsoe, Founder/Executive Director
Student African American Brotherhood
The University of Toledo
P. O. Box 350842
Toledo, OH 43635
419-530-3221
tbledsoe@saabnational.org
2cusaab.org

\* \* \*

## Success—A New Beginning, Inc.

- Works in south central Los Angeles
- Enhances the individual and collective capacity of residents to take more meaningful roles in the policies and systems affecting their own community

**Contact:**
Jah'Shams Abdul-Mu'min
Success—A New Beginning, Inc.
3655 South Grand Avenue, Suite 220
Los Angeles, CA 90008
323-988-5721
jahshams@gmail.com

* * *

## United Teen Equality Center

- Utilizing the popular meeting ground of volleyball, street outreach workers connect with at-risk youth in Lowell, Massachusetts (home to the second largest Cambodian population in the United States)
- Promotes healthier lifestyle choices, increases utilization of health insurance and health care services, and reduces gang violence
- Approaches youth work by blending three components: a "by teens, for teens" safe-haven; youth development programming; and youth organizing

**Contact:**
Gregg W. Croteau
United Teen Equality Center
34 Hurd Street
Lowell, MA 01852
978-441-9949
gregg@utec-lowell.org
utec-lowell.org/about.php

* * *

## Vera Institute of Justice, Inc.

- An innovative approach to preventing violent crime among young men of color
- Recognizes that both violent felony offenders and those they have harmed are traumatized—both require help to break the cycle of violence and engage in developing a just resolution
- District attorneys, judges, and public defenders refer young adults into this program as an alternative to incarceration

Danielle Sered
Common Justice, Vera Institute of Justice, Inc.
233 Broadway, 12th Floor
New York, NY 10279
212-334-1300
dsered@vera.org
vera.org

1100 First Street NE, Suite 950
Washington, DC 20002
202-465-8900
vera.org

546 Carondelet
New Orleans, LA 70130
504-593-0936
vera.org

\* \* \*

## Voices for America's Children

- A national organization established in 1984
- Improves the lives of children in the United States by advocating for effective public policies at the federal, state, and local levels of government
- Commits to speaking out for the well-being of children by supporting child advocates who have achieved policy wins for children in early education, health, juvenile justice, child welfare, and tax and budget decisions

**Contact:**
Sheri Brady
Voices for America's Children
1000 Vermont Ave NW, Suite 700
Washington, DC 20010
202-380-1782
brady@voices.org
voices.org

\* \* \*

## W. Haywood Burns Institute

- A national nonprofit organization with a dynamic and innovative model that proves reducing disparities is a solvable problem
- Aims to protect and improve the lives of youth of color and poor children by ensuring fairness and equity throughout their communities' youth-serving systems
- Has worked in more than 40 jurisdictions nationally and has a 140-member national network
- Provides support to organizations that provide alternatives to detention and helps local organizations to strengthen their programs and engage in policy work

**Contact:**
James Bell
W. Haywood Burns Institute
180 Howard St., Suite 320
San Francisco, CA 94110
415-321-4100 X101
jbell@burnsinstitute.org
burnsinstitute.org

\* \* \*

## The Young People's Project

- Programs in Chicago; Boston; Jackson, MS; Miami; and Ann Arbor, MI

- Uses math literacy to develop young leaders and organizers to change the quality of education and life in communities so children can better reach their potential

**Contact:**
Javier Maisonet
YPP Chicago
3424 S. St., Suite IC3-2
Chicago, IL 60616
773-407-4732
typp.org

Chad Milner
99 Bishop Allen Dr.
Cambridge, MA 02139
617-354-8991
typp.org

Quinn Soto
1452 Dorchester Ave.
Boston, MA 02122
617-822-2400
typp.org

April Dortch
2659 Livingston Road
Jackson, MS 39213
601-987-0015
typp.org

Sharayna Rolle
FIU Center for Urban Education
11200 SW 8th St., Rm. 339A
Miami, FL 33199
305-348-2664
typp.org

Andrea Bachman
2222 LSA Building
500 South State Street
Ann Arbor, MI 48109
734-834-0172
typp.org

* * *

## Youth Advocacy Project (YAP)

- Established in 1992 by the Committee for Public Counsel Services, the Massachusetts public defender agency
- Has grown from one and one-half attorneys to a 20-person team
- Provides advocacy and legal representation for young people who are unable to pay for counsel
- Provides education and training to families and children, youth-serving professionals, and members of the community
- Offers clinical assessment, service planning, and referrals to prevent chronic court involvement and helps high-risk youth lead productive lives
- Uses a multi-disciplinary advocacy model of legal serves, clinical assessment and advocacy, and community outreach

**Contact:**
Joshua M. Dohan
Youth Advocacy Project
10 Malcolm X Boulevard, Suite 2-1
Roxbury, MA 02119-1776
617-989-8100
jdohan@publiccounsel.net
youthadvocacyproject.org

* * *

## YouthBuild USA

- 273 YouthBuild programs in 45 states; Washington, DC; and the Virgin Islands
- 92,000 students have built 19,000 units of affordable housing since 1994
- Senator John Kerry (D-MA) was involved early on; now, there are numerous champions and allies in Congress to ensure funding
- Extends to the broader youth and community development fields to diminish poverty in the United States and internationally

**Contact:**
Charlie Clark
YouthBuild USA
58 Day Street
Somerville, MA 02144
617-623-9900
cclark@youthbuild.org
info@youthbuild.org
youthbuild.org

\* \* \*

## Youth Empowerment Project

- Formed in 2004 by three former employees of the Juvenile Justice Project of Louisiana
- Instrumental in reforming Louisiana's juvenile justice system away from incarceration toward rehabilitation and the development of quality, community-based programs
- Provides intensive case management, mentoring, and educational services to at-risk New Orleans youth
- Helps young people connect with their family and community, thus, laying a foundation for a healthy adulthood

**Contact:**
Donna Wolf
Youth Empowerment Project
1604 Oretha Castle Haley Blvd.
New Orleans, LA 70113
504-207-4588
dwolf@youthempowermentproject.org
youthempowermentproject.org

\* \* \*

## Notes

1. Communities in Schools. http://cisnet.org.
2. One Vision One Life. http://www.onevisiononelife.org/html/About OVOL.html.
3. Project Brotherhood. http://projectbrotherhood.net/.

# Index

# About the Author

Henrie M. Treadwell, PhD, is a Research Professor in the Department of Community Health and Preventive Medicine at the Morehouse School of Medicine. Her published works include *Health Issues in the Black Community* and *The Social Determinants of Health for African American Boys and Men*, as well as contributions to ABC-CLIO's *Prison Privatization*. Treadwell holds a doctorate degree from Atlanta University.